Public Policy and Politics

Series Editors: Colin Fudge and Robin Hambleton

PUBLISHED

Danny Burns, Robin Hambleton and Paul Hoggett, *The Politics of Decentralisation: Revitalising Local Democracy*

Stephen Glaister, June Burnham, Handley M.G. Stevens and Tony Travers, *Transport Policy in Britain*

Christopher Ham, *Health Policy in Britain: The Politics and Organisation of the National Health Service* (fifth edition)

Ian Henry, *The Politics of Leisure Policy* (second edition)

Peter Malpass and Alan Murie, *Housing Policy and Practice* (fifth edition)

Robin Means, Sally Richards and Randall Smith, *Community Care: Policy and Practice* (third edition)

Gerry Stoker, *The Politics of Local Government* (second edition)

Marilyn Taylor, *Public Policy in the Community*

Kieron Walsh, *Public Services and Market Mechanisms: Competition, Contracting and the New Public Management*

FORTHCOMING

Rob Atkinson and Simin Davundi with Graham Moon, *Urban Politics in Britain: The City, the State and the Market* (second edition)

Robin Hambleton, *Reinventing Local Governance*

David Mullins and Alan Murie, *Housing Policy in the UK*

Public Policy and Politics
Series Standing Order
ISBN 0–333–71705–8 hardcover
ISBN 0–333–69349–3 paperback
(outside North America only)

You can receive future titles in this series as they are published. To place a standing order please contact your bookseller or, in the case of difficulty, write to us at the address below with your name and address, the title of the series and the ISBN quoted above.

Customer Services Department, Macmillan Distribution Ltd
Houndmills, Basingstoke, Hampshire RG21 6XS, England.

Also by Christopher Ham

Policy Making in the National Health Service
The Policy Process in the Modern Capitalist State (with M. Hill)
Health Check (with R. Robinson and M. Benzeval)
Management and Competition in the New NHS
Health Care Reform: Learning from International Experience
The Global Challenge of Health Care Rationing (with A. Coulter)
Reasonable Rationing (with G. Robert)

Health Policy in Britain

The Politics and Organisation of the National Health Service

Fifth edition

Christopher Ham

First edition 1982
Second edition 1985
Third edition 1992
Fourth edition 1999

Published 2004 by
PALGRAVE MACMILLAN
Houndmills, Basingstoke, Hampshire RG21 6XS and
175 Fifth Avenue, New York, N.Y. 10010
Companies and representatives throughout the world

PALGRAVE MACMILLAN is the global academic imprint of the Palgrave Macmillan division of St. Martin's Press, LLC and of Palgrave Macmillan Ltd. Macmillan® is a registered trademark in the United States, United Kingdom and other countries. Palgrave is a registered trademark in the European Union and other countries.

ISBN 0–333–96176–5 paperback
ISBN 0–333–96175–7 hardback

This book is printed on paper suitable for recycling and made from fully managed and sustained forest sources.

A catalogue record for this book is available from the British Library.

A catalog record for this book is available from the Library of Congress

10   9   8   7   6   5   4   3   2   1
13   12   11   10   09   08   07   06   05   04

Printed in China

To Ioanna

Contents

List of Figures and Tables

Acknowledgements

The author and publishers would like to thank the following who have kindly given permission for the use of copyright material: The King's Fund for Figure 2.1 taken from *Health Finance: Assessing the Options*, 1988 and Figure 11.1 taken from J. Keen, D. Light and N. Mays, *Public-Private Relations in Health Care*, 2001; Open University Press for Table 11.1 taken from C. Ham, *Health Care Reform*, 1997; Radcliffe Medical Press, Oxford for Figure 2.2 taken from C. Ham, *Management and Competition in the NHS*, 1997; Crown Copyright material is reproduced with the permission of the Controller of Her Majesty's Stationery Office under click licence CO1W0000276: Figure 4.4 taken from Department of Health, *Departmental Report 2003*; Figure 3.1 taken from Secretary of State for Health, *The New NHS: Modern, Dependable*; and Figure 9.2 taken from M. Bajekal and A. Prescott, *Disability. The Health Survey for England 2001*.

Every effort has been made to contact all the copyright-holders, but if any have been inadvertently omitted the publishers will be pleased to make the necessary arrangement at the earliest opportunity.

Preface to the Fifth Edition

This book was originally based on undergraduate and postgraduate courses I taught at Bristol University. The first edition benefited from the comments and suggestions of the students who followed those courses. I am particularly grateful to Laurie McMahon and Andrew Wall for their insights, gained during the first intake of the MSc in Public Policy Studies run by the School for Advanced Urban Studies at Bristol. I would also like to thank former colleagues at the School who commented on draft chapters, most notably Robin Hambleton, Michael Hill, Robin Means, Randall Smith and David Towell. Special mention should also be made of Ken Judge, with whom I jointly taught an undergraduate course in health policy. As editor of the series, 'Studies in Social Policy', in which the first two editions appeared, Ken encouraged me to write *Health Policy in Britain,* and as always was a constructive and critical collaborator.

The fifth edition is based on the same structure as earlier editions but has been completely revised and updated to take account of developments in health services and health policy since 1999. These developments have resulted in the inclusion of two new chapters: one on the impact of political devolution on the NHS, and the other on policy issues for the future. In updating the book, I have benefited from advice from Kevin Woods and Paul Jervis (Chapter 5 on devolution), and from discussions with colleagues in the Department of Health (Chapter 11 on policy issues for the future). Despite the addition of material on Northern Ireland, the book's title has not been changed from Health Policy in Britain, because the title is well-established and recognised in its field.

My thinking on the processes of policy-making and implementation has been influenced by my experience on secondment to the Department of Health between 2000 and 2004, and the effects can be seen throughout the book. During the last five years there have been a wide range of far-reaching initiatives in health policy in Britain and this edition tries to do justice to these initiatives while also putting them in an historical and comparative context.

Last but not least, I would like to thank Ioanna Burnell for her continuing support. The distractions that writing (and revising) a book inevitably create intrudes into home life. Once again, I am pleased to dedicate the book to Ioanna.

I alone am responsible for the final text.

Solihull   CHRISTOPHER HAM

Abbreviations

AHA	Area Health Authority
ASH	Action on Smoking and Health
BMA	British Medical Association
CHAI	Commission for Healthcare Audit and Inspection (known as Healthcare Commission)
CHC	Community Health Council
CHI	Commission for Health Improvement
CPRS	Central Policy Review Staff
CSR	Comprehensive Spending Review
DCMO	Deputy Chief Medical Officer
DGH	District General Hospital
DH	Department of Health
DHA	District Health Authority
DHSS	Department of Health and Social Security
DMT	District Management Team
EU	European Union
FHSA	Family Health Services Authority
FPC	Family Practitioner Committee
GMC	General Medical Council
GP	General Practitioner
HAS	Health Advisory Service
HImP	Health Improvement Programme
HMC	Hospital Management Committee
HMO	Health Maintenance Organisation
ICT	Information and Communication Technology
JCC	Joint Consultative Committee
MAS	Management Advisory Service
ME	Management Executive (of the National Health Service)
MPC	Medical Practices Committee
NAHA	National Association of Health Authorities
NAO	National Audit Office
NHS	National Health Service
NICE	National Institute for Clinical Excellence
NPSA	National Patient Safety Agency
OECD	Organisation for Economic Cooperation and Development
PAC	Public Accounts Committee
PAF	Performance Assessment Framework

PCGs	Primary Care Groups
PCTs	Primary Care Trusts
PESC	Public Expenditure Survey Committee
PFI	Private Finance Initiative
RAWP	Resource Allocation Working Party
RCP	Royal College of Physicians
RHA	Regional Health Authority
RHB	Regional Hospital Board
RL	Regional Liaison
SHA	Strategic Health Authority
SMR	Standardised Mortality Ratio
WHO	World Health Organization

Introduction

This book provides an introduction to health policy in the United Kingdom covering both the substance of health policy and the process of health policy-making and implementation. Its aim is to introduce the organisation of the National Health Service (NHS), its history and development and to the way in which policies for NHS services are made and implemented in central government and in NHS bodies. The book also examines the auditing and evaluation of health policy, and considers which groups have power over policy-making. The main concern of what follows, then, is the politics of health care: who decides, who benefits and who controls health services.

In examining health policy, the focus is not just central government, important as government is in accounting for what happens in the NHS. Rather, the book examines both the macro politics of health policy and the micro politics by reviewing the dynamics of policy-making in health bodies as well as in Westminster and Whitehall. Attention is also given to the influence of the health professions in policy-making, especially doctors, both through their involvement in committees and boards and through the power available to health professionals by virtue of their training and clinical autonomy. Put another way, if formal accounts of the organisation of government and the administration of the NHS provide the starting point of analysis, we seek to test the reality of these accounts by drawing on a wide range of studies and research evidence in the search for a fuller understanding of what actually happens in practice.

One of the characteristics of contemporary debates about health policy is the strength of the views of those who participate in those debates. Controversy is the norm and opinions on what government should do to tackle the problems of the NHS are two a penny. This book endeavours to stand above these debates, reflecting the variety of views that exist in the health policy community but resisting the temptation to take sides. For readers new to this field it is important to be led into the issues that give rise to dispute as dispassionately as possible while not ignoring the conflict that exists. This is therefore not a textbook for those wanting to be persuaded of a particular point of view. Rather, it will have succeeded if the reader is better informed about the terms of the debate about health policy and in a position to make up his or her mind on the issues.

As well as students of health services in the United Kingdom, the book is aimed at those working in the health services and readers from outside the

1

United Kingdom seeking to understand the dynamics of the NHS and health policy. Recognising that an introductory textbook is likely to raise as many questions as it provides answers, suggestions for further reading are offered at the end.

The structure of the analysis

The book is organised into eleven chapters. Chapter 1 examines the way in which the state has increasingly become involved in providing health services in the United Kingdom. Starting with state involvement in public health in the nineteenth century, the chapter traces the development of health insurance measures in the first part of the twentieth century and the establishment of the NHS in 1948. Particular attention is given to events after 1948, including the reorganisation of the NHS in 1974, and its subsequent restructuring in 1982.

Chapter 2 focuses on the development of health policy in the 1980s and 1990s. The chapter begins by describing the efficiency initiatives taken by the Thatcher government during the 1980s and this is followed by an account of the Ministerial Review of the NHS and the White Paper, *Working for Patients*. The process by which the White Paper was translated into law is reviewed, and the impact of the reforms is assessed.

Chapter 3 examines the policies pursued by the Blair government since 1997. The chapter begins with a review of the government's inheritance and goes on to outline the proposals in the White Paper, *The New NHS*. The structure of the NHS to emerge from the White Paper is outlined and the key features of the third way in health care reform are described. This leads into a discussion of *The NHS Plan* and the subsequent changes to the organisation of the NHS in England.

Chapter 4 explores the funding of health services and priority-setting. The growth of NHS expenditure is reviewed and this is followed by a description of the Wanless Review and its outcome. The way in which NHS funds are used is then discussed and this leads into a summary of policies to improve health, develop health care services, and promote integration between health and social care. The process of priority-setting is outlined and the balance between central and local responsibility discussed.

Chapter 5 explains differences between England, Wales, Scotland and Northern Ireland in health and health services before and after political devolution. The impact of devolved government on the structure of the NHS in each country is discussed and emerging divergences in health policy are described. The possible implications of regional government for the NHS in England are also explored.

Chapter 6 considers the organisation of central government in Britain. The functions and powers of Parliament, the Cabinet, the Prime Minister, ministers, civil servants and outside interests are outlined, in order to establish the political context of health policy-making. The development of a number of theoretical approaches to interpret the role of different institutions is also discussed.

Chapter 7 concentrates on the workings of the Department of Health (DH). The way in which the Department is organised is described, and this is followed by an examination of the various influences on health policy-making within central government. The role of pressure groups and other interests is considered, and the chapter concludes with a discussion of attempts within the DH to introduce a greater measure of analysis into the policy process.

Chapter 8 looks at the implementation of health policy, and the local influences on policy-making. A key issue here is the relationship between the DH and NHS bodies. Also significant is the position of the medical profession in the structure of management and as major resource controllers at the local level. These issues are analysed, and the extent to which national policies are implemented is discussed. The chapter also considers the ability of NHS bodies to engage in independent policy-making.

Chapter 9 focuses on audit and evaluation. The development of interest in this area is described and the current arrangements for audit and evaluation are outlined. This includes discussion of the performance assessment framework and the use of star ratings, and an analysis of the role of bodies such as the Audit Commission and the National Audit Office. The extension of audit into the quality of medical care is described and the importance of the Kennedy Inquiry into heart surgery in Bristol is emphasised. This is followed by an assessment of the performance of the NHS in relation to health improvement and access to health care.

Chapter 10 examines the distribution of power in the NHS. Through a discussion of different theories of power, the chapter asks whose interests are served by health services. The relevance of pluralist, structuralist and Marxist theories is assessed, and issues for further research are identified. The chapter seeks to stand back from the detailed discussion of health policy in earlier chapters in order to explore the variety of overarching approaches to understanding the development of health services and power relationships in health care.

Chapter 11 looks to the future. It does so by first examining the performance of the NHS in the international context. This is followed by a review of the place of the private sector in Britain and an analysis of the role of hierarchies, networks and markets in health care. The importance of changing social attitudes and demographic patterns is then considered.

Medical advances hold out the prospect of further improving the health of the population but the cost of these advances creates a challenge in relation to rationing or priority-setting. These issues are reviewed, as are the policies of the main political parties. The chapter concludes by arguing that it will be difficult to take the NHS out of politics, as some have proposed, because politics and the NHS have become more closely intertwined as the importance of the NHS as an issue of public policy has increased.

Chapter 1

The Development of Health Services and Health Policy

The National Health Service came into existence on 5 July 1948 with the aim of providing a comprehensive range of health services to all in need. One hundred years earlier the first Public Health Act was placed on the statute book, paving the way for improvements in environmental health which were to have a significant effect in reducing deaths from infectious diseases. The name of Aneurin Bevan is usually associated with the founding of the NHS, and that of Edwin Chadwick with the public health movement. However, legislation and policy are not made only or mainly by outstanding individuals. It has been said of Bevan that he was 'less of an innovator than often credited; he was at the end, albeit the important and conclusive end, of a series of earlier plans. He "created" the National Health Service but his debts to what went before were enormous' (Willcocks, 1967, p. 104). Much the same applies to other health policy decisions. Individuals may have an impact, but under conditions not of their own making. What is more, most decisions in their final form result from bargaining and negotiation among a complex constellation of interests, and most changes do not go through unopposed. These points can be illustrated through the examples already cited.

Take the 1848 Public Health Act, for example. The main aim of the Act was to provide powers to enable the construction of water supply and sewerage systems as a means of controlling some of the conditions in which infectious diseases were able to thrive and spread. On the face of it, this was a laudable aim which might have been expected to win general public support. In fact, the Act was opposed by commercial interests who were able to make money out of insanitary conditions; and by anxious ratepayers, who were afraid of the public expense which would be involved. It was therefore only after a lengthy struggle that the Act was passed.

Again, consider the establishment of the NHS. The shape taken by the NHS was the outcome of discussions and compromise between ministers and civil servants on the one hand, and a range of pressure groups on the other. These groups included the medical profession, the organisations representing the hospital service, and the insurance committees with their responsibility for general practitioner services. Willcocks has shown how, among these groups, the medical profession was the most successful in achieving its objectives, while the organisations representing the hospital service were the least successful. A considerable part too was played by civil servants and ministers. In turn, all of these interests were influenced by what had gone before. They were not in a position to start with a blank sheet and proceed to design an ideal administrative structure. Thus history, as well as the strength of established interests, may be important in shaping decisions. Let us then consider the historical background to the NHS.

The origins of hospitals and medicine

The origins of hospitals in Britain can be traced back to medieval times when religious foundations established institutions such as St Bartholomew's in 1123 and St Thomas's in 1215. Hospital building took off in the thirteenth century alongside the establishment of universities across Europe and formal medical training. Even at this early stage, three types of doctor began to emerge: physicians, barber-surgeons and apothecaries, the forerunners of general practitioners. Physicians were the elite doctors and their training was based in the universities. In contrast, surgeons served an apprenticeship organised through guilds. Apothecaries were originally shopkeepers who provided basic medical care and administered drugs. Like physicians and surgeons, apothecaries were limited in their ability to offer help to patients by the rudimentary understanding of the causes of disease that existed at that time. Midwives played the major part in childbirth, and childbirth was dominated by women until the eighteenth century.

It was not until 1518 that the College of Physicians of London was formed to exercise control over the licensing and examination of physicians. Subsequently, surgeons separated from barbers and established the London Company of Surgeons in 1745 and this became the College of Surgeons in 1800. The Society of Apothecaries was involved in regulating general practitioners in London, although the extent to which it was effective in this role has been questioned (Porter, 1997). The nature and content of medical education in the eighteenth century was highly variable and many doctors practised without formal qualifications. Only in the nineteenth century with the passage of the Apothecaries Act in 1815 and, more importantly, the Medical Act in 1858, did the state act to regulate medicine.

The Apothecaries Act required apothecaries to have the Licence of the Society of Apothecaries, the receipt of which rested on a combination of training and clinical experience. The Medical Act created the forerunner of the General Medical Council (GMC) with responsibility for licensing doctors and overseeing education and disciplinary matters. In place of a variety of forms of local regulation, a single national register of qualified medical practitioners was created for the first time. Although ostensibly intended to protect the public, the Medical Act also served the interests of doctors by enabling controls to be exercised over the number of doctors in practice. At a time when medical practice was almost entirely private practice, control over entry helped to maintain medical incomes and exclusivity (Stacey, 1992). This was particularly important for general practitioners who were the biggest group of doctors at that time and who sought protection from the unqualified. The important point about the Medical Act was that it led to a system of state-sanctioned self-regulation that has persisted with minor modifications until this day.

The development of hospitals was set back by the dissolution of the monasteries by Henry VIII and the impact this had on institutions for the sick that had had their origins in religious foundations. In London, only St Bartholomew's, St Thomas's and the Bethlem survived until the resurgence of hospitals in the eighteenth century. In parallel there grew up the dispensaries as an early form of outpatient care that also provided drugs for the sick. The role of hospitals developed further in the nineteenth century when specialisation among doctors led to the establishment of specialist hospitals. By 1860 there were at least 66 special hospitals and dispensaries in London concerned with children's health, nervous diseases, orthopaedics and other needs (Porter, 1997). In the second half of the nineteenth century, public infirmaries were created separate from the workhouses that provided relief for the poor, and in this way the basis for state involvement in hospital provision was laid down (see below). Another important development was increasing separation between specialists who controlled care in hospitals and general practitioners who worked in the community. The end of the nineteenth century saw the emergence of the referral system under which specialists became consultants to general practitioners. This division of labour among doctors was to have long lasting implications for the practice of British medicine and the organisation of health services.

Public health services

While the Medical Act of 1858 was a landmark in the development of the medical profession, the most important area of state involvement in the provision of health services during the nineteenth century, in terms of the impact on people's health, was the enactment of public health legislation. Infectious diseases like cholera and typhoid posed the main threat to health at the time. The precise causes of these diseases remained imperfectly understood for much of the century, and the medical profession was largely powerless to intervene. In any event, the main reason for the decline in infectious diseases was not to be advances in medical science, but developments in the system of public health. It was these developments which provided an effective counterweight to the sorts of urban living conditions created by the industrial revolution and within which infectious diseases could flourish.

The 1848 Public Health Act provided the basis for the provision of adequate water supplies and sewerage systems. Behind the Act lay several years of struggle by Edwin Chadwick and his supporters. As Secretary to the Poor Law Commission, Chadwick played a major part in preparing the Commission's *Report of an Inquiry into the Sanitary Conditions of the Labouring Population of Great Britain*, published in 1842. The report, and the ever-present threat of cholera, created the conditions for the Act, which led to the establishment of the General Board of Health. Subsequent progress was variable, with some local authorities keen to take action, while others held back. In practice, a great deal depended on the attitude of local interests, as the Act was permissive rather than mandatory, and the General Board of Health was only an advisory body.

Chadwick's campaign was taken forward by John Simon, first as Medical Officer to the General Board of Health, and later as Medical Officer to the Medical Department of the Privy Council, which succeeded the Board in 1858. Simon's work and the report of the Royal Sanitary Commission, which sat from 1869 to 1871, eventually bore fruit in the establishment of the Local Government Board in 1871, and the Public Health Acts of 1872 and 1875. The 1875 Act brought together existing legislation rather than providing new powers, while the 1872 Act created sanitary authorities who were obliged to provide public health services. One of the key provisions of the 1872 Act was that local sanitary authorities should appoint a medical officer of health. These officers – whose origins can be traced back to Liverpool in 1847 – were significant figures, both in the fight against infectious diseases, and in the campaign for better health. It was mainly as a result of their activities at the local level that more concerted action was pursued.

Mothers and young children

From the beginning of the twentieth century, the sphere of concern of medical officers of health extended into the area of personal health services as the result of increasing state concern with the health of mothers and young children. One of the immediate causes was the discovery of the poor standards of health and fitness of army recruits for the Boer War. This led to the establishment by government of an Interdepartmental Committee on Physical Deterioration, whose report, published in 1904, made a series of recommendations aimed at improving child health. Two of the outcomes were the 1906 Education (Provision of Meals) Act, which provided the basis for the school meals service, and the 1907 Education (Administrative Provision) Act, which led to the development of the school medical service. It has been argued that these Acts 'marked the beginning of the construction of the welfare state' (Gilbert, 1966, p. 102). Both pieces of legislation were promoted by the reforming Liberal government elected in 1906, and the government was also active in other areas of social policy reform, including the provision of retirement pensions.

At the same time action was taken in relation to the midwifery and health visiting services. The 1902 Midwives Act made it necessary to certify midwives as fit to practise, and established a Central Midwives Board to oversee registration. The Act stemmed in part from the belief that one of the explanations for high rates of maternal and infant mortality lay in the lack of skills of women practising as midwives. Local supervision of registration was the responsibility of the medical officer of health, whose office was becoming increasingly powerful. This trend was reinforced by the 1907 Notification of Births Act, one of whose aims was to develop health visiting as a local authority service. The origins of health visiting are usually traced back to Manchester and Salford in the 1860s, when women began visiting mothers to encourage higher standards of child care. The state's interest in providing health visiting as a statutory service mirrored its concern to regulate midwives and provide medical inspection in schools, and the importance of health visiting was emphasised by the Interdepartmental Committee on Physical Deterioration. The 1907 Act helped the development of health visiting by enabling local authorities to insist on the compulsory notification of births. An Act of 1915 placed a duty on local authorities to ensure compulsory notification.

Arising out of these developments, and spurred on by the 1918 Maternity and Child Welfare Act, local authorities came to provide a further range of child welfare services. These services included not only the employment of health visitors and the registration of midwives, but also the provision of infant welfare centres and, in some areas, maternity homes for mothers who required institutional confinements. However, the Ministry of Health, which had been established in 1919, continued to be concerned at the high rate of maternal deaths, as the publication in 1930 and 1932 of the reports of the Departmental Committee on Maternal Mortality and Morbidity demonstrated. Particular importance was placed on the provision of adequate antenatal care. This led to an expansion of antenatal clinics, and, after the 1936 Midwives Act, to the development of a salaried midwifery service.

Health insurance

The 1911 National Insurance Act was concerned with the provision of general practitioner (GP) services. The Act was an important element in the Liberal government's programme of social policy reform, and it provided for free care from GPs for certain groups of working people earning under £160 per annum. Income during sickness and unemployment was also made available, and the scheme was based on contributions by the worker, the employer and the state.

Like other major pieces of social legislation, the Act was not introduced without a struggle. As Gilbert (1966, p. 290) has noted, 'The story of the growth of national health insurance is to a great extent the story of lobby influence and pressure groups'. Gilbert has shown how Lloyd George pushed through the Act to come into operation in 1913, but only after considerable opposition from the medical profession. The doctors were fearful of state control of their work, and of the possible financial consequences. They were persuaded into the scheme when the government agreed that payment should be based on the number of patients on a doctor's list – the capitation system – rather than on a salary, thereby preserving GPs' independence. Also, it was decided that the scheme should be administered not by local authorities, but by independent insurance committees or 'panels'. The insurance companies and friendly societies who had previously played a major part in providing cover against ill-health were given a central role on the panels. The professional freedom of doctors was further safeguarded by allowing them the choice of whether to join the scheme, and whether to accept patients. Finally, the financial fears of the profession were assuaged by the generous level of payments that were negotiated, and by the exclusion of higher-income groups from the scheme. The exclusion of these groups created a valuable source of extra income for GPs. By the mid-1940s around 21 million people or about half the population of Great Britain were insured under the Act. Also, about two-thirds of GPs were taking part. Nevertheless, the scheme had important limitations: it was only the insured workers who were covered, and not their families; and no hospital care was provided, only the services of GPs. Despite these drawbacks, the Act represented a major step forward in the involvement of the state in the provision of health services.

Hospital services

As we noted earlier, public provision of hospitals developed out of the workhouses provided under the Poor Law. The voluntary hospital system had a much longer history, being based at first on the monasteries and later on charitable contributions by the benevolent rich. Of the two types of institution, it was the voluntary hospitals that provided the higher standards of care. As the nineteenth century progressed, and as medicine developed as a science, the voluntary hospitals became increasingly selective in their choice of patients, paying more and more attention to the needs of the acutely ill to the exclusion of the chronic sick and people with infectious diseases. Consequently, it was left to the workhouses to care for the groups that the voluntary hospitals would not accept, and workhouse conditions were often overcrowded and unhygienic. Some of the vestiges of this dual system of hospital care can still be observed in the NHS today.

It was not, perhaps, surprising that workhouse standards should be so low, since one of the aims of the Poor Law was to act as a deterrent. The 'less eligibility' principle underpinning the 1834 Poor Law Amendment Act depended on the creation of workhouse conditions so unattractive that they would discourage the working and sick poor from seeking relief. The Act was also intended to limit outdoor relief: that is, relief provided outside the workhouses. In the case of medical care, this was provided by district medical officers under contract to the Boards of Guardians who administered the Poor Law. Vaccination against smallpox was one of the services for which medical officers were responsible, beginning with the introduction of free vaccination for children in 1840.

There was some improvement in Poor Law hospital services in London after the passing of the 1867 Metropolitan Poor Act. The Act provided the stimulus for the development of infirmaries separate from workhouses, and the London example was subsequently followed in the rest of the country through powers granted by the 1868 Poor Law Amendment Act. However, the establishment of separate infirmaries coincided with a further campaign against outdoor relief. This was despite the fact that in some areas public dispensaries, equivalent to rudimentary health centres, were provided for the first time. Nevertheless, the legislation which encouraged the development of Poor Law infirmaries has been described as 'an important step in English social history. It was the first explicit acknowledgement that it was the duty of the state to provide hospitals for the poor. It therefore represented an important step towards the NHS Act which followed some eighty years later' (Abel-Smith, 1964, p. 82). And as Fraser has commented, 'through the medical officers and the workhouse infirmaries the Poor Law had become an embryo state medical authority providing in effect general practitioners and state hospitals for the poor' (Fraser, 1973, p. 87).

The 1929 Local Government Act marked the beginning of the end of the Poor Law, and was a further step on the road to the NHS. The importance of the Act was that it resulted in the transfer of workhouses and infirmaries to local authorities. County councils and county borough councils were required to set up public assistance committees to administer these institutions, and were empowered to appropriate from them accommodation for the care of the sick. The intention was that this accommodation should then be developed into a local authority hospital service. Although uneven progress in this direction was made before the outbreak of the Second World War, the 1929 Act was important in placing the Poor Law infirmaries in the same hands as the other public health services which were under the control of medical officers of health. These services included not only those already mentioned, but also the provision of specialised hospitals – for example, for infectious diseases and tuberculosis – which local authorities had developed rapidly from the last decades of the nineteenth century. In addition, local authorities had a duty to provide hospitals for people with mental illness and learning disabilities. Local magistrates had been given the power to erect asylums under the 1808 County Asylums Act, but fear of the cost meant that the power was not widely used. The legislation was made mandatory in 1845, leading to a rapid growth in asylums thereafter. By 1930 there were 98 public asylums in England and Wales accommodating about 120 000 patients (Jones, 1972, p. 357).

Accordingly, at the outbreak of the Second World War, local authorities were responsible for a wide range of hospitals. As part of the war effort, public hospitals joined the voluntary hospitals in the Emergency Medical Service (EMS), set up to cope with military and civilian casualties and to provide some coordination of a disparate range of institutions and services. The EMS, with its regional form of organisation, provided a framework for the administration of hospital services after the war. More important, it resulted in senior members of the medical profession seeing at first hand the poor state of local authority hospitals and the smaller voluntary hospitals. At the same time, regional hospital surveys were carried out by the Nuffield Provincial Hospitals Trust, a voluntary body concerned with the quality and organisation of hospital services, and with a particular interest in the regionalisation of hospitals. The surveys were conducted in conjunction with the Ministry of Health, and provided thorough documentation of the widely varying standards which existed (hospitals for the mentally ill and mentally handicapped were not included in the surveys). The summary report of the surveys, published in 1946 as the Domesday Book of the Hospital Services, pointed to considerable inequalities in the distribution of beds and staff between different parts of the country, as well as to the lack of organisation of the service as a whole (Nuffield Provincial Hospitals Trust, 1946). It was in this sense, then, that the experience of war may be said to have created pressure for change, although what form the change should take was very much an issue for debate.

The establishment of the National Health Service

We have seen how, in a variety of ways, responsibility for the provision of health care was increasingly taken over by the state. The key legislative developments were the 1808 County Asylums Act, the 1867 Metropolitan Poor Act and the 1929 Local Government Act, all emphasising the importance of public provision of hospital services; the Public Health Acts and the legislation relating to maternal and child welfare, placing on local authorities a duty to develop environmental and later some personal health services; the 1911 National Insurance Act, recognising the state's responsibility in relation to primary health care; and the Medical Act of 1858 with its provisions on the regulation of the medical profession.

Given the *ad hoc* manner in which these developments occurred, it was not surprising that there should be calls for the coordination and consolidation of service provision. Thus the report of the Dawson Committee, set up in 1919 after the establishment of the Ministry of Health to make proposals for improving health services, recommended the provision of a comprehensive scheme of hospital and primary health care. Later reports from the Royal Commission on National Health Insurance in 1926, the Sankey Commission on Voluntary Hospitals in 1937, and the British Medical Association (BMA) in 1930 and 1938, all pointed to shortcomings in the existing pattern of services, and made various suggestions for change. These included the need for greater coordination of hospitals, and for the extension of health insurance to other groups in the population. The Royal Commission's report also suggested that health service funding might eventually be derived from general taxation instead of being based on the insurance principle.

This view was not shared by the BMA, which, in an important report from its Medical Planning Commission published in 1942, advocated the extension of state involvement in the provision of health services. The BMA suggested that health insurance should be extended to cover most of the population and that the items covered by insurance should encompass the services of hospital specialists and examinations. The same year as the BMA's report appeared saw publication of an even more influential document, the Beveridge Report on Social Insurance and Allied Services. This report made wide-ranging recommendations for the reform and extension of the social security system, together with proposals for a national health service. Coming a year after the government had announced its intention to develop a national *hospital* service at the end of the war, the Beveridge Report added impetus to the movement for change.

The movement gathered momentum in subsequent years, leading to a White Paper containing proposals for a national health service in 1944, the

National Health Service Act in 1946, and the establishment of the Service itself in 1948. Prolonged negotiations accompanied the birth of the Service, and these negotiations at times seemed likely to prevent the birth taking place at all (Webster, 1988). Certainly, the medical profession, as in 1911, fought strongly for its own objectives, and was successful in winning many concessions: retention of the independent contractor system for GPs; the option of private practice and access to pay beds in NHS hospitals for hospital consultants; a system of distinction awards for consultants, carrying with it large increases in salary for those receiving awards; a major role in the administration of the Service at all levels; and success in resisting local government control. The concessions made to hospital doctors led Aneurin Bevan to say that he had 'stuffed their mouths with gold' (Abel-Smith, 1964, p. 480). In fact, Bevan cleverly divided the medical profession, winning the support of hospital consultants and specialists with generous financial payments, and thereby isolating and reducing the power of GPs, who were nevertheless successful in achieving many of their aims.

Far less successful were the local authorities, who lost control of their hospitals, despite the advocacy by Herbert Morrison in the Labour Cabinet of the local government point of view. The main reason for this, apart from the opposition of the doctors, was the unsuitability of local government areas for the administration of the hospital service. As a result, Bevan – and this was one of his personal contributions to the organisation of the NHS – decided to appropriate both the local authority hospitals and the voluntary hospitals and place them under a single system of administration. Another major personal contribution made by Bevan was to persuade the medical profession that the Service should cover all of the population and not just 90 per cent as many doctors wished. Furthermore, the Service was to be funded mainly out of general taxation, with insurance contributions making up only a small part of the total finance.

This, then, is a very brief summary of the debate surrounding the establishment of the NHS. One point to note is the relative unimportance of Parliament in the debate. The policy in this case was more strongly influenced by extra-parliamentary forces, in particular by the major pressure groups with an interest in health services. As we shall argue later, these forces can be seen to comprise a health policy community within which many issues are settled and agreed, either without or with only token reference to Parliament. In this sense, legislation is often little more than a record of the bargains struck in the health policy community. There are exceptions, and parliamentary influence can be important, but to recognise the importance of other factors is a useful corrective to conventional views of British government and politics.

The structure of the National Health Service

The administrative structure of the NHS which came into being in 1948 was the product of the bargaining and negotiation that had taken place in the health policy community in the preceding years. It was therefore a representation of what was possible rather than what might have been desirable. The structure was also shaped by the historical antecedents which have been discussed, with the result that the Service was organised into three parts. First, representing the closest link with what had gone before, general practitioner services, along with the services of dentists, opticians and pharmacists, were administered by *executive councils*, which took over from the old insurance committees. Executive councils were appointed partly by local professionals, partly by local authorities and partly by the Ministry of Health, and they were funded directly by the Ministry. In no sense were executive councils management bodies. They simply administered the contracts of family practitioners (the generic term for GPs, dentists, opticians and pharmacists), maintained lists of local practitioners, and handled complaints by patients.

Second, and again closely linked with the previous system of administration, responsibility for a range of environmental and personal health services was vested in *local authorities*. These services included maternity and child welfare clinics, health visitors, midwives, health education, vaccination and immunisation, and ambulances. The key local

Figure 1.1   *The structure of the NHS in England, 1948–74*

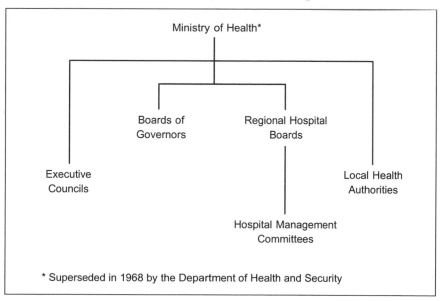

* Superseded in 1968 by the Department of Health and Security

officer continued to be the medical officer of health, and funding of the services was provided partly by central government grants and partly by revenues raised by local authorities. A number of other services previously administered by local authorities, most notably, hospitals, tuberculosis services and cancer schemes, were removed from their control, representing a substantial reduction in the role of public health departments (Lewis, 1986).

Third, hospitals were administered by completely new bodies – *Regional Hospital Boards (RHBs)*, *Hospital Management Committees (HMCs)*, and *boards of governors*. Special status was given to the teaching hospitals – the elite members of the old voluntary hospital system – which were organised under boards of governors in direct contact with the Ministry of Health. This was one of the concessions Aneurin Bevan made to the medical profession. The vast majority of hospitals, though, came under the RHBs, of which there were 14 in England and Wales at first, and 15 later, and HMCs, numbering some 400 in total. RHBs were appointed by the Minister of Health, and they in turn appointed HMCs. Finance for the hospital service was passed down from the Ministry of Health through RHBs and on to HMCs. In the case of teaching hospitals, money was allocated straight from the Ministry to boards of governors. The tripartite structure of the NHS is illustrated in Figure 1.1.

The NHS between 1948 and 1974

One of the assumptions that lay behind the NHS, and which had been made in the Beveridge Report, was that there was a fixed quantity of illness in the community which the introduction of a health service, free at the point of consumption, would gradually reduce. It was therefore expected that expenditure would soon level off and even decline as people became healthier. In fact, the reverse happened. Health service spending in the years immediately after 1948 was much greater than parliamentary estimates had allowed, and supplementary funding was necessary. Concern at the cost of the Service was reflected in the appointment of the Guillebaud Committee of Enquiry in 1953:

> to review the present and prospective cost of the National Health Service; to suggest means, whether by modifications in organisation or otherwise, of ensuring the most effective control and efficient use of such Exchequer funds as may be made available; to advise how, in view of the burdens on the Exchequer, a rising charge upon it can be avoided while providing for the maintenance of an adequate Service; and to make recommendations. (Guillebaud Committee, 1956)

The Committee's report, published in 1956, concluded that there was no evidence of extravagance or inefficiency in the NHS. Indeed, using research carried out by Richard Titmuss and Brian Abel-Smith, the Committee showed that, expressed as a proportion of the gross national product, the cost of the Service had actually fallen from 3.75 per cent in 1949–50 to 3.25 per cent in 1953–54. If anything, the Committee felt that more money, not less, should be allocated to the NHS, particularly to make up for the backlog of capital building works needing to be undertaken. The Committee also considered that more could be done to strengthen the links between the three branches of the Service, although it was not prepared to recommend any major organisational change.

The call for extra resources was echoed by a number of individuals and organisations, and it is not difficult to see why. The 1950s have been characterised aptly as the years of 'make do and mend' in the hospital service, with capital expenditure during the decade amounting to only £100 million. Within this budget, no new hospitals could be built, and critics maintained that doctors were having to practise twentieth-century medicine in nineteenth-century buildings. This was the argument of two hospital consultants, Abel and Lewin, who in a study commissioned by the BMA and published in 1959, argued for greatly increased expenditure (Abel and Lewin, 1959). The response came in the form of the 1962 Hospital Plan, providing for an expenditure of £500 million in England and Wales in the ten years up to 1971. The key concept behind the plan was the District General Hospital (DGH), a hospital of between 600 and 800 beds providing specialist facilities for all but the rarest illnesses for a population of 100 000 to 150 000. Several completely new DGHs were to be built during the decade, while many more existing hospitals were to be upgraded to DGH standard. Thus, after a number of years of restraint, the hospital building programme witnessed a significant expansion.

The 1950s were not, however, wasted years in the hospital service. The amalgamation of local authority and voluntary hospitals soon brought results in terms of a better use of resources. The grouping of hospitals on a district basis under the control of a Hospital Management Committee, and the introduction of a system of regional planning, helped to eliminate some of the shortages and overlaps that had existed before 1948. A good example was the rationalisation of infectious diseases hospitals and the release of beds for alternative uses. Also, there was an increase in the number of medical staff employed, and the services of hospital consultants became much more widely available. Before the establishment of the NHS, most consultants worked in urban areas where there were plentiful opportunities for private practice. After 1948, the introduction of a salaried service for hospital doctors with national salary scales and conditions of service, assisted in bringing about a more even distribution of staff. At the same time, the hospital outpatient service was further developed. These were some of the advantages to accrue from a national hospital service (see Ham, 1981).

As far as general practitioners were concerned, it has been argued that 'it was general practice, sustained for 37 years by National Health Insurance and gaining substantial additional support from the new system, which really carried the National Health Service at its inception' (Godber, 1975, p. 5). A cause of concern, though, was the increasing gulf that developed between GPs and their consultant colleagues, a gulf that had its origins in the referral system established at the end of the nineteenth century (see above). Contact was maintained between the two branches of medical practice through a variety of mechanisms, including part-time hospital appointments for some GPs and allowing GPs direct access to hospital diagnostic facilities. But on the whole, the division between general practice and specialist practice widened, despite recommendations from bodies like the Guillebaud Committee that bridges should be built between the two branches of the NHS.

The most significant developments in general practice did not occur until almost twenty years after the creation of the NHS. These were the growth of health centres, and the emergence of the primary health care team. Equally important was the distribution of GPs between different parts of the country, which was overseen by the Medical Practices Committee, set up under the 1946 NHS Act. The Committee could not direct doctors to work in particular places, but it could designate areas so that well-provided areas did not improve their position at the expense of less well-provided areas. A study carried out in 1971 concluded that:

> the broad pattern of staffing needs have not changed dramatically over the last twenty to thirty years. Areas which are currently facing the most serious shortages seem to have a fairly long history of manpower difficulties, whilst those which are today relatively well supplied with family doctors have generally had no difficulty in past years in attracting and keeping an adequate number of practitioners. (Butler, Bevan and Taylor, 1973, p. 42)

In 1966 a financial inducement, a designated area allowance, was introduced to try to attract doctors to less well-provided areas, and by the 1980s the average list size of doctors practising in designated areas had steadily fallen and the proportion of the population living in such areas had also fallen significantly (Office of Health Economics, 1989). There were, however, a number of outstanding problems in relation to the quality and coverage of general practitioner services, and these are discussed further in Chapter 4.

The third branch of the Service, that provided by local authorities, developed slowly after 1948, with ambulances comprising the main element of expenditure. Care of mothers and young children, home helps and home nurses were the other major items in the local authority health budget. At the opposite end of the scale came vaccination and immunisation, and, until the second half of the 1960s, health centres, which local authorities were responsible for building. It is relevant to note that under the 1948 National Assistance Act and other legislation, local authorities also provided a range of welfare services, including old people's homes and social workers. The division of responsibility for these services and health services became a matter of increasing concern, particularly as long-term plans for both sets of services were developed in the 1960s.

The significance of the 1962 Hospital Plan has already been mentioned. A year later, the Ministry of Health published a parallel document, *Health and Welfare: The Development of Community Care*, setting out proposals for the development of local authority health and welfare services. This was much less of a national plan than the Hospital Plan. It was essentially the bringing together of the ideas of local authorities for the growth of their health and welfare services. The difference between the two documents was a reflection of the greater measure of autonomy enjoyed by local authorities as compared with Regional Hospital Boards and Hospital Management Committees. Nevertheless, the Health and Welfare Plan was important in displaying publicly the directions in which local authority services were intended to develop. One point to emerge was the considerable variation in the plans of authorities, and it was hoped that comparisons would lead to the revision of plans and greater uniformity between areas. This happened to some extent, but the second revision of the Health and Welfare Plan, published in 1966, illustrated that wide differences still existed.

Both Health and Welfare Plans outlined developments in relation to four main client groups: mothers and young children, the elderly, the physically handicapped, and the mentally ill and handicapped (as they were called at the time). As far as the mentally ill and handicapped were concerned, a greater onus was placed on local authorities by the 1959 Mental Health Act, which, among other provisions, heralded a shift from hospital care to community care. The intention was that a range of community services should be developed, including homes and hostels, social clubs, sheltered workshops and social work support. The Health and Welfare Plans indicated what authorities were proposing to provide, and demonstrated that the commitment in central government to the community care policy was not always shared at the local level. Indeed, in a policy document published in 1975, the government noted that 'By and large the non-hospital community resources are still minimal ... The failure ... to develop anything approaching adequate social services is perhaps the greatest disappointment of the last 15 years' (DHSS, 1975a, p. 14).

A further set of ten-year plans for local authority services was prepared in 1972. In this case, the plans covered the newly established social services departments, which were created in 1971 following the report of the Seebohm Committee. The main effect of the Seebohm reforms was to divorce those local authority health services deemed to involve mainly medical skills – such as vaccination and immunisation, and health education – from those services deemed to involve mainly social work skills – such as home helps and residential care. The former were retained by the health departments of local authorities under the control of the medical officer of health, while the latter were transferred to the new social services departments under the director of social services. The new departments comprised a range of services previously provided by the local authority welfare and children's departments, as well as some of those previously administered by the health departments. The main aims of the reforms were to integrate services which had been administered separately in the past, and to provide for the development of a comprehensive family service through the new departments.

One of the points to emerge from the Health and Welfare Plans was the commitment of local authorities to the building of health centres. For a variety of reasons, including the shortage of money and hesitancy among the medical profession, health centres did not develop in the 1950s in the way that had been envisaged by the architects of the NHS. However, local interest in health centres revived in the early 1960s, and was matched by central government attaching greater priority to health centre building. The consequence was that whereas in 1965 in England and Wales there were only 28 health centres from which 215 GPs worked, by 1989 there were 1320 in operation, with almost 8000 GPs. As a result, 29 per cent of all GPs worked in health centres, and many more worked in group practices.

Simultaneously, a greater emphasis was placed on the primary health care team, rather than on the GP working in isolation. This development was very much in line with the thinking behind the Gillie Report on *The Field of Work of the Family Doctor*, published in 1963. Although much less ambitious than either the Hospital Plan or the Health and Welfare Plan, the Gillie Report can to some extent be seen as the GPs' counterpart to these documents. The report argued for more ancillary help to be made available to GPs, and for a closer integration between GPs and other health services, particularly hospitals. The BMA took up the cause of GPs in 1965 with publication of the Charter for the Family Doctor Service. Negotiations with government followed and resulted in the first major changes to the GPs' contract since the inception of the NHS. The most important of these changes were direct reimbursement of the costs of ancillary staff, payment of the costs of practice premises, incentives to encourage doctors to work in areas short of GPs, a postgraduate training allowance, and the provision of loans to enable GPs to work in more modern buildings. The new contract also resulted in a large increase in the pay of GPs.

The theme of integration was taken up in a number of reports as the problem of securing coordination between the three different parts of the NHS gained increasing importance in the 1960s. The nature of the problem could be seen clearly with older people, who might need a short hospital stay followed by a period of convalescence and care in a local authority home, and subsequent assistance at home from the GP, home help and meals-on-wheels service. In a case such as this, there was a need not only to secure close collaboration between the different professional staff involved, but also to ensure the appropriate joint planning of services. The development of long-term plans for the respective services in the early 1960s heightened this, and again pointed to the difficulty of providing a comprehensive and coordinated range of facilities within the existing system of administration, despite exhortations from central government that hospital authorities, local authorities and executive councils should plan and work together.

A second problem which had become apparent by the late 1960s was the poor quality of care provided to certain patient groups. Public attention was drawn to this issue in 1967 with publication of allegations of low standards of service provision and even the ill-treatment of elderly patients at a number of hospitals in different parts of the country (Robb, 1967). This was followed two years later by the report of the official committee which enquired into conditions at Ely Hospital, Cardiff. Ely was a mental handicap hospital, and the committee of enquiry found there had been staff cruelty to patients at the hospital. The committee made a series of recommendations for improving conditions at Ely and for preventing a similar situation arising elsewhere. Subsequently, the Department of Health and Social Security (DHSS), which had been created in 1968 through the amalgamation of the Ministry of Health and the Ministry of Social Security, set aside special money to be spent on mental handicap hospitals, and this was later extended to hospitals for the mentally ill and older people. In addition, the Hospital Advisory Service (in 1976 made the Health Advisory Service) was established to visit and report on conditions at these hospitals. A review of policies was also put in hand, leading to the publication of White Papers on services for the mentally handicapped in 1971, and the mentally ill in 1975. Despite these initiatives, the Ely Hospital 'scandal' was followed by further reports on conditions at other long-stay hospitals, including Whittingham, South Ockenden, Farleigh, Napsbury,

St Augustine's and Normansfield, demonstrating that the process of change in what came to be known as the 'Cinderella' services was often slow, and that significant improvements were difficult to achieve (Martin, 1984).

A third problem, related to the first two, concerned the system of administrative control in the NHS. The neglect of long-stay services was not new, and had been recognised by successive Ministers of Health from the early 1950s onwards. Equally, the need for authorities to work in collaboration had been endorsed and advocated by the Ministry since the establishment of the NHS. The difficulty was in achieving and implementing these policy intentions at the local level. A variety of means of control were available to the Ministry, including circulars, earmarking funds for particular purposes, and setting up special agencies like the Hospital Advisory Service. At the same time, the bodies that were responsible locally for the administration of health services were not just ciphers through which national policies were implemented. They had their own aims and objectives, and, equally significant, they were responsible for providing services where professional involvement was strong. Doctors constitute the key professional group in the NHS, and within the medical profession some interests are stronger than others. In the hospital service it is the consultants in the acute specialties such as surgery and general medicine who have traditionally been most influential. In contrast, consultant psychiatrists and geriatricians have wielded less influence. This helps to explain why it has been difficult to shift resources in favour of services for groups like older people and the mentally ill.

The reorganisation of the NHS

These were some of the problems which had emerged in the NHS some 20 years after its establishment. Suggestions on the best way of tackling the problems varied, but increasingly a change in the tripartite structure of the Service came to be seen as a significant part of the solution. This was the view of the Porritt Committee, a high-status body representing the medical profession, which in a report published in 1962 suggested that health services should be unified and placed under the control of area boards. The first statement of government intentions came in 1968, when the Labour government published a Green Paper which echoed the Porritt Committee's suggestion, and asked for comments on the proposal that 40 to 50 area health boards should be responsible for administering the health services in England and Wales.

One possibility was that a reorganised NHS would be administered by local government, which was itself undergoing reform at the same time.

However, this was discounted in the second Green Paper, published by the Labour government in 1970. The second Green Paper put forward the idea that there should be around 90 area health authorities as the main units of local administration, together with regional health councils carrying out planning functions, and some 200 district committees as a means of local participation. These proposals were developed further in the following year by the Conservative government in the Consultative Document, which strengthened the role of the regional tier of administration and provided a separate channel for local participation in the form of community health councils. The Consultative Document, and the subsequent White Paper, also emphasised the importance of improving management efficiency in the NHS. These proposals were enshrined in the 1973 National Health Service Act and came into operation on 1 April 1974. The reorganised structure in England is illustrated in Figure 1.2.

Reorganisation had three main aims. First, it was intended to *unify* health services by bringing under one authority all of the services previously administered by Regional Hospital Boards, Hospital Management Committees, boards of governors, executive councils and local health authorities. Unification was not, however, achieved in full because general practitioners remained independent contractors, with the functions of executive councils being taken over by family practitioner committees. Also, a small number of postgraduate teaching hospitals retained separate boards of governors.

Figure 1.2   *The structure of the NHS in England, 1974–82*

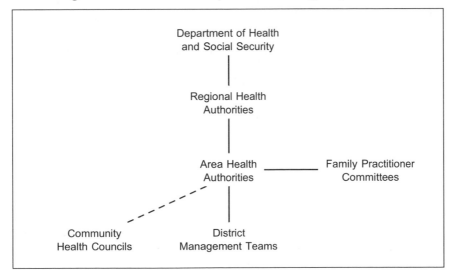

Second, reorganisation was intended to lead to better *coordination* between health authorities and related local government services. To achieve this, the boundaries of the new Area Health Authorities were, in most parts of the country, made the same as those of one or more of the local authorities providing personal social services – the county councils in shire areas, the metropolitan district councils and the London boroughs. In addition, the two types of authority were required to set up joint consultative committees (JCCs) to facilitate the collaborative development of services.

A third stated aim of reorganisation was to introduce *better management*. In fact, important changes in the management of the hospital service had already taken place as a result of the Salmon Report on nursing staff structure, the 'cogwheel' reports on the organisation of medical staff (so called because of the design on the cover of the reports), and the Farquharson Lang Report on the administrative practices of hospital authorities. The Conservative government particularly stressed the need to build on these changes, and one of the outcomes was *Management Arrangements for the Reorganised NHS*, popularly known as the 'Grey Book', which set out in considerable detail the functions of each of the tiers in the new structure, as well as providing job descriptions for health authority officers. Key concepts included multi-disciplinary team working and consensus management, and the medical profession was given an explicit role in the management system. The DHSS also referred to the principle of 'maximum delegation downwards, matched by accountability upwards' to illustrate the spirit behind the new structure. Another significant aspect of the concern to improve management efficiency was the introduction of a national planning system in 1976, two years after the structural reforms (DHSS, 1976c). All of these measures were part of a wider interest within government to borrow ideas from the private sector in the hope of improving performance. It was therefore no coincidence that the new arrangements were devised with the assistance of the management consultants, McKinsey & Co. Ltd. But the changes also reflected the particular concern in the NHS, discussed earlier, to find a more effective means of pursuing national priorities at the local level, and of shifting resources in favour of neglected groups.

The reorganised National Health Service

Thus, after almost 26 years, the NHS underwent a major organisational change. Within the new structure, Regional Health Authorities (RHAs) took over from Regional Hospital Boards, with somewhat wider responsibilities and slightly modified boundaries. The members of RHAs were appointed by the Secretary of State for Social Services, and their main function was the planning of health services. Beneath RHAs there were 90 Area Health Authorities (AHAs) in England, and their members were appointed partly by RHAs, partly by local authorities, and partly by members of the non-medical and nursing staff. The AHA chairman was appointed by the Secretary of State. Some AHAs contained a university medical school and teaching hospital facilities, and were designated as teaching areas. AHAs had planning and management duties, but one of their most important functions was to develop services jointly with their matching local authorities. Both RHAs and AHAs were supported by multi-disciplinary teams of officers. Alongside each AHA was a Family Practitioner Committee (FPC) which administered the contracts of GPs, dentists, pharmacists and opticians. FPC members were appointed by the AHA, local professionals and local authorities. Finance for health authorities and FPCs was provided by the Department of Health and Social Security. Most areas were themselves split into health districts, each of which was administered by a district management team, which in practice became the lowest tier of the Service. At district level were located Community Health Councils (CHCs), introduced as part of the reorganised structure to represent the views of the public to health authorities. There were around 200 CHCs in England.

It is pertinent to note that somewhat different arrangements were made in Wales, Scotland and Northern Ireland, which until reorganisation had had similar structures to those existing in England. The Welsh reorganisation bore the closest resemblance to that of England, the main exception being the absence of RHAs in Wales, where the Welsh Office combined the functions of a central government department and a regional authority. The differences were rather greater in Scotland, where again there was no regional tier of administration. Instead, the Scottish Office dealt directly with 15 health boards, a majority of which were divided into districts. There was no separate system of administration for family practitioner services, and the Scottish equivalent of CHCs were called Local Health Councils. In Northern Ireland, there were four health and social services boards, in direct contact with the DHSS (Northern Ireland), and each of the boards was split into a number of districts. As their name indicated, these boards were responsible for personal social services as well as health services. What is more, as in Scotland, there was no separate system of administration for family practitioner services. District Committees performed the function of CHCs.

These, then, were the administrative changes brought into being in 1974. However, almost before the new system had had a chance to settle down, the reorganised structure became the subject of attack from a number of quarters (Webster, 1996). Criticism centred on delays in taking decisions, the difficulty of establishing good relationships between administrative tiers, and the widespread feeling that there were too many tiers and too many administrators. In fact, the DHSS acknowledged in evidence to the House of Commons Public Accounts Committee that there had been an increase of 16 400 administrative and clerical staff as a result of reorganisation, although some of these staff had previously worked in local authority health services, while others were recruited to the new CHCs (Public Accounts Committee, 1977, p. xvii).

Research on the operation of the new structure pointed to other problems, including the unexpectedly high cost of reorganisation, both in terms of finance and, more particularly, of the impact on staff morale (Brown, 1979; Haywood and Alaszewski, 1980). These issues were the subject of analysis and review by the Royal Commission on the NHS, which was established in 1976 at a time of considerable unrest in the NHS. The unrest stemmed from industrial action by various groups of health service workers, and discontent in the medical profession with the government's policy of phasing out private beds in NHS hospitals. The Commission was asked '[t]o consider in the interests both of the patients and of those who work in the National Health Service the best use and management of the financial and manpower resources of the National Health Service' (Royal Commission on the NHS, 1979), and it reported in 1979. In its report, the Commission endorsed the view that there was one tier of administration too many, and recommended that there should be only one level of authority beneath the region. A flexible approach to change was advocated, and the Commission pointed out that structural reform was no panacea for all of the administrative problems facing the NHS. Other conclusions in a wide-ranging survey were that Family Practitioner Committees should be abolished, and Community Health Councils should be strengthened.

It fell to the Conservative government which took office in May 1979 to respond to the report. In *Patients First*, a consultative paper published at the end of 1979, the government announced its agreement with the proposal that one tier of administration should be removed, and suggested that District Health Authorities should be established to combine the functions of the existing areas and districts. *Patients First* also stated that Family Practitioner Committees would be retained, and that views would be welcomed on whether Community Health Councils would still be needed when the new District Health Authorities were set up (DHSS, 1979a). The Government's final decisions on the main aspects of reorganisation were published in July 1980 (DHSS, 1980a). In large part, they endorsed the *Patients First* proposals, and in addition announced that Community Health Councils would remain in existence, though their functions would be reviewed.

The result was the creation of 192 District Health Authorities (DHAs) in England. DHAs came into operation on 1 April 1982, and within districts emphasis was placed on the delegation of power to units of management. Detailed management arrangements varied considerably, with some units covering services in districts as a whole, such as psychiatric services, while others were limited to a single large hospital. Health authorities were expected to establish management structures within overall cost limits set by the DHSS, and in 1983 it was estimated that the amount spent on management in the NHS had fallen from 5.12 per cent of the total budget in 1979–80 to 4.44 per cent in 1982–83, representing a saving of £64 million. Apart from the reduction in administration, the main change wrought by the reorganisation was the loss in many parts of the country of the principle of coterminosity between health authorities and local authorities. Equally significant was the announcement in November 1981 that Family Practitioner Committees (FPCs) were to be further separated from the mainstream of NHS administration and given the status of employing authorities in their own right. This change was brought into effect by the Health and Social Security Act 1984 and FPCs achieved their independent status on 1 April 1985. In addition, a number of Special Health Authorities were established. Their main responsibility was to run the postgraduate teaching hospitals in London. The structure of the NHS in England after 1982 is shown in Figure 1.3.

Figure 1.3　*The structure of the NHS in England, 1982–91*

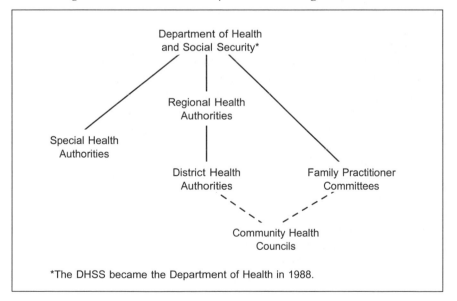

Department of Health
and Social Security*

Regional Health
Authorities

Special Health
Authorities

District Health
Authorities

Family Practitioner
Committees

Community Health
Councils

*The DHSS became the Department of Health in 1988.

In the rest of the United Kingdom different changes were made, reflecting the different administrative structures existing in Scotland, Wales and Northern Ireland. In Wales the main change was the abolition of the district level of management, and the establishment in its place of a system of unit management on a similar basis to that developed in England. In Scotland, a varied approach was pursued initially, some health boards deciding to abolish the district tier, others opting to retain it. However, in 1983 the Secretary of State for Scotland announced that all districts would be abolished and that they would be replaced by a system of unit management from 1 April 1984. As in England and Wales, the importance of delegating power to the local level was stressed. The same principle of delegation applied in Northern Ireland, where the basic structure of health and social services boards was retained. Within boards, district teams were superseded by unit management arrangements.

Conclusion

This chapter has provided an overview of the development of state involvement in the provision of health services in the United Kingdom. It has set out the historical context for discussions in the rest of the book on the dynamics of health policy formulation. Already, however, some key questions about health policy have been raised, if not answered, and they can be summarised as follows:

- First, we have noted the importance of focusing on negotiation and bargaining in the policy community in seeking to understand and explain the detailed processes of health policy-making. In particular, our preliminary analysis has highlighted the significance of identifying the key pressure groups and of examining their interaction with policy-makers. This issue is discussed further in Chapter 7.
- Second, we have noted that there may sometimes be a gap between the intentions of policy-makers and what happens in practice. This was considered in relation to the continued neglect of 'Cinderella' services, and the failure to develop adequate community-based services for the mentally ill. These examples draw attention to the importance of policy implementation, which is examined further in Chapter 8.
- A third question concerns the relationship between policy-makers and service providers. A factor of major significance in the NHS is the position occupied by doctors as service providers and their concern to retain control over their own work. We have seen how the medical profession has fought strenuously to keep its independence, most especially in the campaign by GPs to be independent contractors rather

than salaried employees. Hospital doctors have been equally concerned to maintain their autonomy even though they are in a salaried service. As the DHSS acknowledged in evidence to the House of Commons Expenditure Committee, 'the existence of clinical freedom undoubtedly reduces the ability of the central authorities to determine objectives and priorities and to control individual facets of expenditure' (Expenditure Committee, 1971). The concept of clinical freedom therefore poses peculiar difficulties for policy-makers seeking to change patterns of resource allocation. It also raises central questions about the power structure in the NHS, questions to which we return in later chapters.

- Related to this, a fourth issue not addressed directly so far but of crucial importance, concerns the relationship between health services and society. In other words, what purposes are served by health services, and what is the significance of the dominant position occupied by the medical profession? These issues are rarely discussed explicitly in books on health services and health policy. Instead, implicit assumptions are often made about the benevolent motives underlying state involvement in the provision of health services. Thus, the NHS is viewed as a great social experiment, and as a concrete expression of the development of more humane attitudes to disadvantaged groups in society. In short, the Service is seen as one of the main planks in the welfare state. These are key issues which are considered further in Chapter 10.

Chapter 2

Health Policy under Thatcher and Major

If health policy between 1948 and 1982 was characterised by successive adjustments to the original design of the NHS and a focus on fine tuning its administrative structure, in the following 15 years events took a different turn. The election of the Conservative government under Margaret Thatcher in 1979, coupled with the emergence of major funding pressures, led to the consideration of more radical alternatives. Of particular importance was the introduction of the reforms set out in the White Paper, *Working for Patients,* published in 1989 (Secretary of State for Health and others, 1989a). These reforms in turn followed from the introduction of general management and the implementation of a range of efficiency initiatives. The aim of this chapter is to trace the development of health policy from Thatcher to Major, and in the process to examine the various influences on policy-making and implementation

Increasing NHS efficiency

In reviewing the evolution of health policy in the 1980s and 1990s, it is essential to understand the economic and political context in which the NHS developed. The oil crises of the mid-1970s brought to a halt the rapid expansion of public services and public expenditure that had characterised the postwar era. The Labour government in power at the time was forced to introduce much tighter economic policies bringing it into conflict with its traditional support base in the trade unions and marking the beginning of the end of the corporatist style of politics that had dominated British government in the 1960s and 1970s. These changes were accelerated by the Conservative government elected in 1979 which challenged the prevailing Keynesian orthodoxy and pursued a programme involving the privatisation of state-owned enterprises, reductions in some forms of taxation and controls over public spending. One of the consequences for the NHS was that budgets grew much more slowly than had previously been the case, and attention shifted from the use of increases in resources made available by government to ways of deploying existing budgets more efficiently. As the 1980s wore on, the consensus that had prevailed on health policy broke down and bargaining between government and pressure groups gave way to conflict over plans to introduce market principles into the NHS.

During the first half of the 1980s the main focus of government policy was how to make the NHS more businesslike and efficient. In this respect, health policy illustrated the emergence of what came to be known as the new public management (Hood, 1991) and the priority attached by the Thatcher government to achieving value for money in the use of public resources. In the case of the NHS, the Thatcher government did not come to power in 1979 with a comprehensive and coherent programme of reform. Rather, it introduced a series of policies intended to increase efficiency, and the relationship between these policies was not always apparent. Although the effect was to bring to an end the period of incremental adaptation that had been characteristic of the postwar consensus on the NHS, it was difficult to detect at any stage a clear plan guiding the changes that were made. As Webster has commented:

> The Thatcher reforms represented a long-drawn-out sequence of changes, amounting to a process of continuous revolution, in which the end result was not predictable at the beginning, and indeed the whole process of policy-making was akin to a journey through a minefield, advances being made in an erratic manner, as dictated by the exigencies of political opportunism. (Webster, 1998, pp. 143–4)

Nowhere was this better illustrated than in relation to the wide range of efficiency initiatives launched during the 1980s. One such initiative was a requirement that health authorities should generate efficiency savings every year, which was intended to release funds from existing budgets to support new service developments. Efficiency savings were renamed 'cost improvement programmes' in 1984, and by the end of the decade it was estimated that these programmes had achieved annual savings of almost £1 billion in the hospital and community health services in England. Second, a series of Rayner scrutinies were conducted along the lines of those carried out in the civil service by Sir Derek (later Lord) Rayner and his staff. Rayner was brought in from the retail chain Marks & Spencer to advise the government in 1979 and the approach which bears his name was first applied to the NHS in 1982. The scrutinies were carried out by NHS managers and areas examined included transport services, recruitment advertising and the collection of payments due to health authorities under the provisions of the Road Traffic Act. One of the most controversial studies concerned the use of residential accommodation for NHS staff where it was estimated that up to £750 million could be saved through the sale of property.

Third, performance indicators were developed during 1982 and were first published in the following year. The indicators covered clinical services, finance, manpower and estate management and enabled health authorities to compare their performance with what was being achieved elsewhere. The information used readily available statistics and included variables such as cost per case, length of stay and waiting lists. Ministers emphasised that the indicators were a starting point for a district's assessment of performance and not its conclusion, with health authorities expected to investigate areas in which performance was apparently exceptional and to take remedial action.

Fourth, in 1983 health authorities were asked to test the cost-effectiveness of catering, domestic and laundry services by inviting tenders for the provision of these services from their own staff and from outside contractors. It was estimated that the first round of competitive tendering achieved annual savings of £110 million with most of these savings deriving from contracts won in-house by health authority staff (Social Services Committee, 1990). Some authorities extended competitive tendering to other services such as engineering maintenance and building maintenance.

Fifth, in 1988 the income-generation initiative was launched. This was designed to explore ways in which health authorities could generate additional resources. A total of £10 million was yielded in the first year through schemes such as income from private patients, car parking charges, and the use of hospital premises for retail developments. In addition to these initiatives, a number of other policies were pursued including reductions in manpower, a review of arrangements for audit, and an enquiry into land and property.

Making the NHS businesslike

Of all the policies pursued during this period, the introduction of general management following the Griffiths Report of 1983 had the most significance in the longer term. This report was produced by a small team led by Roy Griffiths, deputy chairman and managing director of the Sainsbury's supermarket chain, and it offered a fundamental critique of NHS management and its failure to ensure that resources were used either efficiently or with the needs of patients in mind. Specifically, the report identified the absence of a clearly defined general management function as the main weakness of the NHS, commenting:

> Absence of this general management support means that there is no driving force seeking and accepting direct and personal responsibility for developing management plans, securing their implementation and monitoring actual achievement. It means that the process of devolution of responsibility, including discharging responsibility to the Units, is far too slow. (Griffiths Report, 1983, p. 12)

Accordingly, the report recommended that general managers should be appointed at all levels in the NHS to provide leadership, introduce a continual search for change and cost improvement, motivate staff and develop a more dynamic management approach. At the same time, the report stated that hospital doctors 'must accept the management responsibility which goes with clinical freedom' (p. 18) and participate fully in decisions about priorities. Another key proposal was that the management of the NHS at the centre should be streamlined and strengthened through the establishment of a Health Services Supervisory Board and an NHS Management Board, with the Chairman of the Management Board being drawn from outside the NHS and the civil service. The report did not attempt to offer a comprehensive analysis of management arrangements in the NHS but rather a series of recommendations for immediate action. As the team concluded:

> action is now badly needed and the Health Service can ill afford to indulge in any lengthy self-imposed Hamlet-like soliloquy as a precursor or alternative to the required action. (p. 24)

This advice was heeded by the Secretary of State who, in welcoming the report, announced that he accepted the general thrust of what the team had to say. Subsequently, the Supervisory Board and Management Board were established within the DHSS, and the government asked health authorities to appoint general managers at all levels in the Service. A phased programme of implementation was planned, beginning with the identification of regional general managers followed by general managers at unit and district levels. Table 2.1 shows the background of general managers appointed in the first round and illustrates that the majority at all levels were administrators from within the NHS. The government also endorsed the Griffiths Report's view that doctors should be involved in

Table 2.1 *Background of general managers, 1986*

	Administrators	Doctors	Nurses	Other NHS	Outside NHS	Total
Regional general managers	9	1	1	1	2	14
District general managers	113	15	5	17	38	188
Unit general managers	322	97	63	16	44	542

Source: Hansard (1986).

management and that they should be given responsibility for management budgets. To this end a number of demonstration projects were established and in 1986 management budgeting was superseded by the resource management initiative. The change in terminology signalled a shift in emphasis away from the development of a budgeting system in isolation towards an approach in which doctors and nurses took on more responsibility for the management of resources as a whole.

Research evidence indicates that the impact of these changes was mixed. In the DHSS, the Supervisory Board was largely invisible and did not provide the leadership that the Griffiths Report had envisaged. The Management Board was more prominent, particularly in leading the implementation of general management and resource management. However, its role initially excluded involvement in the development of policy which continued to be the responsibility of the Department's Policy Group (see Chapter 7). This meant that the Board's influence was limited and its first chairman, Victor Paige, became increasingly frustrated at political interference in his work, resigning from his post in 1986. Griffiths' own assessment was that the changes made at the centre were 'half hearted in their implementation' (Griffiths, 1992, p. 65) and did not succeed in introducing the clarity he and his team had sought.

At a local level, the impact of general management varied with some studies arguing that managers had gained influence in relation to doctors and others maintaining that change had been minimal (Harrison, 1994). In relation to resource management, an evaluation of experience in the demonstration projects indicated that some progress had been made in involving doctors and nurses in management but much remained to be done and the process of change could not be rushed (Packwood, Keen and Buxton, 1991). In reality, the most important effect of the Griffiths Report was to lay the foundations for the introduction of the internal market in 1991. This was because the appointment of what became a cadre of chief executives within the NHS helped to clarify management arrangements and created a group of staff who were largely receptive to the policies that were being pursued.

Dealing with the funding crisis

As the 1980s wore on, a widening gap emerged between the money provided by the government for the NHS and the funding needed to meet increasing demands. This is illustrated in Figure 2.1 which compares actual spending, spending adjusted to include cash-releasing cost improvements, and target spending based on the government's own estimate of the resources needed to fund the demands of an ageing population, advances

Figure 2.1   *Hospital and community health services: trends in spending, targets and shortfalls*

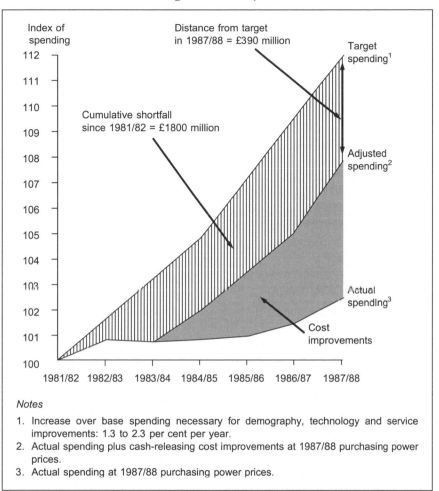

Notes
1. Increase over base spending necessary for demography, technology and service improvements: 1.3 to 2.3 per cent per year.
2. Actual spending plus cash-releasing cost improvements at 1987/88 purchasing power prices.
3. Actual spending at 1987/88 purchasing power prices.

Source: King's Fund Institute (1988).

in medical technology, and rising patient expectations. By 1987/88, the cumulative shortfall in the hospital and community health services since 1981/82 amounted to £1.8 billion, even after allowing for the recurrent savings from cost improvement programmes. For 1987/88 alone, expenditure was almost £400 million below its target level (King's Fund Institute, 1988).

The impact of cumulative underfunding became particularly apparent during the course of 1987. In the autumn of that year, many health authorities had to take urgent action to keep expenditure within cash limits. A survey conducted by the National Association of Health Authorities reported that authorities were cancelling non-urgent admissions, closing wards on a temporary basis, and not filling staff vacancies in order to cope with financial pressures (NAHA, 1987). In the face of a developing crisis in the funding of hospital services, the British Medical Association (BMA) called for additional resources to help meet the funding shortfall. And in an unprecedented move, the presidents of the Royal Colleges of Surgeons, Physicians and Obstetricians and Gynaecologists issued a joint statement claiming that the NHS had almost reached breaking point and that additional and alternative financing had to be provided (Ham, Robinson and Benzeval, 1990).

The government responded in two ways. First, in December 1987, ministers announced that an additional £101 million was to be made available in the United Kingdom to help tackle some of the immediate difficulties that had arisen. Second, Prime Minister Thatcher decided to initiate a far-reaching review of the future of the NHS. The decision was revealed in an interview on the BBC TV programme, *Panorama*, in January 1988 and it was made clear that the results would be published within a year. The Prime Minister established a small committee of senior ministers chaired by herself to undertake the review and the committee was supported by a group of civil servants and political advisers (Timmins, 1995). In a departure from established consultative processes, pressure groups like the BMA were not involved and the analysis of options for change was confined to a small group at the core of government. The leaders of the BMA at the time have subsequently described their exclusion from the policy process (Lee-Potter, 1997).

Although the Review was conducted in private, a large number of organisations and individuals took the opportunity to publish their own views on the direction it should take. Initially, much of the debate centred on alternative methods of financing health services. A variety of proposals were put forward, including suggestions for raising supplementary sources of finance for the NHS, increasing and extending patient charges, encouraging the further growth of private insurance, and switching from taxation to social insurance as the main source of funds for the NHS.

As the Review progressed, it became clear that there was little enthusiasm for a major change in how the NHS was financed. The reasons for this included support for taxation as the principal method of funding and recognition that the alternatives all had drawbacks and might not help in addressing the problems that gave rise to the Review. In other words, the same factors identified by Norman Fowler as precluding a move to private insurance in the early 1980s again served to maintain the status quo (Fowler, 1991). This was confirmed by the Chancellor of the Exchequer at the time of the Review who has recalled in his memoirs:

we looked ... at other countries to see what we could learn from them; but it was soon clear that every country we looked at was having problems with its provision of medical care. All of them – France, the United States, Germany – had different systems; but each of them had acute problems which none of them had solved. They were all in at least as much difficulty as we were, and it did not take long to conclude that there was surprisingly little that we could learn from any of the other systems. To try to change from the Health Service to any of the other sorts of systems in use overseas would simply be out of the frying pan into the fire. (Lawson, 1992, p. 616)

As the financing debate took a back seat, greater attention was paid to how resources could be used more efficiently through changes to the delivery of health services. Of particular importance was the proposal that hospitals should compete for resources in an internal market. This proposal had originally been advocated by Alain Enthoven in 1985 (Enthoven, 1985) and it was taken up and developed by right-wing think-tanks such as the Adam Smith Institute and the Centre for Policy Studies. The debate about delivery also included proposals to make doctors more accountable for their performance and to involve doctors more effectively in management. In parallel, suggestions were put forward for strengthening the management of health services by building on the introduction of general management.

During the Review, the Prime Minister decided to split the DHSS into two and to move the Secretary of State, John Moore, to the Department of Social Security. This decision was prompted by the difficulty experienced by Moore in managing one of the biggest government departments, and the need to ensure that health issues received the undivided attention of a senior minister at a time of critical importance for the government. Before his departure, Moore indicated that he intended to pursue a path of evolutionary reform, and this was reinforced by the appointment of Kenneth Clarke as the new Secretary of State for Health. Clarke took up his post in July 1988, and he played a major part in the preparation of the White Paper, *Working for Patients*, which was published in January 1989 (Secretary of State for Health and others, 1989a).

Working for Patients

In the White Paper, the government announced that the basic principles on which the NHS was founded would be preserved. Funding would continue to be provided mainly out of taxation and there were no proposals to extend patient charges. Tax relief on private insurance premiums was to be made available to those aged over 60, apparently at the Prime Minister's insistence

(Lawson, 1992), but the significance of this was more symbolic than real. For the vast majority of the population, access to health care was to be based on need and not ability to pay. The main changes in the White Paper concerned the delivery of health services. These changes were intended to create the conditions for competition between hospitals and other service providers, through the separation of purchaser and provider responsibilities and the establishment of self-governing NHS trusts and GP fundholders.

As well as these changes, the White Paper aimed to strengthen management arrangements. In the new Department of Health (DH), this was to be achieved by appointing a Policy Board and NHS Management Executive in place of the Supervisory Board and NHS Management Board. At a local level, the composition of health authorities was to be revised along business lines. Managers would sit as members of authorities for the first time and would be joined by a small number of non-executive directors appointed for their personal contribution and not because they were drawn from designated organisations. Similar changes were planned for the family practitioner services, involving the replacement of Family Practitioner Committees by Family Health Services Authorities (FHSAs).

Another important aim of the White Paper was to make doctors more accountable for their performance. In part, this was to be achieved by general managers playing a bigger part in the management of clinical activity. This included participating in the appointment of consultants, in drawing up job plans for each consultant, and in deciding which consultants should receive distinction awards (increases in salary intended to reward clinical excellence). In addition, new disciplinary procedures would be introduced for hospital doctors to enable disciplinary matters to be dealt with expeditiously. Considerable emphasis was also placed on the involvement of doctors and nurses in management through an extension of the resource management initiative, and on making medical audit a routine part of clinical work in both general practice and hospitals.

The reform of primary care and community care

In parallel with the Review, the government developed equally far reaching proposals for the future of primary care and community care. The primary care changes stemmed from a consultative document issued in 1986 and a White Paper, *Promoting Better Health,* published in 1987 (Secretary of State for Social Services and others, 1987). The stated aims of the changes were to raise standards of health and health care, to place greater emphasis on health promotion and disease prevention, and to offer wider choice and information to patients. A key element in the changes was the introduction of new contracts for GPs and dentists.

The contract for GPs, which was published at the same time as *Working for Patients,* included provision for health checks for new patients, three-yearly checks for patients not otherwise seen by a GP, and annual checks of patients aged 75 or over. In addition, targets were set for vaccination, immunisation and cervical cancer screening, encouragement was given to the development of health promotion clinics and the provision of minor surgery, and GPs were expected to become more closely involved in child health surveillance. Other features of the new GP contract included extra payments for doctors practising in deprived areas, additional money to employ practice staff and improve practice premises, and a request that practices produce an annual report and information leaflets for patients. The procedure through which patients change their doctors was also simplified. Overall, the proportion of a GP's income that derives from capitation payments was increased from 46 per cent to 60 per cent. This was designed to act as an incentive to GPs to provide services demanded by patients. The new contract came into operation in April 1990.

In the case of family dentists, the new contract emphasised the need for dental care to include preventative work as well as restorative treatment. Regular patients would be entitled to more information about their treatment in a treatment plan, emergency cover arrangements, and replacement of certain restorations which failed within a year. As far as children were concerned, dentists were to receive a capitation payment for each child instead of being paid by item of service for treatment given. Part of the cost of these changes was met by introducing a charge for adult dental examinations and by removing most adult eye tests from the NHS. The new contract for dentists came into operation in October 1990.

The government's plans for the future of community care were developed in response to a report prepared by Sir Roy Griffiths in 1988 (Griffiths Report, 1988). The community care White Paper, *Caring for People,* published in 1989, contained the government's proposals (Secretary of State for Health and others, 1989b) which in large part endorsed the recommendations of the Griffiths Report. Local authorities were given the lead responsibility in the planning of community care and were required to prepare community care plans in association with NHS authorities and other agencies. It was expected that local authorities would become enablers and purchasers, coordinating the provision of care in different sectors, and providing some services directly themselves. These changes went hand in hand with new funding arrangements. Under these arrangements, the income support available to people in need of assistance from public funds was be the same whether they lived at home or in voluntary or private sector residential care. In this way, it was hoped to target more effectively public support of people in residential care.

Implementing the reforms

The proposals set out in *Working for Patients* aroused strong feelings on all sides. Opposition to the government's proposals was led by the medical profession. The BMA launched a fierce campaign, and this was directed as much against the new contract for GPs as against the programme set out in the White Paper. Organisations representing patients shared many of the concerns of the medical profession as did bodies speaking for other staff groups. There was more support for the reforms from managers and health authorities, although the timetable for implementing some of the changes was widely perceived to be unrealistic. Despite opposition, the government's large majority in Parliament meant that the NHS and Community Care Bill received the Royal Assent in June 1990. The determination of the Secretary of State, Kenneth Clarke, was particularly important in this process.

In comparison with the NHS reforms, the discussion of the changes to community care provoked much less controversy. The Griffiths Report had attracted considerable support at the time of its publication and the fact that the government accepted most of the recommendations of the Report helped to smooth the process of reform. The one major concern about the changes was whether local authorities would be allocated enough money to develop adequate services in the community. This issue was complicated by the reform of local government finance with the community charge or poll tax replacing domestic rates in 1990. Mainly because of this, the government decided to delay implementation of the changes to community care until 1993.

The structure of the NHS in England as it emerged from these changes is illustrated in Figure 2.2. In the rest of the United Kingdom similar changes were implemented, although the timetable for reform in both Scotland and Northern Ireland was somewhat slower than in England and Wales. There were also detailed differences in the composition of health authorities in each country.

At the heart of the NHS reforms was a shift from an integrated system in which District Health Authorities (DHAs) both held the budget for health care and managed hospital and community health services, to a contract system in which responsibility for purchasing and provision was separated. This was achieved by the creation of entirely new organisations – self-governing NHS trusts – to manage services thereby enabling DHAs to focus on purchasing health care for the populations they served. Alongside DHAs, GP fundholders purchased a limited range of services for their patients, the budgets they received being deducted from the resources allocated to DHAs. Under these arrangements, DHAs and GP fundholders negotiated contracts with NHS trusts to provide services, and these

Figure 2.2   *The structure of the NHS in England, 1991–96*

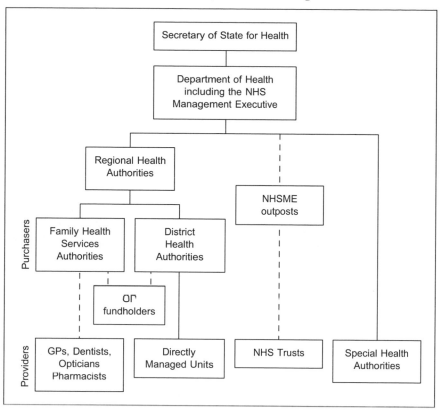

Source: Ham (1997a).

contracts (or service agreements as they were often known) specified the cost, quantity and quality of care expected by purchasers. One of the purposes of separating responsibility for purchasing and provision was to stimulate competition between providers in what was often referred to as an 'internal market'. Through competition, the Thatcher government argued that there would be a strong incentive to increase efficiency within the NHS and to enhance responsiveness to patients.

Implementation of *Working for Patients* differed from previous reorganisations in that the reformed structure was not put in place on a single appointed day. Rather, in recognition of the complexity of the changes and political anxieties about their feasibility, implementation was phased in. This was particularly apparent in the case of the two major organisational innovations contained within the reforms, NHS trusts and GP fundholders, whose numbers increased every year between 1991 and 1996 (see Table 2.2).

Table 2.2   *The implementation of GP fundholding and NHS trusts*

	NHS trusts	GP fundholders
1991	57	306
1992	99	288
1993	136	600
1994	140	800
1995	21	560
1996	–	1200

Note: Figures are for number of new entrants each year in England.

At the outset, there was some uncertainty about the degree of interest there would be in NHS trusts and fundholding in view of the strength of opposition to *Working for Patients* on the part of the medical profession. In the event, a combination of commitment by general managers, the leadership provided by the NHS Management Executive, and financial incentives that made it attractive for managers and doctors to put themselves forward meant that support for these innovations was greater than expected.

In the course of implementation, the proposals in *Working for Patients* were progressively modified to enable all NHS providers to seek trust status (not just acute hospitals with over 250 beds as the White Paper had specified) and to encourage smaller as well as bigger general practices into fundholding. These developments were possible because the broad framework set out in the White Paper omitted many of the details of how the internal market would operate in practice, and what details there were changed in the light of debate and experience. Further guidance was given in a series of working papers issued after publication of *Working for Patients,* but to a considerable extent it was left to NHS staff to make the reforms work on the ground. The contrast with the 1974 reorganisation of the NHS which derived from a highly detailed design developed by the DHSS could not have been greater.

The lack of detail reflected the speed with which *Working for Patients* was produced, the absence of any coherent proposals on the part of those involved in the Ministerial Review, and a concern to avoid more radical alternatives because of the risk of unpopularity. The consequence of these gaps in the government's thinking was an impression that Ministers and civil servants were 'making it up as they went along' (Timmins, 1995, p. 467). It also meant that managers and health service professionals were left to discover the importance of the separation of purchaser and provider roles, NHS trusts, GP fundholding and contracts in the process of implementation. In some respects, therefore, national policy was shaped by the local response as well as vice versa. To be sure, on certain issues the Department of Health did publish prescriptive guidance which appeared at odds with the emphasis on the devolution of responsibility within the internal market, but in many areas policy was made on the hoof as part of an emergent strategy (Ham, 1997a).

Alongside the phased approach to change and the emphasis on an emergent strategy, implementation was affected by the changing political context. Even before the reforms were launched in April 1991, Margaret Thatcher had had doubts about whether they would work and she asked a number of businessmen to assess the state of readiness within the NHS (Timmins, 1995). Despite their advice that the reforms were unlikely to succeed, Kenneth Clarke persuaded the Prime Minister to allow him to proceed, although with a general election imminent strenuous efforts were made to ensure that change was introduced in a planned fashion. In the code language favoured by ministers and civil servants, the emphasis was placed on a 'steady state' and a 'smooth take off' for the reforms in order to avoid hospitals running into financial difficulties as a result of the operation of the internal market in the run up to the election. The risks were perceived to be particularly great in London where purchasers had an incentive to move contracts and resources from relatively expensive teaching hospitals in inner London to providers with lower costs. Partly in anticipation of problems arising, in 1991 the government appointed Professor Sir Bernard Tomlinson to lead an inquiry into the future of health services in London and to make recommendations. Outside London these issues were handled less through Tomlinson-style inquiries than by health authorities working with each other and with providers to plan the changes in provision that the market necessitated. Whatever the preferred approach, the outcome was the same: the internal market became a *managed* market in which competition and planning went hand in hand.

By intervening to determine the future of health care in London and other areas, ministers were acknowledging the realities of a health service in which the ultimate responsibility for decisions rested with them. Yet, in so doing, they ran the risk of weakening the competitive incentives designed to drive down costs and raise standards. This applied particularly to NHS trusts whose freedoms as self-governing organisations were increasingly constrained by central guidance from the Department of Health. As one of the civil servants most closely involved in this process has observed:

> ministers and the centre are finding it difficult to reconcile devolved accountability with the demand for detailed monitoring created by parliamentary interest in operational issues. In consequence, the centre is

drawn into a whole range of issues, from hospital catering standards to the freedom of speech of hospital staff that it once expected to leave to the discretion of local management. The dilemma is that without substantial operating freedom, Trust management cannot be expected to produce a better performance than the old directly managed units, but that with such freedom there is bound to be a diversity of behaviours and performance. The existence of outliers is then seen – by the press, auditors and politicians – as a cause for central regulation. (Smee, 1995, p. 190)

In practice, market management and regulation developed in an *ad hoc* manner and it was not until the end of 1994 that national guidance was published (DH, 1994). In the event, the guidance had little influence in practice, coming too late to change ways of working that were already established and to alter the imperatives facing politicians in circumstances where providers were threatened with closure or major change of use. It was partly for this reason that ministers altered their approach to the presentation of their policies, describing them as a programme of *management reforms* and not an internal market.

The impact of the reforms

In assessing the impact of the reforms, it is as well to remember the title of the White Paper from which they derive. *Working for Patients* may have been a response to the funding problems facing the NHS at the end of the 1980s, but its declared purpose was to improve services to patients. In this it was following the lead set in the Griffiths Report on general management which was critical of the failure of the NHS to develop a customer orientation and which recommended that greater attention should be given to surveying the experience of users and making services more responsive to their needs. The emphasis on patients was maintained after John Major replaced Margaret Thatcher as Prime Minister in 1990 with the publication of the *Patient's Charter* which set out a range of rights and standards and provided the basis for the development of performance tables showing how NHS trusts compared in areas such as waiting times and cancelled operations.

In taking stock of progress in implementing the reforms, ministers maintained that increases in the number of patients treated provided a clear indication that patients were benefiting, although independent analysts pointed out that these increases were probably the result of substantial increases in funding for the NHS between 1990 and 1993 rather than due to the reforms *per se*. Ministers also used reductions in the longest waiting times for treatment to argue that the NHS was becoming more responsive. While the evidence on waiting times was stronger than that in relation to the number of patients treated, critics contended that patients waiting under a year for their operations were waiting longer to enable the government to deliver its promise in the *Patient's Charter* that no patient should wait longer than two years. Other assessments were equally inconclusive with the British Social Attitudes' survey reporting in 1994 that levels of dissatisfaction with the NHS had fallen at the same time as the Health Services Commissioner or Ombudsman criticised the record of the NHS in responding to patient complaints and argued that the more fragmented structure introduced as a consequence of the reforms had made it more difficult to coordinate the provision of care. Later evidence from the British Social Attitudes' Survey confirmed the concerns of the Health Services Commissioner with figures from 1996 indicating the highest ever level of reported dissatisfaction with the NHS (Judge, Mulligan and New, 1997).

Researchers have offered a variety of judgements on the impact of the internal market experiment. The most comprehensive early assessment detected relatively few changes in the first stages of implementation and argued that more time was needed to reach an informed judgement (Robinson and Le Grand, 1994). A more positive judgement was made by the Organisation for Economic Cooperation and Development (OECD, 1994a) which found much to commend in the changes that had been introduced, highlighting fundholding in particular as an example of success, and pointing to encouraging early results from the performance of NHS trusts. These conclusions were challenged by Bloor and Maynard (1994) who pointed to the inadequacies of the evidence on which they were based. In a separate review, Maynard and Bloor (1996) argued that the success of the reforms had been mixed, a view supported by Klein (1995) in his assessment.

Studies by economists underline the difficulty of demonstrating productivity or efficiency gains as a consequence of the internal market. For example, Soderlund and colleagues concluded that competition between hospitals had no significant effect on productivity (Soderlund *et al.*, 1997), whereas Propper (1996) found some evidence that the degree of competition was related to the prices charged by trusts. In a later analysis, Propper and colleagues examined the impact of competition on the quality of care (Propper, Burgess and Gossage, 2003). Using data on hospital death rates after heart attack within 30 days of admission, this analysis reported that hospitals in competitive areas had poorer outcomes than hospitals in areas with little or no competition. Propper and colleagues qualified this finding by noting that competition may have had other beneficial effects, and they cautioned against using data from only one area of service provision to draw overall conclusions about the impact of markets in health care.

The most thorough analysis of the evidence to date concluded that overall little change – positive or negative – could be detected (Le Grand, Mays and Mulligan, 1998). This analysis systematically reviewed the findings from a large number of research studies, seeking to assess the impact of the reforms under five broad headings: efficiency, equity, quality, choice and responsiveness and accountability. Like other researchers, these authors emphasised the difficulty of separating the effects of the reforms from other changes in policy occurring at the same time and from increases in NHS funding. Given this caveat, they noted some evidence of improvements in efficiency, indications that equity was affected adversely by the differential access achieved by GP fundholders, no evidence that trust status had an impact on quality, minimal change to choice and responsiveness, and no real difference in accountability arrangements. The main explanation of these findings offered by these authors is that the incentives contained within the internal market were too weak. Le Grand and colleagues emphasised that their analysis was concerned primarily with *measurable* change, and they added that there was some evidence of cultural change as a result of the reforms which may not have been adequately captured in the research studies they reviewed.

In relation to cultural change, the findings of Ferlie and colleagues lend support to the argument that *Working for Patients* did have an impact on roles and relationships within the NHS (Ferlie *et al.*, 1996). Among the changes reported by these researchers was a reorientation of hospital specialists towards GPs and some evidence that the influence of managers and of clinicians in management roles was increasing. These findings echo the author's own assessment based both on research into the reforms and experience of working with a wide range of NHS bodies throughout this period (Ham 1996 and 1997a). What this indicated was that the traditional influence of providers, especially those located in acute hospitals, was challenged by health authorities in their new purchasing role and by GP fundholders. As a consequence, more attention was given to public health issues, a development that was reinforced by the publication of a national health strategy for England (see Chapter 4). Primary care also received higher priority as health authorities and fundholders undertook a reassessment of established expenditure patterns. This included GPs offering extra services in their practices and in some cases hospital specialists seeing patients in the community on an outreach basis. The impact on resource allocation may have been at the margins (Klein, Day and Redmayne, 1996) but the change in behaviour and culture was nevertheless tangible. The cause of this was less the operation of the internal market, which as we have seen was tightly constrained, than the reorientation of purchasers to populations and patients. Put another way, the separation of purchaser and provider responsibilities altered the organisational politics of the NHS leading to changes in the balance of power both within the medical profession and between doctors and managers.

Streamlining the structure

As implementation of the reforms progressed, it became apparent that a contract-based system was more expensive to administer than the integrated system it replaced. The scale of increase in management costs was difficult to quantify with precision, although one estimate suggested that the reforms had resulted in an additional expenditure of £1.5 billion on management. Much of this increase derived from the need to employ staff to negotiate and monitor contracts and to supply information to purchasers and providers. Ministers responded by establishing a review of functions and manpower in 1992 which started as an examination of the respective roles of Regional Health Authorities (RHAs) and NHS Management Executive regional outposts in England, but turned into a comprehensive assessment of management arrangements at all levels. This became necessary because, in the spirit of an emergent strategy, it was clear that the structure of the NHS was no longer in tune with the requirements of the reforms.

The outcome was a decision to merge the functions of RHAs and the regional outposts in eight regional offices of the renamed NHS Executive. In addition, the roles of District Health Authorities and Family Health Services Authorities were combined in unified health authorities and action was taken to reduce management costs. Taken together, these changes amounted to nothing less than a further reorganisation of the NHS, and the new structure is illustrated in Figure 2.3. Subsequently, an efficiency scrutiny set out a number of ways in which paperwork and regulation could be reduced, including moving towards longer-term contracts or service agreements (NHS Executive, 1996). In making this proposal, the scrutiny was reflecting developments already occurring within the NHS, illustrating once again the extent to which national policy was shaped during the course of implementation.

To return to the starting point of this chapter, the reorganisation of the NHS that took place in 1996 and the organic nature of the reforms lend support to Webster's observation that developments in health policy under Margaret Thatcher and John Major involved a continuous revolution. Yet, unlike Webster, it is not necessary to subscribe to the view that ideological imperatives were the main driving force (1998, pp. 142–8) behind the reforms to explain what happened. As Klein (1995, p. 176) has suggested, there are many different ways of telling the story of *Working for Patients*

Figure 2.3   *The structure of the NHS in England, 1996–99*

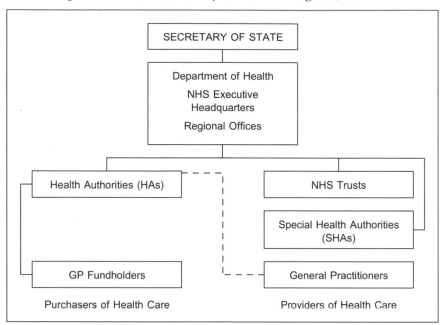

Source: NHSE.

and its aftermath, ranging from a response to the changing state of the economy to an exercise in policy learning. All versions of the story put politicians at the heart of the reform of the NHS, but other influences were also at work. What is clear is that the evolution of health policy in the 1980s and 1990s sheds further light on the dynamics of the policy process and in the conclusion we draw out the main lessons.

Conclusion

In this chapter we have seen how changes in the economic context in which the NHS functions and in political debate exerted a significant influence on health policy. The election of a Conservative government under Margaret Thatcher and the adoption by the government of policies to control public expenditure and achieve greater efficiency in public services led to radical reforms to the NHS. The incremental pattern of policy development that dominated the first 30 years of the NHS was replaced by the implementation of changes that were neither the product of political consensus nor the outcome of bargaining between government and pressure groups. This is a reminder of the need to seek explanations of the development of health policy beyond the health sector, a theme we return to in later chapters.

One of the most striking observations on health policy in this period is that a government with a parliamentary majority was able to drive through changes in the face of strong opposition. This testifies to the power of the executive in the British system of government and shows that even unpopular policies can be promulgated if the government has the political will to do so. The involvement of Prime Minister Thatcher in the most radical of these policies undoubtedly contributed to this as did her adherence to the school of conviction politics. Yet Margaret Thatcher was not alone in this regard as the determination of Kenneth Clarke to face down the medical profession amply demonstrated. To this extent, health policy during the 1980s and 1990s showed that ministers matter and make a difference.

The corollary is that the power of even the most well-placed pressure groups may not always be sufficient to defeat proposals put forward by ministers. This lesson emerges not just from the failure of the BMA and other groups to stop the government proceeding with the implementation of *Working for Patients,* but also from the inability of doctors to prevent the imposition of a new contract for GPs in 1990. In both instances, ministers overcame resistance to their policies and were not afraid to risk unpopularity in the process. The established rules of conduct in the health policy community were suspended (although not abandoned), and in place of bargaining and negotiation with key groups ministers decided among themselves what they wanted to do and acted accordingly. Notwithstanding this, pressure groups were closely involved in the implementation of policy and on many issues apart from *Working for Patients* and the new contract for GPs they continued to exert influence.

Finally, it is clear that the implementation of policy feeds back into policy-making, making it difficult to draw hard and fast distinctions between these activities. This is particularly evident from experience in the 1990s when doctors and managers in the NHS shaped the implementation of *Working for Patients* and in so doing influenced how national policy itself developed. A number of examples of this have been identified in this chapter, indicating how the broad framework set out in *Working for Patients* was adapted and refined in practice. In this respect, the impact of political ideology was modified by managerial pragmatism and judgement of what was likely to be acceptable to the public and the health professions. And as we note in later chapters, the need to secure the cooperation of the medical profession to ensure effective implementation of policy meant that the BMA was excluded from the corridors of power for only a short period.

Chapter 3

New Labour and the NHS

The election of a Labour government under Tony Blair in 1997 brought to an end 18 years of Conservative government under Margaret Thatcher and John Major and appeared to offer the prospect of a return to quieter times for the NHS. In practice, this was not to be as the Blair government developed its own policies for the modernisation of the NHS and in the process published proposals which were just as radical as those contained in *Working for Patients*. These proposals centred on what ministers described as a 'third way' of reform, different from both the internal market of the Thatcher government and the application of centralised planning by previous Labour governments. The aim of this chapter is to analyse this third way and to explore its evolution.

The inheritance

The way in which successive Conservative Health Ministers changed the language used to present their reforms by placing less emphasis on competition was noted in the previous chapter. This change was initiated as early as 1991 when the Secretary of State for Health, William Waldegrave, explained in an interview that the NHS market:

> isn't a market in a real sense ... it's competition in the sense that there will be comparative information available. It's not a market in that people don't go bust and make profits and all that, but it's using market-like mechanisms to provide better information. (quoted in Smith, 1991, p. 712)

Waldegrave's comments were echoed by his successor Virginia Bottomley in a 1995 speech reviewing the development of the reforms. Like Waldegrave, Bottomley emphasised the importance of competition by comparison and she argued for:

> [a] long-term and strategic view. A great deal can and will be achieved through the purchaser/provider system. As that relationship matures, I want to see greater use of longer-term contracts between health authorities, fundholders and NHS Trusts ... The new NHS requires a

strategic oversight ... There are many issues ... where it is important to take a broad view. The implementation of our strategy for developing cancer services is just one example of where we shall achieve a long-term goal by working together within the framework offered by the new NHS. (Bottomley, 1995, p. 7)

Bottomley's replacement, Stephen Dorrell, also played down the role of markets in health care and focused instead on using what he described as the *management reforms* to increase efficiency and raise standards. In his view, there was a need to encourage collaboration between purchasers and providers and long-term relationships, in part because of the policy of reducing management costs. Dorrell's position was expressed most clearly in a White Paper on the NHS published in 1996, restating the government's commitment to the founding principles of the NHS, and outlining a future in which priority would be given not to the development of the market but to information and information technology, professional development and managing for quality (Secretary of State for Health, 1996). Viewed in retrospect, the White Paper was an important stepping stone between the application of market principles in the early 1990s and the explicit rejection of these principles at the end of the decade.

Yet if competition and markets were words that rarely crossed the lips of politicians, experience within the NHS was more variable. The development of partnership-working and long-term contracts evolved in parallel with continuing and in some cases increasingly competitive behaviour on the part of purchasers and providers. This was apparent in the movement of contracts by purchasers between providers, and the efforts of NHS trusts to increase their income by attracting contracts from purchasers in the NHS and the private sector. To this extent, there was a dissonance between the policy message articulated in government, and practice within the NHS. Put another way, with the competitive genie out of the bottle, politicians experienced difficulties in squeezing it back in, at least in those parts of the NHS where there was both scope for competition and an inclination to use the levers that had been introduced to bring about improvements in performance.

With competition out of favour among Ministers, a new policy agenda began to emerge in the latter stages of the Major government. This owed less to a belief in market forces than a desire to use the organisational changes brought about by *Working for Patients* to achieve other objectives. Specifically, the separation of purchaser and provider roles refocused attention on the public health agenda as health authorities developed strategies for meeting the needs of the populations they served in line with the national health strategy published by the government (see Chapter 4). There was also increasing interest in primary care as the shift in the balance of power that resulted from *Working for Patients* turned the spotlight on services in the community and ways in which these services might be strengthened. The other main strand in the new policy agenda was the establishment of a research and development programme for the NHS, including the encouragement given within the programme to evidence-based health care. None of these policies was in place at the time *Working for Patients* was published, but all rose to prominence as a consequence of the reforms.

The emphasis placed on public health, primary care and evidence-based health care and the shift away from competition had the effect of narrowing the differences between the Thatcher government and the Labour Party. In reality, the common ground between the Conservatives and Labour became larger as a result of movement on both sides. From a position of outright opposition to the internal market in 1989, the Labour Party came to acknowledge that there had been some benefits from the changes contained within *Working for Patients* while promising to reverse those elements of the changes which it disliked. This pragmatic approach was evident in the first restatement of Labour's policy published in 1995, *Renewing the NHS* (Labour Party, 1995), which accepted the value of the separation of purchaser and provider responsibilities, although as a means of ensuring that providers were held to account for their performance rather than a vehicle for promoting competition. *Renewing the NHS* also proposed to abolish GP fundholding because of its expense and inequity and to replace it with a system of GP commissioning. And, consistent with developments already taking place, Labour announced that annual contracts would be replaced by longer-term comprehensive health care agreements.

The willingness of the Labour party to accept some of the policies initiated by its political opponents was symptomatic of the changes to Labour's approach that occurred throughout the 1990s. Having lost four general elections in succession, the Labour party undertook a fundamental review of its programme and developed a series of proposals in different areas of public policy designed to make it more attractive to the electorate. These proposals drew on the philosophy of leaders like Tony Blair and were distinctive both in the acceptance that some of the changes made under the Thatcher and Major governments should be supported and in the rejection of policies associated with what became known as old Labour. This helps to explain why the election of the Blair government in 1997 did not entail a return to the *status quo ante*, but rather a further period of reform in which the organisation of the NHS was altered yet again. Put another way, health policy in the late 1990s was shaped by the changing face of British politics with developments in the NHS paralleling changes made in other sectors such as education and social care.

The New NHS

On its arrival in office the Blair government had developed the outlines of its approach to the NHS but this approach was much stronger in relation to the principles that should guide change than the detail of how to convert these principles into practice. It was also the case that the new government was clearer about what it was opposed to – the fragmentation of the NHS market – than what it was for. The government's position reflected frequent changes among Labour Party shadow health ministers and continuing internal debates between the modernisers who were willing to accept some of the changes initiated by the Thatcher government and the traditionalists who were much more sceptical and whose influence was still important. The appointment of a traditionalist, Frank Dobson, as Secretary of State for Health, and a moderniser, Alan Milburn, as Minister of State, had the effect of internalising this debate within the Department of Health.

The first six months of the new government were therefore taken up with elaboration of the policy position articulated by the Labour party in opposition, and it was not until December 1997 that the government's proposals were published. The White Paper setting out these proposals, *The New NHS*, identified six principles behind the government's plans:

- to renew the NHS as a genuinely national service;
- to make the delivery of health care against these new national standards a matter of local responsibility;
- to get the NHS to work in partnership;
- to drive efficiency through a more rigorous approach to performance and by cutting bureaucracy;
- to shift the focus onto quality of care so that excellence is guaranteed to all patients;
- to rebuild public confidence in the NHS.

The White Paper went on to state:

> In paving the way for the new NHS the Government is committed to building on what has worked but discarding what has failed. There will be no return to the old centralised command and control system of the 1970s ... But nor will there be a continuation of the divisive internal market system of the 1990s ... Instead there will be a 'third way' of running the NHS – a system based on partnership and driven by performance. (Secretary of State for Health, 1997, p. 10)

This statement and others in the White Paper indicated that the Blair government was at pains to distance itself from both Conservative policies towards the NHS and the approach of previous Labour governments. In this respect, developments in health policy mirrored those across government as a whole, with 'new Labour' seeking to carve out a niche in the marketplace of political ideas that was both distinctive and electorally attractive. The 'third way' was used to describe the position.

The central and recurrent description of the government's stance in *The New NHS* White Paper was 'new', with the modernisation of the NHS identified as the main objective. Ministers emphasised that they were adopting a pragmatic approach based on the belief that 'what counts is what works' (p. 11). It was for this reason that the White Paper included a commitment to retain what it described as 'the separation between the planning of hospital care and its provision' (p. 12) as well as the decentralisation of responsibility for operational management to NHS trusts and the priority attached to primary care. Indeed, in relation to primary care, the government announced that while fundholding *per se* would be abolished, it wanted to extend the principles of fundholding to all family doctors and community nurses through a system of primary care groups (PCGs). Equally important, the White Paper included a clear commitment to bring an end to what was left of the market and to promote collaboration and partnership. In this sense it was seeking to 'go with the grain' (p. 11) of developments already under way, for example by moving towards longer-term service agreements and further reducing the paperwork and bureaucracy associated with annual contracting.

The Blair government's approach was eclectic as well as being pragmatic. Whereas the Thatcher government's reforms were based on a single core idea – the use of the market to improve NHS performance – the White Paper included a number of different mechanisms to increase efficiency and to enhance responsiveness (Ham, 1999). For example, there was a return to greater central involvement in the NHS in the aspiration to develop a 'one nation NHS' (p. 55), and to reduce variations in performance through the development of national service frameworks and the creation of agencies like the National Institute for Clinical Excellence. In parallel, the White Paper placed considerable emphasis on the freedom available to GPs and others in the new PCGs to make decisions on the use of resources at a local level and to bring about improvements in services for patients.

Similarly, ministers pointed out that their plans included a wide range of incentives for NHS staff to increase efficiency and raise standards alongside the use of sanctions to penalise poor performance. The incentives focused on the flexibilities available to PCGs to move resources around and to redeploy savings; the sanctions on new arrangements for visiting hospitals and other providers through the proposed Commission for Health Improvement, and the threat of intervention by ministers and civil servants in the event of performance failures. The eclectic nature of the government's approach was particularly apparent in the framework for performance management set out in the White Paper which demonstrated that in future performance would be assessed not only in relation to efficiency (the preoccupation of the Thatcher and Major governments), but also health improvement, fair access, effective delivery, patient experience and health outcome.

In putting forward these proposals, ministers explained that they represented a ten-year programme for the modernisation of the NHS. The aim was to encourage 'evolutionary change rather than organisational upheaval' (p. 5) and in the process to address weaknesses in the system the government had inherited. This entailed shifting the focus to integrated care for patients as a reaction against the fragmentation of the market, and out of a concern to promote continuity of care and collaboration between different agencies and staff. Although not primarily about the funding of the NHS, the White Paper included a commitment to continue paying for health care through taxation and to increase spending on the NHS in real terms every year. In making this commitment, the government emphasised that it expected to see 'major gains in quality and efficiency' (p. 15), including quicker and more convenient access to services through a reduction in waiting lists for treatment and the application of information technology to deliver services in different ways.

The new structure

Figure 3.1 illustrates the structure of the NHS in England as it emerged from the White Paper. The White Paper emphasised that health authorities would give strategic leadership at a local level with a particular focus on developing health improvement programmes (HImPs) in conjunction with NHS bodies, local authorities and other partner organisations. HImPs were intended to be local health strategies and a means of translating national targets for the improvement of health and health services into practice. Health authorities were also given a major role in the development and support of PCGs. This included establishing groups and helping them take on more responsibility for commissioning and service provision, thereby freeing up health authorities to concentrate on their strategic functions. PCGs were held to account by health authorities through annual accountability agreements which provided the framework for monitoring and performance review.

The number and configuration of PCGs was determined locally by health authorities in discussion with GPs and others involved in primary care, subject to the approval of regional offices. In the event, 481 groups were set up in England in April 1999 serving populations ranging from

Figure 3.1   *The structure of the NHS in England, 1999–2002*

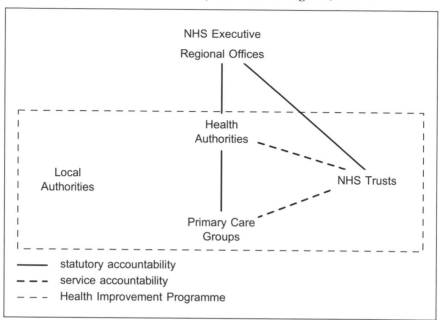

Source: Secretary of State for Health (1997).

46 000 to 257 000. Each PCG was run by a board comprising four to seven GPs, one or two community or practice nurses, one social services nominee, one lay member, one health authority non-executive, and the group's chief executive. PCG chairs were almost invariably GPs and were supported by a small management team. While membership of PCGs was a requirement for all GPs, there was flexibility over the degree of responsibility they wished to assume. All PCGs were initially established as advisory bodies and it was envisaged that over time they would take on a wider range of functions, including becoming primary care trusts accountable for commissioning care and providing community services for the population.

Guidance issued after publication of the White Paper contained further details on the functions of PCGs. Three core functions were identified:

1. To improve the health of their community by:

    • addressing the health needs of the population;
    • promoting the health of the population; and
    • working with other organisations to deliver effective and appropriate care.

2. Develop primary and community health services through:

- clinical governance to develop high quality primary and community services;
- professional development, education and training; and
- investing in improving primary care services.

3. The commissioning of secondary care services:

- over time, take on responsibility for commissioning the majority of hospital services;
- develop appropriate mechanisms and structures to commission services; and
- seek long-term investment in care by developing NHS service agreements.

NHS trusts were the other main organisations in the structure that was developed by the Blair government. While many of the responsibilities of trusts continued as before, the government underlined its expectation that trusts would work in partnership with health authorities in the spirit of collaboration that lay behind the changes. To this end, health authorities were expected to involve trusts fully in the preparation of HImPs and they were given reserve powers to ensure that capital investment and new consultant medical staffing decisions of trusts did not cut across the strategy set out in HImPs. In parallel, new statutory duties for partnership and quality were created, the latter finding expression in the emphasis placed on clinical governance. Under these duties, chief executives of trusts were held accountable for the quality of the services they provided, and the White Paper proposed that each trust should establish a sub-committee chaired by a senior clinician to lead work on quality.

It was significant that the structure set out in the White Paper included local authorities alongside NHS bodies. This reflected the concern in the government's plans to break down barriers between agencies and to encourage partnerships not only within the NHS but more widely. The consultative document on public health published early in 1998 underlined this concern with its proposal that HImPs should be the means of translating national health targets into action, and that health action zones should be established in which NHS bodies would come together with local authorities and others to tackle the root causes of ill-health and develop new ways of involving local people (Secretary of State for Health, 1998a). The consultative document also announced that the government intended to place a duty on local authorities to promote the economic, social and environmental well-being of their area.

Implementation

Taken together, these proposals amounted to a further period of radical change within the NHS. Although ministers emphasised that the proposals were to be implemented gradually over a ten-year period, the continuous revolution initiated by the Thatcher government was perpetuated under the Blair government which showed no wish to slow the process of change. A further similarity with the reforms that followed from *Working for Patients* was that *The New NHS* set out a broad framework rather than a detailed blueprint. The guidance that was issued after publication of the White Paper filled in many of the gaps but, as with the Thatcher reforms, there was scope for NHS bodies to take the framework developed by the government and adapt it in the process of implementation.

The establishment of primary care groups was the most important innovation made by the government and signalled a clear commitment to maintain the move towards a primary-care-led NHS initiated by the Conservatives. Indeed, by involving all GPs in commissioning and offering the opportunity to primary care groups to take on the management of community health services and to become primary care trusts, the government was taking the Conservatives' reforms a good deal further and was holding out the prospect of an NHS in which doctors and nurses in primary care would exercise increasing influence. The decision to give PCGs control of resources and to unify different elements in the budget, thereby allowing resources to be transferred between hospitals and the community, was particularly important, creating an incentive for as much work as possible to be done in primary care and to reduce the use of hospital services. In pursuing this approach, the government was seeking, in the words of the White Paper, to 'align clinical and financial responsibility' (p. 9), drawing on the experience of fundholding and extending this to primary care as a whole.

The proposals on public health and health improvement were also significant. Although previous governments had given priority to these issues, the commitment of the Blair government was indicated by the appointment of the first Minister for Public Health and by the focus on the role of health authorities in improving the health of the population and not just developing local health services. The decision to maintain the separation between planning and service provision was motivated by a concern to avoid health authorities being drawn into the management of services, thereby enabling them to concentrate on the public health agenda. Similarly, the proposal to give PCGs responsibility for commissioning most health services for their patients was intended to free up health authorities to assess the health needs of the populations they served and to make a reality of the national health strategy at a local level. In this sense, health authorities were expected to become public health agencies, leading the development of local health strategies and harnessing the contribution of different agencies in so doing.

As far as health services were concerned, the attention given to the quality of care in the government's plans emerged as a particularly high priority. Again, improving quality was not a new policy objective, but the combination of strong political commitment and a series of incidents which highlighted failures of performance meant that the momentum behind this objective was of a different order than under other governments. This was illustrated by publication of a document, *A First Class Service*, setting out the government's plans in detail and explaining the link between the various initiatives that had been set in train (Secretary of State for Health, 1998b). These plans centred on the establishment of clear national standards through the National Institute for Clinical Excellence and national service frameworks; the introduction of clinical governance to ensure the delivery of these standards at a local level; and the setting up of the Commission for Health Improvement to monitor delivery. The significance of these initiatives lay in recognition that self-regulation by the health professions was no longer sufficient to ensure consistently high standards, and that new mechanisms were needed to promote quality within the NHS.

One of the themes linking these changes was the concern to reduce variations in performance. The policies of the Blair government were initially designed to reduce these variations primarily by seeking to change behaviour rather than changing the structure of the NHS. Of course, structural change did occur following publication of the White Paper, but the reforms that followed immediately from *The New NHS* were unlike those that occurred in the 1974 and 1982 reorganisations when introducing a new structure was the central objective of government policy. The Blair government sought to bring about changes in behaviour through a variety of mechanisms, including new forms of regulation, the use of information to compare performance, the application of incentives, and the further development of peer review among health professionals.

It was this eclectic mixture of instruments that made up the 'third way' and that constituted new Labour's alternative to the use of competition to improve performance. In reality, notwithstanding the rhetoric of politicians, the market did not entirely disappear under the government's plans. The residue of competition was most evident in the commitment to collect and publish data on the comparative performance of providers. It was also apparent in the ability of PCGs to move services from one provider to another as a last resort if improvements in performance could not be achieved in other ways. This meant that there was still a degree of 'contestability' in the new NHS, a word used by Labour politicians to describe their plans in opposition and in government.

Integrated care

The establishment of PCGs was in many ways the cornerstone of the Blair government's policy. The rationale behind PCGs was that they would empower GPs, community nurses and others to bring about improvements in health and health services for their patients in the process of moving 'beyond fundholding'. By aligning clinical and financial responsibility in PCGs, ministers sought to create an incentive for health professionals and managers to tackle weaknesses in service provision and to overcome some of the obstacles of previous arrangements when budgets were divided into separate compartments. Of particular importance was the opportunity to move resources between hospitals and the community where this was seen to be appropriate.

PCGs also included an incentive to review variations in performance among GPs in that groups operated within a fixed budget and the decisions of GPs on prescribing, referrals and patient treatment had an impact on the PCG as a whole. Ministers were in this way establishing a mechanism intended to promote not only peer comparison and peer review, but also peer pressure to change performance where this was deemed to be unacceptable. The significance of PCGs was that action to reduce variations was to be taken by health professionals rather than by managers or politicians. Only if this failed would external regulation come into play whether through the involvement of existing bodies such as the General Medical Council and the Audit Commission, or through the intervention of newly-established institutions like the tpgoto 55
Commission for Health Improvement.

The wider significance of PCGs was that they signalled a further move towards a system of clinically managed care in which the staff in day-to-day contact with patients became the main agents of change. In this respect, there were parallels with the work of health maintenance organisations (HMOs) which have led the development of managed care in the United States. Key features of HMOs include an emphasis on the prevention of illness and the provision of information to patients to encourage self-care; the promotion of quality through the adoption of clinical guidelines and protocols; the use of nurses and other health care professionals in place of doctors where appropriate; and the encouragement given to doctors from different backgrounds to work together in networks as part of multispecialty groups.

The opportunity available to PCGs to become primary care trusts (PCTs) held out the prospect of a 'one-stop shop' model of service delivery in which all but the most highly specialised forms of care would be offered by PCTs. Not only this, but also the pilot projects initiated under the 1997 Primary Care Act (see Chapter 4) suggested that GPs in PCTs might choose to be salaried rather than independent contractors, and indeed that nurses might take on some of the functions traditionally performed by doctors. The subsequent involvement of a number of HMOs in working with PCTs underlined the interest in developing managed care techniques within the NHS. The establishment of PCGs and PCTs were examples of the Blair government's aim of developing integrated care. By bringing together the services of primary care teams and those of nurses and other staff working in the community services, and by linking the provision of care with a large measure of responsibility for commissioning, these new organisations were an attempt to overcome the fragmentation of previous arrangements.

The comprehensive spending review

The New NHS White Paper was published at the mid-point of the comprehensive spending review (CSR) initiated by the Blair government on coming into office. The purpose of the review was to take stock of public expenditure as a whole and the balance between spending programmes in the light of the government's election commitments. In advance of the completion of the review in July 1998, extra resources were allocated to the NHS to deal with winter pressures and to assist in the achievement of the targets that had been set for reducing waiting lists. But it was the CSR that provided the first real indication of the Blair government's approach to public spending in general and NHS spending in particular. The significance of the CSR was threefold. First, it resulted in education and health receiving substantial increases in expenditure at a time when lower priority was attached to other spending programmes. Second, the CSR was based on plans for three years rather than the usual period of one year. And third, the additional resources allocated by the government were intended to produce specified improvements in performance. The watch-words of the White Paper which announced the results of the CSR were 'money for modernisation' and 'investment for reform' in recognition that ministers expected public services to become more efficient, equitable and responsive as a result of the commitment made by the government (Chancellor of the Exchequer, 1998). To ensure that this happened, departments were required to negotiate public service agreements with the Treasury setting out performance targets for different services.

In the case of the NHS, the CSR led to a planned increase in expenditure of £21 billion between 1999 and 2002. This amounted to an annual increase of 4.7 per cent in real terms. The targets to be achieved with this money included the reduction of waiting lists by 100 000 to fulfil the promise made by the Prime Minister before the election. The public service agreement subsequently negotiated with the Treasury set out a range of other targets. These included objectives relating to the national health strategy, the policy of improving quality and access, and the emphasis on primary care. Consistent with the CSR and the priority attached by the Blair government to partnership working, a number of targets included a commitment to collaboration between the NHS and other agencies.

The increases in expenditure that resulted from the CSR appeared to relieve some of the pressure within the NHS. Yet on closer inspection, the priority attached to the NHS was not as impressive as first appeared, in part because the increase of £21 billion was calculated by adding together the extra spending planned over three years, and in part because pay awards made to NHS staff in 1999 eroded the value of the real-terms increase assumed in the CSR White Paper. The claim of both Conservative and Labour governments in their respective 1996 and 1997 White Papers on the future of the NHS that rationing was unnecessary and that there was no reason to believe that the NHS could not cope with the demands of demography, technology and rising expectations appeared increasingly untenable. This was underlined by the difficulty experienced by the Blair government in achieving its target of reducing waiting lists, dealing with the pressures of emergency hospital admissions during the winter months, and finding the resources to pay for new drugs and medical technologies.

These difficulties came to a head in the winter of 1999/2000 when hospitals found themselves under considerable pressure from an outbreak of flu. Media reporting of patients being forced to wait on trolleys for beds to become available brought to public attention the consequences of capacity constraints. The plight of Mavis Skeet, a patient with cancer whose operation was cancelled until the point when her condition was inoperable, came to symbolise the shortcomings of the NHS. Influential figures like Lord Winston, a Labour peer, expressed their dissatisfaction with government policies, with Winston drawing on his mother's experience of using the NHS to compare the United Kingdom unfavourably with other countries. In a television interview in January 2000 the Prime Minister made a commitment to increase spending on health care to bring it up to the average of the European Union. This commitment was reinforced by the decision in the March 2000 budget to increase NHS spending in 2000/01 by £2 billion more than the plans set out in the CSR and by around one third in real terms in five years. This decision reflected the outcome of the 2000 spending review and particularly recognition by both the Prime Mnister and the Chancellor of the Exchequer that there needed to be a sustained commitment to increase NHS funding.

The NHS Plan

In responding to its critics, the government emphasised that it would take time to improve the performance of the NHS, and work was put in hand to prepare a ten-year plan for the future of the NHS. A series of Modernisation Action Teams were set up to analyse the challenges facing the NHS and to come up with proposals for reform. The teams comprised NHS staff, patients' representatives, and people drawn from professional associations, the research community and other sectors. The results of the work of the Modernisation Action Teams were brought together with the views of Ministers and officials in the Department of Health in *The NHS Plan: a plan for investment, a plan for reform*, published in July 2000 (Secretary of State for Health, 2000). The preface to the plan set out the core principles of the NHS and contained a commitment from the leaders of twenty-five national organisations to these principles. The plan itself described how the resources made available to the NHS would be used to deliver 'a health service designed around the patient' (p. 10).

The emphasis on investment and reform in *The NHS Plan* followed from the analysis undertaken in its preparation. The results of this analysis were presented in chapter two of the plan which summarised the outcome of consultation with the public and staff. This analysis showed that both the public and staff attached high priority to more and better paid staff. For the public, reduced waiting times for treatment were important, while staff identified the need for more training and 'joined up working' with social care at community and primary care levels. In its analysis, the government highlighted the failure of the NHS to provide services centred around the needs of individual patients, notwithstanding its many achievements. This failure was attributed to an under-invested system, a lack of national standards, demarcations between staff, a lack of clear incentives, barriers between services, a lack of support and intervention, over-centralisation, and disempowered patients. The plan emphasised that the values and principles that lay behind the NHS still held good, but that its practices had to change to meet contemporary expectations.

A major theme of *The NHS Plan* was the need to increase spending on the NHS to enable capacity to be expanded. Specific commitments included the provision of 7000 extra beds in hospitals and intermediate care, over 100 new hospitals by 2010 and 500 new one-stop primary care centres, over 3000 GP premises modernised and 250 new scanners, 7500 more consultants, 2000 more GPs, 20000 extra nurses and 6500 extra therapists. *The NHS Plan* also emphasised the need for investment to be accompanied by reform. Reform was to be achieved through a new relationship between the Department of Health and the NHS in which local NHS organisations that performed well would be given more freedom to run their own affairs and a Modernisation Agency would be established to spread best practice. The Modernisation Agency would build on existing work to redesign care around patients in order to improve access and raise standards. Its main purpose was to provide advice and external expertise to NHS staff 'to support continuous service improvement' (p. 60).

The plan contained a large number of specific commitments in a wide range of areas. These included the use of additional resources to ensure that hospitals were clean and hospital food was of higher quality; improved pay for NHS staff and a commitment to improve the working lives of staff; the development of intermediate care and partnership working between the NHS and social care; new contracts for GPs and consultants; the appointment of 'modern matrons' with authority on hospital wards; and changes for patients that included more information, greater choice, and the development of a patient advocacy and liaison service. Of particular importance were the commitments to cut waiting times for treatment, including the establishment of targets to reduce maximum times for outpatient appointments to three months and inpatient treatment to six months by 2005. A waiting-time target was also set for primary care with patients being guaranteed access to a primary care professional within 24 hours and to a primary care doctor within 48 hours by 2004. These and other key objectives were brought together in the public service agreement included as an annex to the plan.

Throughout *The NHS Plan* there was reference to the need for better systems for improving performance to enable the investment of additional resources to be used to good effect. Although no longer using the 'third way' rhetoric, the plan echoed the analysis in *The New NHS* white paper in noting the weakness of the internal market and of the 'top down government model' (p. 57). In place of these approaches, a new delivery model was outlined in which the Department of Health would set national standards and put in place a framework to support delivery of those standards. Arrangements for inspection through the Commission for Health Improvement would be strengthened and the performance of NHS organisations would be assessed and made public. High performing organisations would be rewarded with extra funding and greater autonomy. Failing organisations would be given additional support and would be subject to a rising scale of interventions. The Department of Health would change its role to support these developments.

The NHS Plan can be seen both as a restatement of new Labour's commitment to the NHS, and as a declaration of its determination to reform the service to overcome the weaknesses that had brought it back into the public gaze. The involvement of stakeholders in the development of the plan, and their support for the core principles on which it was based, was designed to create a coalition to support implementation, although this did not prevent critics expressing scepticism about whether the commitments contained in the plan could be delivered. In particular, it was argued that the NHS was based on an outdated structure – the postwar nationalised model – that had been superseded in other sectors, and was unlikely to work in health care even with additional investment accompanied by reform. For its part, the government argued that a long-term commitment to increase NHS funding, at levels not achieved in the past, would enable the consequences of under-investment to be addressed, provided that staff were willing to embrace reform. In making this case, ministers emphasised that the changes taking place in the NHS were consistent with the principles of public service reform articulated by the prime minister, and applied in other sectors such as education, policing and social care.

Shifting the Balance of Power

Further detail on the new relationship between the Department of Health (DH) and the NHS emerged in 2001 as part of an initiative known as *Shifting the Balance of Power* (DH, 2001a). This initiative was intended to move power and control over budgets to front-line staff and patients. At the heart of the change was the decision to establish primary care trusts (PCTs) throughout the NHS, reduce the number of health authorities from 95 to 28, and replace the eight regional offices of the DH with four Directorates of Health and Social Care. As part of these developments, the NHS Executive within the DH lost its separate identity as part of a programme to streamline the work of the Department under the leadership of a combined permanent secretary and NHS chief executive.

The new structure of the NHS in England came into effect in 2002 and is illustrated in Figure 3.2. The aim was to give PCTs control over 75 per cent of the NHS budget by 2004 in an effort to ensure that staff in close contact with patients were able to influence how resources were used. This initiative was consistent with the approach set out in *The New NHS* White Paper in 1997 but took the development of PCTs further and faster than had been anticipated. The decision to reduce the number of health authorities, focus their role on strategic issues and replace regional offices was intended to enable PCTs to assume greater responsibility for commissioning and service provision. One of the consequences was a period of further structural upheaval at a time when the NHS was in the early stages of implementing *The NHS Plan*.

Figure 3.2   *The structure of the NHS in England after 2002*

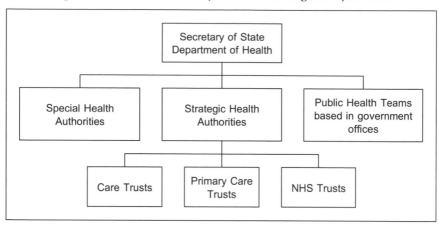

NHS trusts were not directly affected by these developments but their future was brought into question by the announcement early in 2002 of plans to create NHS Foundation Trusts. The original intention behind NHS Foundation Trusts was to give high performing NHS trusts the opportunity to manage their services with less interference from the DH and with greater involvement of local communities, staff and other stakeholders. In the event, the government announced that all NHS trusts were expected to become NHS Foundation Trusts in time and a programme for improving performance in the NHS was put together to enable this to happen. Even more importantly, ministers decided to establish NHS Foundation Trusts as public benefit corporations overseen by a new regulator rather than line managed by the DH. The freedoms available to NHS Foundation Trusts were more circumscribed than had been planned by health ministers, largely because of objections by the Treasury, but nevertheless they represented potentially the most radical organisational innovation in the history of the NHS since its inception.

Delivering the NHS Plan

The significance of NHS Foundation Trusts became clear on publication of *Delivering the NHS Plan* in April 2002. (Secretary of State for Health, 2002). *Delivering the NHS Plan* was issued at the time of the 2002 budget and it described how the new relationship between the DH and the NHS was expected to evolve. The main new elements in *Delivering the NHS*

Plan were the emphasis on patient choice and the commitment to develop greater plurality of provision. Although patient choice had been mentioned in *The NHS Plan*, it was now identified as a key priority in the reform of the NHS. *Delivering the NHS Plan* invoked experience in Sweden and Denmark to support the argument that choice for patients could be delivered in a tax-funded system. Patient choice was to be supported by a new system of payment by results under which hospitals were to be funded on the basis of the work they undertook.

The policy of developing greater plurality of provision was also foreshadowed in *The NHS Plan* but was taken further in *Delivering the NHS Plan*. The latter document included commitments to maximise the use of spare capacity in private hospitals, bring in overseas clinical teams to establish services for the NHS, and develop new public–private partnerships to support the rapid development of diagnostic and treatment centres. Proposals to establish NHS Foundation Trusts included in *Delivering the NHS Plan* (described in the document as NHS Foundation Hospitals) were consistent with the policy of developing greater plurality of provision, and with the drive to shift the balance of power to the front line.

The April 2002 budget was the occasion on which the Chancellor of the Exchequer announced the outcome of the spending review for 2002. The NHS was one of the principal beneficiaries of the spending review, securing increases in funding of over 7 per cent per year in real terms between 2002/03 and 2007/08 as a result of the Wanless Review (see Chapter 4). The plans announced in the budget envisaged expenditure on the NHS in England increasing from £56 million to £90 million over this period. The 2002 spending review was particularly important in making a commitment to increase funding over five years compared with the three year planning period covered in previous spending reviews. And unusually for a budget, taxes were raised to pay for these spending increases.

A return to the market?

Taken together, the policies set out in *Delivering the NHS Plan* were similar in a number of respects to those that lay behind the internal market. This was particularly apparent in the emphasis placed on patient choice, the system of payment by results in which money would follow patients to providers, and the commitment to establish NHS Foundation Trusts. As in the 1990s, these policies were intended to create stronger incentives to improve performance and to ensure that the NHS really did work for patients. A further similarity was the willingness to use the private sector and to develop new forms of public–private partnerships. The approach displayed in *Delivering the NHS Plan* in this area signalled a marked departure from new Labour's early period in office when the NHS was actively discouraged from working with the private sector. As such, it represented a triumph for the modernisers over the traditionalists, exemplified by the opposition of the former Secretary of State for Health, Frank Dobson, to the policies developed by his former junior minister and successor, Alan Milburn.

At the same time, there were important differences between the policies set out in *Delivering the NHS Plan* and the internal market. To begin with, patient choice, provider diversity and payment by results were introduced in a context in which NHS funding was increasing at a much faster rate than in the 1990s. In addition, the government had started the process of establishing national standards for the NHS through national service frameworks and National Institute for Clinical Excellence guidance, and it had established an independent mechanism for inspecting providers in the form of the Commission for Health Improvement. These differences meant hospitals were seeking to increase their share of a rapidly rising budget rather than competing in a zero sum game, and they were doing so in an environment where there were safeguards against quality of care being sacrificed as a result of competition. And unlike in the internal market where there was price competition, under the payment by results system the aim was to reimburse hospitals according to a fixed tariff modelled on experience in countries where case mix funding was well developed.

Having made these points, there is no doubt that the wheel had turned, if not full circle, then at least part of the way back to new Labour's 1997 inheritance. The reason for this has to be sought in the limited impact of the policies set out in *The New NHS* White Paper in the first two years of implementation and the recognition in government that other approaches were needed to produce improvements in performance. This did not entail abandoning the commitment to develop PCTs, a more explicit approach to improving quality, and a systematic framework of national standards and inspection. Rather, it meant supplementing these instruments through greater plurality of provision and patient choice. These policies were adopted in response to the weaknesses of attempts to run the NHS on a centralised basis, and reflected recognition that more emphasis needed to be given to incentives and contestability than had been appreciated in the early phases of new Labour's tenure in government. A further influence was the competition for political ideas with the government pre-empting some of the policies advocated by opposition parties.

Viewed in the wider context, *The NHS Plan* and *Delivering the NHS Plan* can be seen as an attempt to move the NHS from a hierarchically managed to a regulated health care system. It was this that lay behind the commitment in *The NHS Plan* to develop a new relationship between the DH and the NHS. At the heart of this relationship was devolution of power to PCTs and to clinical teams; a more limited role for the Department centred on setting priorities and promulgating standards; and an increasing role for the Commission for Health Improvement in inspecting providers and improving quality. One of the changes heralded in *Delivering the NHS Plan* was the establishment of a new Commission for Healthcare Audit and Inspection (known as the Healthcare Commission) with responsibility for inspecting both the public and private health care sectors, and this symbolised the greater emphasis placed on regulation.

One of the drivers of these changes was the high political cost involved in running the NHS as a centralised system. With accountability for NHS performance residing with the Secretary of State, responsibility for failures as well as credit for successes gravitated towards a single point in the system. In an era of ever closer media scrutiny of the NHS, the imperatives confronting the government of the day to respond to reports of performance failures grew stronger, even if the ability of government to address the causes of these failures remained limited. And with NHS staff complaining about the adverse consequences of micro management by government, ministers had a strong incentive to find a way of devolving as much responsibility as possible within the NHS, thereby distancing themselves from matters over which in practice they had little control. Strengthening the role of inspectors and placing more emphasis on regulation were a logical consequence of these developments.

As a final comment, it is worth emphasising that in the debate between Labour's modernisers and traditionalists, the Chancellor of the Exchequer occupied an ambiguous position. Treasury concerns about NHS Foundation Trusts mean that the radicalism of the DH had to be modified to enable this policy to be pursued. The concerns of the Treasury found expression in a major speech by the Chancellor in which he argued the case for competition as the engine to drive economic prosperity, while emphasising the limits to markets in areas like education and health care (Brown, 2003). Yet in noting the weaknesses of markets in health care, he also gave support to policies designed to decentralise power in the NHS and promote contestability between providers. This included endorsement of the policies set out in *Delivering the NHS Plan*. While the Chancellor's speech seemed to indicate that differences within government on the direction of reform were directed at the detail rather than the principle of reform, in practice there were lingering suspicions that the occupants of the Treasury remained to be convinced that greater patient choice and plurality of provision could be reconciled with equity and other established NHS values.

The impact of the reforms

Various assessments of the impact of new Labour's health policies have been offered. One of earliest was the review of the Blair government's first five years in office prepared by the King's Fund (Appleby and Coote, 2002). The authors of this review identified a number of achievements, including the government's continued commitment to tax financing and the allocation of additional resources to the NHS. They also offered a positive verdict on the development of national service frameworks and the establishment of the Commission for Health Improvement. In the King's Fund's view, the government had managed to achieve closer integration of health and social care, and had succeeded in putting health inequalities on the policy map. Against these achievements, a number of failures were identified. These included the early focus on cutting waiting lists rather than waiting times, the over-emphasis on stuctural change, and weaknesses in the implementation of policy. Overall, the review concluded that 'the direction of travel seems to us to be well judged and much of the detail is admirable. More credit is due than is currently paid' (Appleby and Coote, 2002, p. 7).

A broadly similar judgement was reached by two government audit bodies, the Audit Commission and the Commission for Health Improvement, in reviews published in 2003. In its assessment, the Audit Commission focused particularly on the implementation of *The NHS Plan*, drawing on the views of local auditors in its review of progress (Audit Commission, 2003). The Audit Commission reported that there had been significant progress in some areas, particularly the reduction of inpatient and outpatient waiting times. At the same time, it noted that there were some major challenges confronting the NHS, including implementation of national service frameworks for older people and mental health. For its part, the Commission for Health Improvement (CHI) judged that the performance of the NHS was improving, while also noting that improvement was often limited to particular areas or services (CHI, 2003). The main issues of concern to CHI included staff shortages in some areas, the continuation of mixed sex wards, and the lack of time for staff learning. CHI also highlighted the importance of leadership in NHS organisations and the need in particular to strengthen medical leadership.

The most comprehensive and independent assessment of the government's record was the review funded by the Nuffield Trust (Leatherman and Sutherland, 2003). This review was presented as a mid-term evaluation of the ten-year quality agenda. Like the other reviews summarised above, the Nuffield Trust's analysis noted achievements as well as challenges. In particular, it gave the government credit for embarking on a comprehensive and ambitious programme of quality improvement and summarised a range of evidence to support its judgement that progress had been made. The challenges highlighted in the review included problems of data quality and the lack of coordination of different initiatives. In summary, Leatherman and Sutherland concluded:

> Qualitative and quantitative data indicate that mid-term overall performance is trending in the right direction, most particularly in those areas on which attention and effort has been focused by policy mandates, performance-reporting requirements and extrinsic incentives. Legislation, increased NHS funding, new organisational capacity, regulatory structures and targeted quality-improvement interventions appear to be demonstrating some generalised salutary effect. However, although quality data indicates improvement, there is no assurance of forward momentum. The Government's ambitious aims will not be met easily (Leatherman, and Sutherland, 2003, p. 265).

Conclusion

In this chapter we have described the policies of the Blair government towards the NHS. In the process we have noted the strong element of continuity between the latter stages of the Conservative government and the approach pursued by the new Labour government. There were of course differences between politicians but these were much less significant than might have been expected in view of the debate that took place on *Working for Patients* a decade earlier. Continuity was born out of convergence which resulted from movement on both sides. The third way pursued by the Blair government incorporated important elements of the reforms initiated by the Thatcher and Major governments and was facilitated by the retreat on the part of Conservative politicians from the pro-market policies of the early 1990s. It also illustrated the extent of the change that had occurred within the Labour Party itself involving the development of policies to modernise public services as a whole and not just the NHS.

To this extent, the evolution of health policy in the 1990s indicates the influence of learning in the policy process. On the one hand, Conservative ministers adjusted course in the light of experience and feedback on what was working (and what was acceptable) and what was not working in the implementation of *Working for Patients*. On the other hand, Labour politicians were willing to take a pragmatic approach, emphasising that 'what counts is what works' and avoiding the temptation to engage in knee-jerk opposition to policies initiated by their opponents. The scope for learning extended to the implementation of *The New NHS* which like

Working for Patients provided a broad framework only and offered the opportunity for policy to be shaped and remade as it was carried into action.

To make this point is to underline the argument of Heclo (1974) and others that policy-making is both an arena in which there is bargaining between different interests and a focus for puzzling about ways of tackling social problems. The balance between bargaining and puzzling varies between issues and over time. In the case of health policy in Britain the political struggles of the late 1980s and early 1990s gave way to a greater degree of analysis and reflection as the decade wore on. To be sure, there remained disagreements between the government and pressure groups about the detail of policy and to some degree the direction of change, but after the sound and fury that greeted *Working for Patients* these disagreements were relatively unimportant. Having emphasised the politics of policy-making in the previous chapter, the focus on learning in this chapter draws attention to another important aspect of the policy process.

While the changes to the organisation of the NHS initiated by the Blair government were being implemented, the debate about NHS funding and rationing simmered in the background. This debate was not new but it assumed particular intensity in this period as the ability of the NHS to continue providing universal and comprehensive services came under scrutiny. To understand the context of this debate we now go on to review long-term trends in the funding of the NHS and the way in which rationing occurs.

Chapter 4

Funding Health Services and Setting Priorities

The aim of this chapter is to describe key issues in the funding of health care and to review areas of current importance in health policy. The chapter begins with an analysis of trends in NHS expenditure and an assessment of the sources of funding and its distribution. This leads into a discussion of current policy issues in relation to public health, health care and social care. The chapter concludes with a review of priority-setting or rationing.

The growth of NHS expenditure

One of the assumptions made in the Beveridge Report was that expenditure on health services would decline once the backlog of ill-health which was thought to exist in the community had been eradicated by the introduction of a health service free at the point of use. This assumption turned out to be false and, far from declining, expenditure increased steadily in the years after the establishment of the NHS. As Table 4.1 shows, whereas in its first full year of operation the Service cost £437 million to run, by 2003 expenditure in the United Kingdom had risen to an estimated £74 billion. Over the same period the real cost of the NHS increased sevenfold, and the NHS share of total public expenditure rose from 11.8 per cent in 1950 to an estimated 17 per cent in 2001 (Office of Health Economics, 2003).

These increases were necessary to enable the NHS to meet the demands created by changes in demography, technology and society. Analysts of health services pointed out that there was not a fixed quantity of disease, as the idea of a backlog of ill-health implied, but rather there was potentially infinite demand (Thwaites, 1987). This was because of the greater use of services by older people and their increasing numbers in the population; the opportunities for diagnosis and treatment opened up by developments in medical technology; and the emergence of a new generation of service users with higher expectations of the standard of care to be provided. Although the importance of these factors varied from year to year and were difficult to quantify, taken together they added to

Table 4.1   *NHS expenditure in the UK, 1949–2003*

Calendar year	Total (£m)	Total NHS cost at 1949 prices (£m)
1949	437	437
1954	539	434
1959	792	528
1964	1 137	667
1969	1 733	814
1974	3 835	1 151
1979	8 855	1 255
1984	16 080	1 447
1989	25 690	1 765
1994	39 715	2 200
1999	52 264	2 518
2003 (est)	74 343	3 229

the pressures confronting the NHS and helped fuel the increase in expenditure over time. Another way of expressing this increase is shown in Figure 4.1 which illustrates the share of the gross domestic product consumed by the NHS rising from 3.5 per cent in 1949 to over 6 per cent in 2003. In the same year, total health expenditure accounted for around 7.7 per cent of gross domestic product, just below the EU average.

The size of the NHS budget is shaped by the state of the economy and government decisions on the priority to be attached to different spending programmes. High rates of growth in the 1960s and early 1970s gave way to lower increases in the late 1970s and 1980s. This change was stimulated by escalating oil prices which fuelled inflation and caused successive governments to take action to control public expenditure. One of the mechanisms used was cash limits which capped expenditure on most areas of NHS spending and imposed a strict financial discipline on those responsible for running services. The election of the Thatcher government in 1979 meant that spending continued to be tightly controlled as monetarist policies began to bite. The government gave priority to achieving economic prosperity through privatisation and competition, and social policy expenditure was subjected to close scrutiny. A strong emphasis was placed on using expenditure on public services like the NHS more efficiently, and we noted in Chapter 2 the wide range of efficiency initiatives launched during this period. The purse strings were subsequently loosened as more money was allocated to the NHS between 1990 and 1993 to ease the introduction of the proposals set out in *Working for Patients*. Growth rates were then much lower until the election of the Blair

Figure 4.1 *The cost of the NHS as a percentage of GDP, 1985–2003*

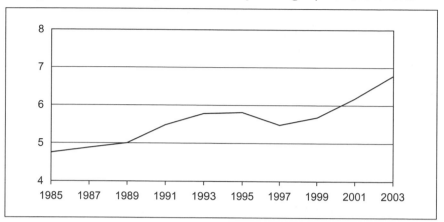

government in 1997 and the comprehensive spending review initiated by the government which from 1999 resulted in a return to higher increases (see Chapter 3).

Alongside public expenditure on health care, private spending accounts for around 18 per cent of total health care expenditure. Private expenditure is made up of the charges paid by patients for NHS prescriptions, dental care and ophthalmic services, as well as spending on services that are provided privately. The latter may be paid for out of pocket or under the terms of private medical insurance. Over 6 million people or around 11 per cent of the population are covered by private medical insurance in the United Kingdom. The number of people with insurance has increased steadily throughout the lifetime of the NHS and expansion was particularly rapid in the early 1980s. The majority of subscribers are in group schemes, especially those offered by companies as fringe benefits, and the main services provided are outpatient appointments with specialists and quicker access to non-urgent surgery than is available within the NHS. In recent years there has been a substantial growth in the numbers of people paying for private hospital treatment out of their own pocket with some estimates suggesting a threefold increase between 1997 and 2002 (Timmins, 2003), alongside reductions in the number of individuals taking out insurance.

International comparisons show that expenditure on health care in the United Kingdom as a proportion of gross domestic product is lower than in many other developed countries (OECD, 2003a). This is illustrated in Figure 4.2. Analysis of variations in health service expenditure between countries indicates that levels of spending are closely related to levels of national income and that the United Kingdom spends about what would be expected given the pattern of economic development in the postwar period. The main difference between the United Kingdom and other countries is in the composition of health service spending, with private expenditure making up a smaller proportion of the total in the United Kingdom than the average for OECD countries. This has led some commentators to argue that the funding pressures under which the NHS operates should be addressed by encouraging private expenditure to increase to the levels found elsewhere.

Whatever the merits of these arguments, it is clear that the NHS is an effective mechanism for controlling expenditure on health care. The corollary is that this may create problems, as when a series of years of expenditure constraint require staff in the NHS to cut back or delay the provision of services in order to balance their budgets. This is precisely what happened in 1987, and the funding crisis in that year forced the Thatcher government to set up its review of the NHS. These funding pressures reappeared in the late 1990s and were accompanied by debates about the rationing of health services and the denial of treatment to patients. We noted in the previous chapter the decision of the Blair government to increase NHS funding in response to these pressures and we now discuss the Wanless Review set up subsequently to examine the long term funding requirements of the NHS.

Figure 4.2   *International comparison of expenditure on health care, 2001*

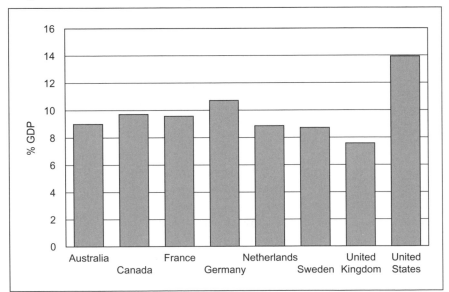

The Wanless Review

In March 2001 the Chancellor of the Exchequer, Gordon Brown, announced the establishment of a review of the long-term funding needs of health care led by Derek Wanless, former Group Chief Executive of NatWest Bank. The terms of reference of the review were:

1. To examine the technological, demographic and medical trends over the next two decades that may affect the health service in the UK as a whole.
2. In the light of (1), to identify the key factors which will determine the financial and other resources required to ensure that the NHS can provide a publicly funded, comprehensive, high quality service available on the basis of clinical need and not ability to pay.
3. To report to the Chancellor by April 2002, to allow him to consider the possible implications of this analysis for the Government's wider fiscal and economic strategies in the medium term; and to inform decisions in the next spending review in 2002. (Wanless, 2001, p. 1)

The link between the setting up of the Wanless Review and the 2002 spending review was important in signalling the intention of using the results of the work undertaken by Wanless to inform future decisions on NHS spending.

Wanless published an interim report in November 2001 as a basis for consultation. In a wide ranging analysis, the report concluded that there was no evidence that tax financing of health care should be replaced either by social insurance or private funding. In so doing, it confirmed the analysis set out in *The NHS Plan*. The interim report went on to note that the United Kingdom lagged behind some other countries in health outcomes and argued that this was in part because of the relatively low level of expenditure on health care in the United Kingdom. It identified a number of factors likely to increase spending on health care over a 20-year period including rising patient and public expectations and advances in medical technology, although the scale of the increase was not estimated. One of the issues emphasised in the report was the potential for the NHS to make better use of information and communication technology (ICT).

The final Wanless report was published in April 2002 and largely confirmed the conclusions of the interim report. The main additional points to arise from consultation on the interim report were the need for stronger links between health and social care, and for greater emphasis on health promotion and disease prevention. Unlike the interim report, the final Wanless report provided estimates of the costs of achieving its vision of a health service better able to meet the public's expectations of accessible, convenient and high quality care. These estimates were based on three alternative scenarios, described as:

> scenario 1: *solid progress* – people become more engaged in relation to their health. Life expectancy rises considerably, health status improves and people have confidence in the primary care system and use it more appropriately. The health service becomes more responsive, with high rates of technology uptake, extensive use of ICT and more efficient use of resources;
>
> scenario 2: *slow uptake* – there is no change in the level of public engagement. Life expectancy rises, but by the smallest amount in all three scenarios. The health status of the population is constant or deteriorates. The health service is relatively unresponsive with low rates of technology uptake and low productivity; and
>
> scenario 3: *fully engaged* – levels of public engagement in relation to their health are high. Life expectancy increases go beyond current forecasts, health status improves dramatically and people are confident in the health system and demand high quality care. The health service is responsive with high rates of technology uptake, particularly in relation to disease prevention. Use of resources is more efficient.
>
> (Wanless, 2002, p. 9)

Figure 4.3 displays spending estimates for these three scenarios. As the figure shows, the final Wanless report argued for higher rates of spending increases in the first five years of the period reviewed to enable the United Kingdom to *catch up* with other countries. Beyond the first five years, lower rates of spending increases were recommended to enable the United Kingdom to *keep up* with other countries. In making these recommendations, the report emphasised the importance of resources being used effectively. This included proposals for a role for the National Institute for Clinical Excellence in examining older technologies and practices that might no longer be appropriate and effective, the extension of national service frameworks to areas not already covered, and a major programme of investment in ICT based on central standards.

The final Wanless report confirmed that 'the current method of funding the NHS through taxation is relatively efficient and equitable' (p. 13) but added that 'there may be some scope to extend charges for non-clinical services. This would potentially help provide more choice for patients' (p. 13). In practice, this recommendation received relatively little attention in the context of the report's main finding that there was a need for a very substantial increase in resources for health care over the long term. This finding was accepted by the government and was reflected in the outcome of the 2002 spending review: an increase in NHS funding averaging over 7 per cent a year in real terms in the period up to 2007/08. The 2002

Figure 4.3 *Average annual real growth proposed by Wanless (percentage)*

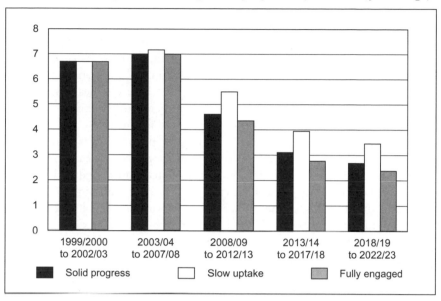

spending review also resulted in a substantial increase in social care spending. This was in part to compensate for previous spending reviews that had not benefited social care to the same extent as the NHS, and which as a consequence had contributed to the problems of discharging patients from hospital and achieving key targets.

The Wanless Review did not break new ground but it did serve an important function in making the case for a sustained increase in health care funding. In so doing, Wanless reinforced the direction set in previous spending reviews, and provided the NHS with a degree of certainty in relation to funding that was unprecedented. Although the government's critics argued that Wanless was appointed by the Chancellor to lend legitimacy to decisions already taken, the manner in which the review was conducted, including consultation with outside experts and the use of research on international experience of health care financing (Dixon and Mossialos, 2002), meant that Wanless could claim a degree of independence that an internal review could not. In any case, there was little serious dissent from the conclusion that additional resources were required, even if there remained differences as to how these resources should be raised and doubts about the ability of the government to achieve a fundamental change in the performance of the NHS. These doubts were reinforced by evidence that appeared to show declining efficiency in the NHS in the late 1990s (Le Grand, 2002) which was itself part of a broader trend affecting public services as a whole during this period.

Raising and spending money in the NHS

NHS funds come from three sources. In 2003/04, almost three-quarters of NHS funds derived from taxation, and around one-fifth were raised through national insurance contributions (DH, 2003a). The remainder came from charges and other receipts, including income from land sales and the proceeds of income generation schemes. User charges have always comprised a small proportion of total NHS expenditure and this continues to be the case, notwithstanding increases made in the 1980s and 1990s.

How is the NHS budget spent? The biggest proportion is allocated to current expenditure on hospitals, community health services and family health services. The remainder is allocated to capital expenditure on hospitals and community health services, departmental administration and central health and miscellaneous services. A more detailed breakdown of hospital and community health services current expenditure shows that the largest share of expenditure (52 per cent) goes on acute services, followed by mental health (13 per cent), services for older people (9 per cent), learning disability (5 per cent) and maternity (4 per cent). Administration comprises around 5.6 per cent of the budget (DH, 2003a, p. 67).

In the case of family health services expenditure, the biggest proportion of the budget goes on pharmaceuticals (46 per cent) followed by payments to general practitioners (31 per cent), dentists (14 per cent), pharmacists and opticians (2.5 per cent each). Another way of looking at how the money is spent is to analyse expenditure by different age groups. As Figure 4.4 shows, expenditure is particularly high at the time of birth and among older people. The rising trend of expenditure with age explains why the ageing population adds to the demands facing the NHS.

Staff salaries and wages are the largest single item of expenditure in the NHS as a whole, comprising around two-thirds of the total. Approximately 1.2 million people were employed in the NHS in 2002, and around half of these staff were professionally qualified. They included 368 000 nurses, midwives and health visitors, 73 000 hospital and public health doctors, 117 000 scientific, therapeutic and technical support staff, and 16 000 qualified ambulance staff. As well as these directly employed staff, there were around 32 000 general practitioners, 21 000 dentists, 11 000 pharmacists and 7000 opticians working as independent contractors. The number of staff working in the NHS is increasing as part of the expansion outlined in *The NHS Plan*.

While almost all of the NHS budget is allocated according to a weighted capitation formula, some resources are set aside for specific purposes. Earmarking funds in this way has been used by the Blair government to ensure that priority is given to particular services and needs. The NHS modernisation fund established by the government included money to cut

Figure 4.4   *Distribution of hospital and community health services*
expenditure by age group

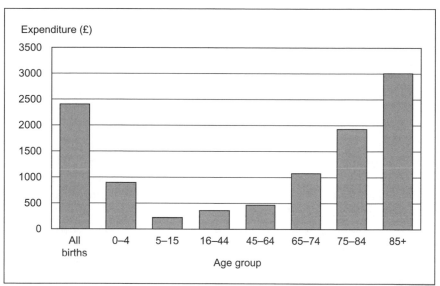

Source: DH (2003a).

waiting lists, improve primary care, develop drug advisory services, support health action zones, and invest in information technology initiatives.

NHS capital expenditure has traditionally been provided and controlled by the Treasury in the same way as current expenditure. In the first decade of the NHS, funds for capital development were limited and only on publication of the Hospital Plan in 1962 did this change. More recently, NHS trusts have been encouraged to seek resources through the private finance initiative (PFI). This is a scheme under which public sector capital projects like new hospitals are paid for via money loaned by banks. Initially, PFI was used for minor NHS schemes such as car parks and incinerators, but it is now applied to major projects including the rebuilding of entire hospitals. Private sector involvement in these projects encompasses not only the provision of capital, but also facilities management and the development of services in partnership with the NHS.

By 2002, PFI had resulted in the completion of 11 major capital schemes and work had started on site at a further 13. As well as the programme for major acute hospitals, PFI was used to support small and medium sized schemes in mental health and community health services. A sister initiative, the NHS Local Improvement Finance Trust (LIFT), was set up to support the development of public–private partnerships in relation to primary care premises. The costs and benefits of funding NHS capital developments through PFI and similar mechanisms have been widely debated.

In raising finance for hospital building from the private sector, PFI is attractive for governments seeking to limit public borrowing. On the other hand, the costs of PFI schemes have to be met through annual payments to those providing private finance, and the high level of these payments puts pressure on NHS budgets. The supporters of PFI argue that the costs of these schemes are more than offset by the speed with which they are completed and the innovation and quality that they offer. For their part, critics of PFI maintain that hospitals financed in this way may be too small to enable them to function effectively. They also contend that PFI commits the NHS to the provision of hospital-based care over the long term (typically around 30 years) when a shift should be taking place to the provision of services in the community.

The Department of Health gives guidance to the NHS on the use of resources in circulars, White Papers and related documents. Of particular importance is the guidance on planning and priorities which brings together advice from different sources to set out priorities for both health and social services. For the sake of convenience, current priorities may be grouped under three main headings: policies in the field of public health and health improvement; policies to develop health care services; and policies to promote integration of health and social care. Each will be discussed in turn.

Public health and health improvement

The priority attached to health improvement since the mid-1970s reflects the rediscovery of public health and recognition that factors like poverty, employment and housing are often more important than health care services in reducing morbidity and premature mortality. The consultative document, *Prevention and Health: Everybody's Business* (DHSS, 1976d), noted that improvements in health in the previous century had resulted largely from the public health movement rather than specific medical interventions, and argued that further gains were dependent on people taking care of themselves by changing their lifestyle. Individuals were urged to stop smoking, take more exercise and adopt an appropriate diet in order to reduce the risk of ill-health and death. These views were reiterated in a White Paper on *Prevention and Health*, published a year later (DHSS, 1977a), and a series of other publications gave advice on issues such as safety during pregnancy, eating for health and avoiding heart attacks.

A rather different approach was taken in the Black Report, *Inequalities in Health,* published in 1980. This report resulted from the deliberations of a working group set up to assemble information about differences in health status among the social classes and factors which might contribute to these differences. Following a comprehensive review of the available data, the working group concluded 'we wish to stress the importance of differences in material conditions of life' (Black Report, 1980, p. 357) in explaining social class inequalities in health. On this basis, the working group made a series of recommendations for reducing inequalities, in particular emphasising the importance of factors outside the NHS. The Thatcher government was not persuaded by the analysis and recommendations of the Black Report, and it was not until almost 20 years later that the Report was taken seriously by policy-makers (see Chapter 9).

During the 1980s, particular attention was paid to the development of policies to limit the spread of HIV/AIDS. Earmarked funds were set aside to support work in this field with priority being given to preventing HIV/AIDS through changes in behaviour and the provision of information to the public about risk factors. This emphasis on changes in lifestyle was also reflected in the work of the Health Education Authority, the body responsible at the time for campaigns to improve health. The Authority initiated programmes on cigarette smoking, alcohol abuse and healthy eating, including the 1987 'Look After Your Heart' campaign. In parallel, the Thatcher government put forward proposals for preventing illness by strengthening the role of GPs, dentists and other providers of primary care (Secretary of State for Social Services and others, 1987). As we noted in Chapter 2, this included the implementation of new contracts for GPs and dentists which contained incentives to encourage health checks, vaccination and immunisation, screening, health promotion, and preventative dentistry.

In a White Paper entitled *The Health of the Nation* (Secretary of State for Health, 1992), the Major government set targets for the improvement of health in five key areas including HIV/AIDS. A Cabinet Committee was appointed to oversee implementation of the strategy in government as a whole, while at a local level health authorities through their directors of public health were expected to work with other agencies to counteract the conditions which give rise to ill-health and to attach higher priority to prevention within the NHS. *The Health of the Nation* was superseded by the consultation paper *Our Healthier Nation,* issued by the Blair government shortly after coming into office. Although similar in some respects to *The Health of the Nation,* the consultation paper differed in placing greater emphasis on the social, economic and environmental causes of illness and in explicitly acknowledging the importance of inequalities in health. *Our Healthier Nation* identified two aims of the health strategy, namely:

> To improve the health of the population as a whole by increasing the length of people's lives and the number of years people spend free from illness. To improve the health of the worst off in society and to narrow the health gap. (Secretary of State for Health, 1998a, p. 5)

It went on to propose a national contract for better health in which government, local communities and individuals would work in partnership to improve health. The contract set out action by different agencies and the consultation paper also identified three settings for action: schools, workplaces and neighbourhoods. In relation to targets, *Our Healthier Nation* again differed from *The Health of the Nation* by proposing four priority areas instead of five, and by restricting the number of targets to be pursued. Specifically, the consultation paper suggested the following aims for the year 2010:

- *Heart Disease and Stroke*: to reduce the death rate from heart disease and stroke and related illnesses amongst people aged under 65 years by at least a further third;
- *Accidents*: to reduce accidents by at least a fifth;
- *Cancer*: to reduce the death rate from cancer amongst people aged under 65 years by at least a further fifth;
- *Mental Health*: to reduce the death rate from suicide and undetermined injury by at least a further sixth.

The public health White Paper, *Saving Lives: Our Healthier Nation* (Secretary of State for Health, 1999), was published in 1999 together with a report setting out how the government was planning to respond to the Acheson inquiry on health inequalities. The White Paper confirmed the four priority areas as those identified in the consultation paper: coronary heart disease and stroke, cancer, mental health, and accidents. Greater emphasis was placed on improving health in later life, for example by setting targets for health improvement in people aged under 75 and not under 65 as in the consultation paper. An overall aim of preventing up to 300 000 untimely and unnecessary deaths was set, and the government announced it was establishing a Health Development Agency to raise the standards and quality of public health provision. The White Paper reiterated the importance of action by government, communities and people to achieve these targets, and it noted the role that local authorities could play in support of the strategy. The need for action across government was also emphasised in the response to the Acheson inquiry which enumerated actions being taken to address the inquiry's recommendations (see Chapter 9).

One of the factors that contributes to health inequalities is the higher level of smoking in lower socio-economic groups compared with higher socio-economic groups. A White Paper on smoking published in 1998 set out a wide range of measures designed to cut the number of people smoking by 2010. Although rejecting a ban on smoking in public places, the White Paper included plans to develop smoking cessation clinics, restrict tobacco advertising and protect young people and children. The Tobacco Advertising and Promotion Act 2002 created powers to ban press, billboard and most internet advertising of tobacco products and to bring an end to the promotion of tobacco products through the sponsorship of sporting and other events.

The public health agenda assumed renewed importance in response to the threat of global terrorism and the emergence of new infectious diseases such as sudden acute respiratory syndrome (SARS). The establishment of the Health Protection Agency in 2003 was in part a response to these challenges. The Agency brought together a number of bodies working in the field of health protection and emergency planning to provide a single focus for action in this area of public health.

Health care services

Access and standards

Policies to develop health care services encompass a wide range of initiatives. Underpinning many of these initiatives is a concern to raise standards of health care provision and to improve access and convenience. Publication of the *Patient's Charter* in 1991 exemplified this concern and was the first attempt since the establishment of the NHS to define the rights of patients and the standards of service they should expect from the NHS (DH, 1991). The *Patient's Charter* was one of a series of charters published by the Major government as part of its policy to improve the performance of public services and it reflected recognition among policy-makers of the importance of rising public expectations of the NHS.

Table 4.2 summarises the standards and guarantees in the *Patient's Charter* including additions contained in the enlarged and updated version published in 1995. As this shows, particular emphasis was placed on reducing waiting times for hospital treatment. A maximum waiting time of 18 months was promised for inpatient treatment and 26 weeks for the first outpatient appointment. A maximum waiting time of 12 months was also set for coronary artery bypass grafts. Performance tables showing how providers were performing on a number of the *Patient's Charter* standards were published from 1994, and over time greater attention was given to

Table 4.2   *The Patient's Charter*

Ten rights were included in the *Patient's Charter* published in 1991:

- to receive health care on the basis of clinical need, regardless of ability to pay;
- to be registered with a GP;
- to receive emergency medical care at any time through a GP or through the emergency ambulance service and a hospital accident and emergency department;
- to be referred to a consultant, acceptable to a patient, when a GP thinks this is necessary, and to be referred to a second opinion if a patient and GP agree this to be desirable;
- to be given a clear explanation of any treatment proposed, including any risks or alternatives;
- to have access to health records, and to know that those working for the NHS are under a legal duty to keep their contents confidential;
- to choose whether or not to take part in medical research or medical student training;
- to be given detailed information on local health services, including quality standards and maximum waiting times;
- to be guaranteed admission for treatment by a specific date no later than two years from the day when a patient is placed on a waiting list;
- to have any complaint about NHS services investigated and to receive a full and prompt written reply from the chief executive or general manager.

The updated and enlarged *Patient's Charter* published in 1995 set out new rights and standards including:

- 90 per cent of outpatients to be seen within 13 weeks for their first appointment and everyone within 26 weeks;
- all patients waiting for an operation to be guaranteed admission for treatment no later than 18 months from the day of being placed on a waiting list;
- a three- to four-hour standard for 'trolley waits' in accident and emergency departments, to be reduced to two hours from April 1996;
- urgent home visits by community nurses within four hours and for non-urgent patients within two days.

---

measures of clinical performance alongside indicators of access and responsiveness.

The policy of raising standards was given added impetus after the election of the Blair government in 1997. Following a review of the *Patient's Charter*, the government published *Your Guide to the NHS* giving people advice on how to stay healthy, and how to use the NHS. This document also set out what people could do to use the NHS responsibly. More importantly, the strategy that was developed in relation to quality of care and clinical performance in *A First Class Service* (see Chapter 3) led to the establishment of two new organisations, the National Institute for Clinical Excellence (NICE) and the Commission for Health Improvement (CHI).

The role of NICE is to produce authoritative national guidance on the use of new and existing technologies, while the Commission for Health Improvement has the job of scrutinising standards and advising on action needed to strengthen quality. The work of these institutions is supported by the development of national service frameworks setting out national standards and models for services such as coronary heart disease and mental health. In addition, a framework of clinical governance was introduced to strengthen existing systems for quality control. Subsequently, the government established the National Patient Safety Agency to run a mandatory reporting system for logging all failures and errors, and the National Clinical Assessment Authority to provide a fast response to concerns about doctors' performance. The priority attached to these issues by the Blair government was in part a response to evidence of failures of clinical performance within the NHS, and a concern to underpin self-regulation within the medical profession with other mechanisms of quality assurance.

The Blair government also gave priority to policies designed to improve access and convenience within the NHS. Of particular significance was the reduction of waiting lists for hospital treatment in the light of the pledge made by the Prime Minister when in opposition to cut the number of people on waiting lists by 100 000. Extra resources were allocated to implement this pledge and a national waiting-list action team was established to ensure delivery of the target that had been set. The emphasis on access and convenience was seen too in the establishment of a number of pilot projects to introduce booked admission systems in place of waiting lists and to test out a 24-hour telephone nurse helpline known as NHS Direct. In addition, an annual survey of patient and user experience was set up to provide regular feedback on how well the NHS was serving its customers. A related initiative was the encouragement given to the use of new technologies to improve access to care, as in the more widespread application of telemedicine within the NHS.

Both NHS Direct and the booked admissions pilots soon became part of mainstream policy development and they featured prominently in *The NHS Plan*. Achievement of the waiting list target led to the establishment of new targets for cutting waiting times for treatment as policies to improve access took centre stage. Alongside the aim of reducing the maximum waiting times for outpatient appointments to three months and inpatient treatment to six months by 2005, even more ambitious targets were set for high priority areas like cancer services and heart operations.

Effort was also directed at improving access to emergency services to achieve the target set in *The NHS Plan* that by 2004 no patient should wait more than four hours in accident and emergency from arrival to admission, transfer or discharge. To achieve the access targets, the government gave priority to increasing hospital capacity, including making greater use of spare capacity in the private sector and paying for some NHS patients to be treated in hospitals in other European countries. In parallel, the Modernisation Agency provided support to the NHS in reforming services to enable waiting times to be cut and booked admissions to be rolled out. As waiting times came down, the government also emphasised the need to increase patient choice, and this is discussed further in Chapter 9.

Primary care

The position of primary care as the first point of contact for patients and the gateway to hospital and specialist services has long been seen as a strength of the NHS. This position was reinforced by the 1965 Charter for the Family Doctor Service and the new contract for GPs that followed in 1966. Subsequent developments focused on the extension of group practice and primary care teams and the improvement of premises. Notwithstanding these developments and the improved distribution of family doctors around the country, the Royal Commission on the NHS highlighted a number of weaknesses in primary care, including the poor quality of services in certain declining inner city areas (Royal Commission on the NHS, 1979). Many of these weaknesses persist and there continue to be concerns about variations in standards and performance.

Only with the 1997 Primary Care Act were powers created to encourage new approaches to be developed. These centred on a series of pilot projects, including the employment of salaried family doctors and nurse-led schemes. The Act emerged from a process of consultation and debate started under the Major government and it was passed into law with the support of opposition parties. Its main significance was in offering greater flexibility and choice in the provision of primary care. This entailed the continuation of independent contractor status for GPs who prefer this option, and the ability to negotiate local personal medical services contracts for GPs who wish to do so. Alongside changes to arrangements for providing cover for GPs in the evenings and at weekends, often involving the creation of cooperatives in which doctors support each other in delivering services out of hours, the personal medical services pilots opened up a new chapter in the development of primary care. This involved not only the choice of different kinds of working arrangements but also the emergence of new primary care organisations.

Many of these organisations build on initiatives taken in the light of *Working for Patients*. The establishment of GP fundholding and GP commissioning in different forms marked a move away from the GP practice as the principal form of primary care organisation to the establishment of multifunds, total purchasing projects, locality commissioning groups, out-of-hours cooperatives and related agencies. The effect was to break down the isolation of individual doctors and practices and to encourage increased collaboration. This was reinforced by setting up GP commissioning pilots under the Blair government, and subsequently the introduction of primary care groups and primary care trusts across the NHS in England. The GP practice continues to be of fundamental importance in these arrangements, but increasingly practices are working within a local framework of primary care and in so doing are comparing their approach with that of peers. As an example, variations in the use and cost of pharmaceuticals are being examined by the new primary care organisations as part of a shift towards managed primary care.

In line with developments in other areas of health policy since 1997, primary care has been under pressure to improve access for patients. This has been pursued in two main ways. First, new forms of primary care provision have been developed alongside the GP practice. The most important new forms have been NHS Direct, discussed earlier, and walk in centres. Around 60 walk in centres have been set up in England to deal with minor ailments and they are often located in high street premises. Walk in centres are staffed by experienced nurses and they provide treatment for minor injuries and illnesses. Second, policies to improve access to primary care have focused on reducing the time patients may have to wait to see a GP. *The NHS Plan* set a target that by 2004 patients should be able to have a GP appointment within 48 hours, and GP practices have received help from the National Primary Care Collaborative to redesign their services to achieve this target. A related policy was the encouragement given to the development of GPs with special interests, who would be able to treat patients without referral to hospital.

In 2003 agreement was reached on a new contract for GPs. Under the new contract, primary care practices, rather than individual GPs, are commissioned by primary care trusts to provide services to patients. Three funding streams are available, including a global sum to cover practice costs, enhanced service payments to fund the provision of additional services, and quality rewards designed to provide an incentive for practices to achieve higher standards of care. These quality rewards apply to conditions such as heart disease, diabetes and asthma. The other important element in the contract is the opportunity for practices to decide not to provide a service out of hours. When this happens, the primary care trust is responsible for the provision of this service

Acute hospital services

Policy on acute hospital services has developed in a piecemeal fashion and with the exception of waiting lists has not received the same attention as policy in other areas. The organisation of acute services was first addressed systematically in the 1962 Hospital Plan which set out a vision of a network of district general hospitals (DGHs) serving populations of 100 000 to 150 000, and each containing between 600 and 800 beds. The programme of hospital building that occurred after the Plan resulted in the building of many completely new DGHs and the upgrading of several existing hospitals to DGH standard. The Bonham Carter Report of 1969 (Central Health Services Council, 1969) proposed that even larger DGHs should be built to serve bigger populations but these proposals were not accepted. Instead, policy moved in favour of smaller DGHs supported by community hospitals (DHSS, 1980b). Despite this, the changing pattern of medical staffing in hospitals, with junior doctors spending more time undergoing training, consultants playing a bigger part in the delivery of services, and specialisation requiring a larger number of consultants to work together to offer the full range of services to a high standard, threatened the viability of smaller DGHs and led to moves to link and integrate services at adjacent hospitals (Ham, Smith and Temple, 1998).

Changing patterns of use of acute services have resulted in more patients being treated in fewer beds. This has been made possible by advances in medical technology, including the increased use of day surgery, developments in anaesthetics, and the use of new drugs. The average length of stay of patients in acute hospitals has fallen as a consequence and NHS hospitals typically operate with high levels of bed occupancy and little spare capacity. This has caused problems in recent years, especially during the winter months when increases in emergency admissions have put pressure on a system already working close to its limits. In some cases this has meant patients having to wait on trolleys until beds have become available. Policy on acute services has sought to deal with this by allocating additional resources to assist with winter pressures and by encouraging the development of alternatives to hospital care in the community and in nursing homes. The government has also acted to increase the provision of intensive care facilities as rising demands have exposed inadequacies in capacity.

An inquiry into NHS hospital beds was undertaken by the Department of Health and published in 2000 (DH, 2000a). The inquiry found that there was a mismatch between patients' needs and available resources. In particular, it highlighted evidence of significant inappropriate or avoidable use of acute hospital beds and of shortages of service alternatives to hospitals that could reduce admissions and bring care closer to patients' homes. Looking ahead to the next 10 to 20 years, the inquiry developed three scenarios: maintaining the current direction, acute bed focused care, and care closer to home. In the event, the government opted for the third scenario in which the main emphasis was placed on the development of intermediate care services to prevent avoidable admissions to acute care and to facilitate the transition from hospital to home. *The NHS Plan* announced that provision was being made for 5000 extra intermediate care beds and an extra 1700 intermediate care places.

Subsequently, the government carried out a review of the organisation of acute hospitals in the light of trends to centralise some services in fewer, larger facilities. The report of the review (DH, 2003c) challenged the view that 'biggest is best' and argued that it was important to maintain local access to acute hospitals through a greater emphasis on these hospitals operating as part of networks of care. The review argued for a whole systems and integrated approach to service requirements in which hospitals were planned in relation to primary and social care as well as other specialist facilities. It was anticipated that small acute hospitals would have a continuing role, even though they might not provide the full range of services. One of the factors driving change in acute hospital organisation was the European Working Time Directive which made it difficult to maintain 24-hour medical cover in small hospitals. The review argued that networking between hospitals and the development of extended roles for nurses and non-medical practitioners were essential to address these challenges.

Cancer and heart disease

In recent years, high priority has been given to improving services for people with cancer and heart disease. The priority attached to these conditions reflects the contribution made by cancer and heart disease to morbidity and premature mortality, and the opportunity this presents to improve population health through more effective prevention and treatment. Successive public health white papers have given priority to reducing premature deaths from these causes and have set targets for improvement (see p. 84). In addition, the Blair government has published national strategies aimed at strengthening the approach taken to the prevention, diagnosis, treatment and care of these conditions.

Policy on cancer services derives from the Calman-Hine report which set out a framework for commissioning high quality cancer care (Calman-Hine, 1995). The central proposal of this report was that care should be organised at three levels – primary care, cancer units and cancer centres – linked together to offer a network of appropriate services to patients.

The NHS Cancer Plan, published in 2000, built on the Calman-Hine report, announcing significant investment in cancer services and new targets for improving access and raising standards (DH, 2000b). *The NHS Cancer Plan* noted that one-third of the population of England would develop cancer at some stage of their lives and one-quarter would die of cancer. The plan went on to note that progress had been made in reducing deaths from some cancers but England still lagged behind other European countries, particularly in poorer survival rates from lung, colon, prostate and breast cancer. These differences were attributed in part to delays in diagnosis resulting from waiting times to see a specialist, and decades of under-investment in staff and equipment. The plan also acknowledged the importance of variations in cancer services and outcomes and the need to address the postcode lottery of cancer care.

Among the challenges set out in the plan, the need to improve prevention was strongly emphasised. This included further action to tackle smoking and improve diet, and to improve screening. At the heart of the plan was a commitment to reduce waiting times for diagnosis and treatment to overcome the delays that contributed to poorer outcomes. A series of targets were specified in the plan including a maximum one-month wait from diagnosis to treatment for all cancers by 2005, and a maximum two-month wait from urgent GP referral to treatment for all cancers by 2005. These targets were to be achieved through increased investment in staff and equipment involving the appointment of an extra 1000 cancer specialists by 2006, and the provision of 50 new magnetic resonance imaging scanners and 200 new CT scanners. Consistent with the approach taken in *The NHS Plan,* this extra investment was to be accompanied by reform. Specifically, the plan announced that the Cancer Services Collaborative would be rolled out across the country as part of the expanding work programme of the Modernisation Agency.

In the case of heart disease, a national service framework was published in 2000 (DH, 2000c) This framework noted that heart disease was the commonest cause of premature death in the United Kingdom, and that there were wide variations between social classes, ethnic groups, and geographical areas. The national service framework argued that timely, effective treatment could reduce the suffering and risk associated with heart disease, and it drew on available evidence to suggest how this might be done. Twelve service standards were identified in the framework encompassing prevention, treatment and rehabilitation. Specific areas for improvement included the provision of smoking cessation clinics and rapid access chest pain clinics, reducing call-to-needle time for clot-busting drug treatment, improving the use of effective medicines after heart attack, and increasing the number of revascularisation procedures undertaken. As in the case of cancer, emphasis was also placed on reform and service redesign, and this was subsequently pursued through the coronary heart disease collaborative which again came under the Modernisation Agency. Particular priority was attached to the reduction of waiting times for heart operations, and a patient choice pilot was launched in 2002 enabling patients who had been waiting for longer than six months to travel to another hospital for surgery.

One of the effects of both *The NHS Cancer Plan* and the national service framework for heart disease was to increase the costs of drug prescribing in the NHS. In the case of cancer, prescribing was affected by the decisions of the National Institute for Clinical Excellence (NICE) on the use of new drugs for the treatment of cancer. In the case of heart disease, prescribing costs rose as a result of the greater use of statins to reduce cholesterol levels. These investments and the other changes that flowed from *The NHS Cancer Plan* and the national service framework resulted in a number of improvements for patients and for the population. For example, it was estimated that more effective prescribing had saved up to 6,000 premature deaths from heart disease (DH, 2003d). In relation to cancer, a review by the Audit Commission and the Commission for Health Improvement reported progress since 1995 in improving cancer services. The review also noted variations between different parts of the country and cancer types, and continuing delays in patients getting access to diagnosis and treatment (CHI, 2001). The government's own three year progress report on implementing the cancer plan, published in 2003, noted the improvements in outcomes that had been achieved and it highlighted the impact of additional investment, inlcuding the acquisition of additional equipment and the appointment of 940 extra cancer consultants since 1997. An independent assessment published at the same time was more critical, arguing that more patient choice and greater private sector involvement were needed to achieve the government's targets (Sikora and Bosanquet, 2003).

Health and social care integration

Policies on health and social care over the last 40 years have focused particularly on the expansion of care in the community. In the case of older people and people with mental illness, learning disabilities and physical disabilities, there has been a move away from providing care in hospitals and residential institutions to offering support in the home and in home-like settings. Implementation of this policy has pointed up the importance of effective joint planning between the NHS and local authorities who are responsible for social care services. Successive governments have placed high priority on the integration of health and social care but with the exception of Northern Ireland, where these services are the responsibility of a single agency, progress in achieving integration has been variable.

The 1959 Mental Health Act signalled the intention to develop community-based services, spurred on by developments in the treatment of mental illness and in social attitudes which made it possible to begin the run down of the large old psychiatric hospitals or asylums which had been the main source of care until that point. The White Paper, *Better Services for the Mentally Ill* (DHSS, 1975a), continued this trend and encouraged the integration of hospital services for people with mental illness in DGHs. The White Paper also included norms for the provision of services by local authorities, encompassing day centres, hostels and long-stay accommodation. In practice, public expenditure restrictions served to slow the development of these services, and the availability of comprehensive mental health care remained uneven. This again demonstrated the gap between the intentions of policy and implementation.

The care programme approach developed in the 1990s was intended to ensure that health and social care needs were assessed systematically and agreed services provided. This was supplemented by guidance on the components of care the government expected to be offered to people with mental illness. In view of concerns about patients discharged from hospital without adequate support, supervised discharge was introduced in 1996 to provide more control over certain categories of patients considered to pose risks either to themselves or the community. The rapid succession of policy initiatives in this period culminated in publication of a White Paper, *Modernising Mental Health Services,* in 1998 setting out the Blair government's plans for the future. The White Paper highlighted the failures of the community care policy and indicated that additional resources would be provided not only to address these failures but also to fund extra beds. To this extent, the White Paper recognised the need for a range of services to be available to people with mental illness and it reflected both public and political recognition of the continuing role of hospitals in the treatment of mental illness.

A national service framework for mental health was published in 1999 (DH, 1999). This set standards in five areas: health promotion, primary care and access to services, services for people with severe mental illness, carers, and the prevention of suicide. Additional resources were allocated to mental health services to support implementation of the national service framework. Examples of good practice were included in the framework and the standards that were set were based on a review of the evidence on the effectiveness of different services and interventions. The proposals in the framework on the prevention of suicide were intended to support the achievement of the target set in the public health White Paper that the suicide rate should be reduced by at least one-fifth by 2010.

Policies for people with learning disabilities have undergone significant change following the White Paper, *Better Services for the Mentally Handicapped,* published in 1971 (DHSS, 1971). The main objective of the White Paper was to bring about a reduction of about one-half in the number of hospital beds provided for mentally handicapped people (as they were known at the time), and to expand local authority services in the community. Standards in hospital were also to be improved to overcome the deficiencies noted in the *Report of the Committee of Enquiry into Ely Hospital, Cardiff* (Ely Report, 1969) which found evidence both of the neglect of patients and their abuse. A review published in 1980 indicated progress in meeting these objectives and proposed an even greater reduction in hospital provision and the need for care to be provided in smaller units (DHSS, 1980c). The review went on to stress the importance of developing local authority services and integrating these services with those provided by health authorities. These developments were taken further by the increasing emphasis placed on enabling people with learning disabilities to live an ordinary life in the community through supported living programmes and similar initiatives. In recognition that social care is often more important for people with learning disabilities than health care, in some parts of the country health authorities and local authorities have agreed to pool budgets, with local authorities taking the lead responsibility for the commissioning of these services.

In 2001 the government published a White Paper, *Valuing People: a new strategy for learning disability for the 21st century* (DH, 2001b). The White Paper reviewed the full range of needs of people with learning disabilities, including health care, and set out a vision based on four principles: rights, independence, choice and inclusion. The major problems identified in the White Paper included poorly coordinated services for families with disabled children, insufficient support for carers, limited housing and employment opportunities, and few examples of real partnership between health and social care. Additional funding was announced in the White Paper, including a Learning Disability Development Fund of up to £50 million per annum, and an Implementation Support Fund. Help was also provided for advocacy services and for carers. In the case of the NHS, the White Paper emphasised that people with learning disabilities should have the same right of access to mainstream health services as the rest of the population.

Services for older people were subject to a major policy review in 1981 (DHSS, 1981b), and since then have been through a series of changes driven largely by shifting policies in respect of public funding of care in private and voluntary sector residential and nursing homes. These changes centred on the availability of resources through the social security budget to pay for care in these homes during the 1980s. Expenditure increased rapidly, reaching £2.5 billion a year by 1993, leading to an expansion of the private nursing home provision. It was partly in response to this that the government acted to cap spending and to make local authorities the lead agencies in arranging social care. The shift in policy was also stimulated by a desire to move resources away from residential and nursing home provision by giving local authorities greater flexibility to develop home care and other services in line with the recommendations of the Griffiths Report on community care (see Chapter 2).

One of the consequences was that the role of the NHS in the provision of care declined significantly, focusing mainly on acute services rather than long-term or continuing care, and continuing a trend established in the 1950s (Bridgen and Lewis, 1999). This happened by default rather than design and it represented a major shift in policy that was never debated or agreed (Audit Commission, 1997). Under the new funding arrangements, people above a certain income level were required to pay for continuing care themselves instead of having access to such care in the NHS. In 1994 the Health Service Commissioner or Ombudsman upheld a complaint from the wife of a man suffering brain damage who argued that the NHS should have provided continuing care to her husband. This led the Department of Health (DH) to issue guidance to health authorities and local authorities asking them to develop local policies and eligibility criteria on continuing care and indicating that health authorities in some areas would need to increase expenditure on these services to enable the NHS to meet its obligations in the light of the Ombudsman's judgement.

The election of the Blair government resulted in the establishment of a Royal Commission to explore options for the future funding of long-term care against a background of increasing dissatisfaction with the progressive shift of responsibility from the public to the private sector and the blurred boundary between the NHS and social care. The Royal Commission reported in 1999 with the majority recommending that all nursing and personal care in care homes, and all personal care in people's own homes, should be provided free. The provision of accommodation and food would be means tested and it was estimated that the cost of making these changes would be around £1 billion initially. The minority on the Commission dissented from these proposals, arguing that they would involve the use of public funds to support better-off members of society at the expense of those most in need. Instead, the minority proposed that the existing rules on means testing should be relaxed and nursing care only should be free.

The government responded to the Royal Commission at the same time as it published *The NHS Plan*. Many of the recommendations of the Royal

Commission were accepted but not the central proposal that all care should be provided free. Rather, the government decided to make NHS nursing care free in all settings, and to maintain means testing for personal care. Additional resources were allocated to support the development of services for older people with the main emphasis being on the development of intermediate care. The establishment of the National Care Standards Commission in 2002, in response to the report of the Royal Commission, was intended to provide stronger safeguards for quality. One of the effects was to put pressure on the care homes market as providers were caught between requirements to meet new standards laid down by the National Care Standards Commission and revenues that were held down by the level of fees paid by local authorities. In some parts of the country, closures of care homes threatened to destabilise services for older people, and representatives of providers argued for fee increases to enable them to continue providing services.

Subsequently, the national service framework for older people set out a comprehensive strategy for the provision of fair, high quality, integrated health and social care services (DH, 2001c). The framework included standards for the improvement of health and social care services in areas such as hospital care and health promotion. A report on progress in implementing the framework published by the DH in 2003 identified a number of improvements that had occurred, including the expansion of intermediate care and intensive home care. A further report from the Ombudsman published at around the same time as the progress report on the national service framework drew attention to the failure of the NHS to meet its obligations to provide continuing care to older and disabled people (Health Services Commissioner, 2003). The report was based on investigations into four cases and concluded that some health authorities and trusts had misinterpreted DH guidance on eligibility criteria for NHS funding, developed in response to the Coughlan judgement in the Court of Appeal in 1999. This judgement found that the NHS was responsible for meeting the costs of care of patients whose needs were primarily health needs. The Ombudsman recommended that the DH should review its guidance on eligibility again and be more active in checking that local criteria followed the guidance. The decision of the Scottish Parliament to fund the costs of personal care as well as nursing care (see Chapter 5) underlined the restrictive nature of the policy developed in England and led to pressure on the government to reconsider the recommendations of the majority on the Royal Commission.

A theme that runs through discussions of policies for priority groups such as older people, people with learning disabilities, and people with mental illness is the importance of joint planning and provision between the NHS and local government in making a reality of community care. A series of reports over the years have reviewed arrangements for integration and have made proposals for strengthening links between services. Of particular importance were the arrangements for joint planning and joint finance put in place in the 1970s. While some progress has been made in achieving better integration, political, professional and organisational differences have not facilitated joint approaches, and more radical proposals for change such as placing health and social care under the control of a single agency have been considered but rejected. The most recent policy document to address these issues similarly maintained that 'Major structural change is not the answer' (DH, 1998b, p. 5).

Under the Health Act 1999, health authorities and local authorities have been placed under a duty to work in partnership. The Act provided for new flexibilities through pooled budgets, lead and joint commissioning, and integrated provision. One way in which integration is going forward is through the creation of Care Trusts. These trusts are formed when primary care trusts or NHS trusts make a joint application with local councils to commission and provide services in an integrated way. The first four Care Trusts were formed in April 2002. Three focus on mental health services and the fourth on primary care and adult social care services. In many parts of the country, intermediate care services have been developed jointly by the NHS and local authorities and there has been increasingly close collaboration in planning for and dealing with winter pressures on the NHS. The Department of Health has exerted strong pressure on the NHS and local authorities to avoid a repetition of the crisis that confronted the NHS in the winter of 1999/2000 and has allocated extra resources to tackle the problem of delayed transfers between hospitals and the community. Under the Community Care (Delayed Discharges etc) Act 2003, local authorities are required to pay NHS bodies for the care of people in hospital who could appropriately be looked after in the community with effect from 2004.

Service integration has also emerged as an important issue in relation to children's services. In this area of service provision, the government responded to the inquiry into the death of Victoria Climbie (Laming Report, 2003) by announcing the biggest reorganisation of children's services in 30 years. The reorganisation included the appointment of an independent commissioner to protect the rights and wellbeing of children, the appointment of a children's director in each local authority, and the establishment of Children's Trusts to bring together local authority, health and some government services for children. It is expected that Children's Trusts will be set up by 2006. These proposals built on the plans for strengthening children's services included in the national service framework published in 2003.

Priority-setting

Priority-setting or rationing is not new and in the first phase of the NHS debate centred on the adequacy of the funding made available by the government and the decision to introduce charges for some services. As time went on, the lengthening of waiting lists for hospital treatment came to exemplify rationing by delay and there was also evidence that doctors rationed access to specialist services such as dialysis for the treatment of kidney failure (Halper, 1989). The latter example illustrates the more general point that NHS rationing tended to be implicit and a matter of clinical judgement rather than a process that occurred out in the open. Only in the 1970s when expenditure constraints began to bite and growth rates slowed did governments address the issue of priority-setting systematically.

The high point of priority-setting at a national level occurred in 1976 when the Labour government published a consultative document on *Priorities* setting out quantified targets for the development of different services (DHSS, 1976b). In the following year there was a retreat from this approach with the White Paper, *The Way Forward* (DHSS, 1977b), indicating in broad terms, as illustrative projections only, the kinds of developments that might occur. This process was taken to its logical conclusion in *Care in Action* (DHSS, 1981c), the first statement on priorities produced by the Thatcher government, which gave a general account of government policies for different services and client groups, and argued that priority-setting was a matter for local decision and local action.

How then do health authorities arrive at decisions on priorities? Research evidence indicates that local decisions are shaped by inherited commitments and by bargaining between different interests. National guidance on priorities plays a major part in this process and account is also taken of the views of local people and the preferences of providers. The outcome tends to involve incremental adjustments to existing budgets rather than major changes of direction as health authorities spread resources around in seeking to reconcile the demands placed upon them (Ham, 1993; Klein, Day and Redmayne, 1996). Decisions are informed by the application of techniques and evidence on cost-effectiveness, but it is the judgement of local policy-makers and their weighing of different claims that is decisive. Put another way, priority-setting is an arena in which the politics of the NHS are played out at a local level and in Chapter 8 we explore further the dynamics of the micro politics of health care.

The reluctance of governments to take a lead in setting priorities derives from the political costs involved in taking unpopular decisions. This was illustrated by the response to the 1976 *Priorities* document and the opposition of groups representing services identified as low priorities to the approach taken by the government. In these circumstances, it is not surprising that politicians prefer to pass responsibility to health authorities or seek to mask the effects of their policies. As Klein (1995) has observed, the diffusion of blame is an enduring feature of the NHS and helps to explain why decision-makers at a local level are given the responsibility of making choices between different services. An example that illustrates this was the case of Child B, a 10-year-old girl denied funding for an experimental treatment for leukaemia by the Cambridge and Huntingdon Health Authority (Ham and Pickard, 1998). The case received extensive publicity and the senior staff of the health authority were responsible for accounting to the media and the public for their decision.

Similarly, politicians may resort to subterfuge and evasion in reconciling limited budgets and growing demands. The withdrawal of long-term care from the NHS through a series of incremental decisions (see above) is a clear illustration of this, demonstrating how care may be rationed even in the absence of public debate. Restrictions on the availability of dental services within the NHS indicate a different kind of approach, with care that was once seen as part of the core of NHS provision being withdrawn as a consequence of dissatisfaction on the part of dentists with NHS terms and conditions. In this case, the failure of successive governments to respond to the decision of dentists in some areas to no longer offer to provide services within the NHS meant that dental care *de facto* became a private service in these areas.

In relation to services other than long-term care and dentistry, local responsibility for priority-setting results in variations between areas in the availability of services within the NHS. This has become known as 'rationing by postcode'. Access to care then depends on where people live and this has raised questions about the claim of the NHS to be a national service in which care is available on the basis of need. Examples include the priority attached to new drugs such as beta interferon for the treatment of multiple sclerosis, and access to services like infertility treatment. In both of these cases there are variations between areas reflecting differences between health authorities in the importance given to competing claims on the use of resources. The decision of the Blair government to establish the National Institute for Clinical Excellence and to develop national service frameworks was an attempt to address the so-called postcode lottery. These developments signalled the willingness of the government to take on a bigger role in priority-setting and to ensure greater equity in the provision of services. Ultimately, however, responsibility for implementing national service frameworks rests with primary care trusts and NHS bodies at a local level, and the existence of these bodies means that there will always be divergence between national aspirations and local service delivery. The dynamics of policy-making in NHS bodies is explored further in Chapter 8.

Conclusion

In this chapter we have noted that the size of the NHS budget is shaped by the state of the economy and government decisions on priorities between spending programmes. Periods of growth have been interspersed with years of relative famine as economic imperatives and political bargaining have combined to determine the allocation of resources to different sectors. Policies for specific services have been developed in relation to public health and health improvement, health care, and health and social care integration and evidence indicates that there has often been a gap between aspiration and achievement. Responsibility for reconciling the many priorities identified by government and allocating resources between competing claims rests with health authorities and primary care trusts.

The paradox of a national health service in which NHS bodies and doctors play a major part in resource allocation is explained by the political costs involved in explicit priority-setting at a national level, and the quest for alternative ways of diffusing blame and avoiding accountability. This point has not been lost on health authorities and the medical profession, hence the clamour for government to take a lead on these issues. In the next phase of development, primary care trusts will be expected to take a greater responsibility in priority-setting. The major unresolved question is the balance that will be struck between the role of these trusts and the guidance emerging at a national level from NICE, national service frameworks and other sources.

Chapter 5

Scotland, Wales and Northern Ireland

In this chapter, we describe the organisation and politics of the NHS in Scotland, Wales and Northern Ireland. The chapter begins with a description of differences in organisation and management before devolution. This is followed by an account of the changes that followed from devolution, both in NHS structures and in systems of national government. The limited impact of devolution on health policy is discussed and the chapter concludes by exploring the prospects for regional government in England (the chapter draws extensively on Hazell, 2003; Jervis and Plowden, 2003; and Woods, 2002).

Differences before devolution

In its review of the funding of the NHS, the Wanless report drew attention to differences within the United Kingdom. These differences, illustrated in Figure 5.1, include the size and age structures of the populations of England, Scotland, Wales and Northern Ireland; the health of these populations; and the availability of health service resources. Analysis has shown that NHS expenditure per capita is lowest in England and highest in Scotland, whereas health indicators tend to be best in England and worst in Scotland. With the extra resources available, the Scottish NHS buys more hospital beds and staff per capita than the English NHS and has higher rates of both inpatient and outpatient activity than England. The position in Northern Ireland and Wales is generally between these extremes (Dixon, Inglis and Klein, 1999). The absence of a direct relationship between health service spending and health outcomes reflects the importance of non-medical factors in influencing the health of the population, and we discuss this further in Chapter 9.

We noted in earlier chapters that the structure of the NHS in Scotland, Wales and Northern Ireland differs from that in England in certain respects. Differences in structure became even greater following the election of the Blair government. *The New NHS* White Paper in England was preceded by the publication of a White Paper in Scotland, *Designed to Care,* proposing the establishment of primary care trusts bringing together

Figure 5.1   *Health and health care in England, Scotland, Wales and Northern Ireland*

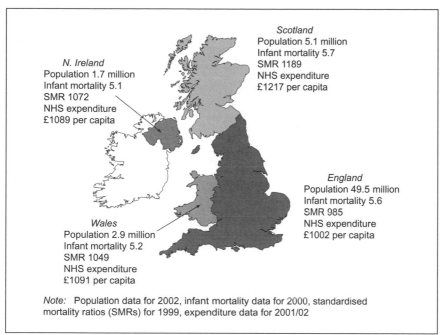

Scotland
Population 5.1 million
Infant mortality 5.7
SMR 1189
NHS expenditure
£1217 per capita

N. Ireland
Population 1.7 million
Infant mortality 5.1
SMR 1072
NHS expenditure
£1089 per capita

England
Population 49.5 million
Infant mortality 5.6
SMR 985
NHS expenditure
£1002 per capita

Wales
Population 2.9 million
Infant mortality 5.2
SMR 1049
NHS expenditure
£1091 per capita

Note: Population data for 2002, infant mortality data for 2000, standardised mortality ratios (SMRs) for 1999, expenditure data for 2001/02

all services other than acute care (Secretary of State for Scotland, 1997). Primary care trusts were established in 1999 and they were given full responsibility for primary care and community health services, and services for people with mental illness and learning disabilities. Under the Scottish plans, local health care cooperatives were set up to involve GPs in developing the provision of services, although participation in these cooperatives was voluntary and GPs lost control of budgets as both fundholding and GP commissioning came to an end. In the new structure of the NHS in Scotland, there was a distinction between the strategic and planning roles of Health Boards and the operational management responsibility of trusts. As in England, an important objective in Scotland was the development of integrated care, and joint investment funds were intended to facilitate integration between primary care trusts and acute trusts.

The White Paper for Wales, *NHS Wales: Putting Patients First,* differed from the English White Paper in proposing the establishment of local health groups instead of primary care groups. These were set up on a coterminous basis with local authorities and as subcommittees of health authorities. Initially, the White Paper indicated that local health groups would be advisory bodies but would take on greater responsibility for commissioning services over time. These groups were established in 1999 and they brought together GPs, other primary care contractors, health professionals such as nurses and other local interests. The configuration of NHS trusts in Wales was reviewed in parallel with debate on the White Paper and as a result the number of trusts was reduced from 25 to 16. Similar changes took place in Scotland as part of the move towards acute trusts and primary care trusts.

The position in Northern Ireland was reviewed in the consultation document *Fit for the Future,* whose proposals reflected the unique features of Northern Ireland, in particular the integration of health and social care. Two options were outlined in the consultation document, the first following the approach set out in England and centring on the establishment of primary care groups, the second entailing the creation of local care agencies which would comprise primary care partnerships to commission care and trusts to manage services. Under both options, it was proposed that the structure of health and social services should be streamlined to reduce the number of organisations involved and to simplify the management of services. A paper published in 1999 set out the results of consultation on *Fit for the Future* and proposed that 5 health and social care partnerships should take over the functions of both the health and social services boards and fundholders, and that the number of trusts should be halved. Continuing uncertainty about the political future of Northern Ireland meant that these proposals were not implemented.

Differences after devolution

One of the most significant changes made by the Blair government during its first term was to devolve power to Scotland, Wales and Northern Ireland. The elections that took place in May 1999 led to the creation of a 129-member parliament in Scotland and a 60-member assembly in Wales. While the Westminster Parliament retained power over the constitution, defence, the economy and other major areas, devolution gave the Scottish and Welsh governments control over areas such as health and social care. The Scottish Parliament has greater powers than the Welsh Assembly because of its ability to enact primary legislation and to vary the rate of income tax by up to 3 per cent but in both countries there is an opportunity to develop policies that are adapted to different needs. A similar opportunity exists in Northern Ireland where the 108-member Assembly elected in June 1998 had powers devolved to it in December 1999.

One of the immediate effects of devolution was to change the way in which the NHS is governed in Scotland, Wales and Northern Ireland. The electoral systems adopted in Scotland and Wales, involving proportional representation rather than Westminster-style first-past-the-post elections, resulted in the formation of minority or coalition governments that depended on cooperation between the political parties. The Labour party was the senior partner in these governments but was dependent on the support of the Liberal Democrats. A different situation prevailed in Northern Ireland where the electoral system required parties representing nationalists and republicans to share power. The complex system of checks and balances adopted in Northern Ireland was designed to bring groups with a long tradition of conflict into government, rather than as a means of securing policy reform. Together with the interruption of devolved government by the resumption of direct rule from Westminster in the light of continuing disagreements between the parties in the government of Northern Ireland, the result was a period in which change in health and social care was the exception rather than the rule.

Divergences in NHS structures

Devolution did result in some departures from the policy direction taken in England in both Scotland and Wales. As an example, the Scottish and Welsh governments produced their own versions of *The NHS Plan* shortly after the Blair government published its intentions. In Scotland, *Our National Health* (Scottish Executive, 2000) emphasised the importance of health improvement as well as service improvement, building on the approach set out in the public health white paper, *Towards a Healthier Scotland*, published a year earlier. Like its English counterpart, *Our National Health* identified improving services to patients by reducing waiting times and improving standards of care in clinical areas such as cancer and heart disease as high priorities. It also proposed further changes to the structure of the NHS in Scotland, involving the creation of unified health boards. These plans for structural change were elaborated in a further document, *Rebuilding our NHS* (Scottish Executive, 2001), and the new unified boards came into operation in 2001. In most cases, each board contained one primary care trust and one acute trust. Subsequently, *Partnership for Care* (Scottish Executive, 2003), proposed the abolition of NHS trusts and the establishment of community health partnerships in place of local health care cooperatives.

In Wales, *Improving Health in Wales* (National Assembly for Wales, 2001) was similar to the NHS plan for Scotland in highlighting the importance of health improvement and reducing health inequalities. In this respect, it built on the public health white paper, *Better Health: Better Wales*, and emphasised the need for partnership between the NHS and other organisations in improving health. *Improving Health in Wales* also contained proposals for changing the structure of the NHS in Wales, involving the abolition of health authorities to enable the role of the Assembly and that of local health groups (later renamed local health boards) to be strengthened. Unlike in England, community health councils were retained in Wales. As far as service improvement was concerned, *Improving Health in Wales* echoed many of the priorities set out in *The NHS Plan*, although there was less emphasis on specific targets and quantified objectives than in the English plan.

There was no equivalent of *The NHS Plan* in Northern Ireland where the structure inherited by the Assembly remained largely unchanged. The main exception was in respect of general practitioner fundholding which was eventually abolished in 2002 and superseded by local health and social care groups that operate as committees of the health and social services boards. Table 5.1 describes differences in the structure of the NHS in the four countries that make up the United Kingdom.

Systems of national government

Prior to devolution, the Secretary of State for Scotland was the political head of the NHS in Scotland, and responsibility for the NHS rested with the Scottish Office. After devolution, the Scottish Executive and the Scottish Parliament took over this role. The Scottish Executive refers both to the government of Scotland and the civil servants supporting it. The minister for health and community care in the Cabinet, supported by a chief executive and around 600 civil servants and other staff seconded from the NHS and local government, is responsible for the NHS in Scotland. The Scottish Parliament takes a close interest in the NHS and the Health and Community Care Committee of the Parliament is involved in scrutinising the performance of the NHS as a whole in Scotland and the affairs of individual trusts.

A similar transition occurred in Wales where, prior to devolution, the Secretary of State for Wales was the political head of the NHS in Wales, and was supported by the Welsh Office. The Minister for Health and Social Services in the Welsh Assembly Government is one of the members of the Cabinet and is responsible for the NHS in Wales. She is held to account by the Health and Social Services Committee of the Assembly. The Minister for Health and Social Services is supported by the Director of NHS Wales and around 250 civil servants. In Northern Ireland, a Sinn Fein member of the Assembly became Minister for Health, Social Services and Public Safety, and the Committee on Health, Social Services and Public Safety was established to scrutinise health and social care issues. The Department of Health, Social Services and Public Safety employs 1000 staff.

In both Scotland and Wales, devolution had the effect of increasing parliamentary scrutiny of NHS matters (Woods, 2002). The result was to

Table 5.1 Differences in the NHS in the UK, April 2004

	Central Management	Regional Structure	Health Authorities	NHS Trusts	Primary Care
England	Department of Health	Public health teams are located in the government offices of the regions	28 strategic health authorities	c.280 NHS trusts	c. 300 primary care trusts
N. Ireland	The Department of Health, Social Services and Public Safety	–	4 health and social services boards	19 health and social services trusts	5 local health and social care groups
Scotland	Scottish Executive Health Department	–	15 health boards	–	c. 40 community health partnerships
Wales	NHS Directorate in the Welsh Assembly Government	3 regional offices of the NHS Directorate	–	14 NHS trusts	21 local health boards and 1 unified health care board

Source: format of table based on earlier version in Ham (2001).

increase the influence of politicians *vis-à-vis* civil servants and NHS managers. There have also been some divergences in health policy. The most important difference involved the decision in Scotland to provide free personal care for older people needing long term care. The Welsh Assembly Government put pressure on Westminster to enable the same approach to be pursued in Wales but without success (Osmond, 2003). This means that the main example of policy divergence in Wales is the decision to extend free prescriptions and eye tests and to make a commitment to phase out prescription charges entirely by 2007.

There appeared to be divergence too in the stronger commitment to partnership working in Scotland and Wales compared with England, although studies of the new systems of government indicate that the aspiration to achieve more 'joined up' government was difficult to realise in practice. Indeed, if anything devolution reinforced the separation of services because of the appointment of ministers to head each service, and the scrutiny of these services exercised by legislative committees (Jervis and Plowden, 2003). Similar tendencies were at work in Northern Ireland where the structure of government and the sharing of ministerial posts between political parties whose views were often strongly opposed militated against integrated approaches, notwithstanding the rhetoric of policy documents. The main issues of health policy debate in Northern Ireland since devolution have concerned the siting of maternity units and the configuration of acute services. In 2002, work started on a 20-year strategy for the future of health and social services in Northern Ireland, and this included a commitment to extensive consultation with the public and professional organisations.

One of the unexpected consequences of devolution was that the main source of divergence in health policy was to be found in Whitehall, particularly as the Blair government entered its second term. The willingness of the government to make greater use of the private sector as a provider of services to NHS patients, its policy of expanding the range of choices available to patients, and its active support of approaches that were similar to those used during the internal market experiment, meant that there was a widening gap in policy between different parts of the United Kingdom. To be sure, the commitment to the founding values and principles of the NHS was not affected by these developments, but the way in which these principles were applied and expressed increasingly diverged. A good example of divergence was the policy on NHS Foundation Trusts that was pursued actively in England and not at all in the other three countries.

One of the constraints on the devolved governments is the way in which resources are allocated within the United Kingdom. The distribution of public expenditure is governed by the Barnett formula and this results in the allocation of blocks of expenditure to the Scottish, Welsh and Northern Ireland governments. In view of the higher levels of public spending in these countries historically in comparison with England, the increases made available to the devolved governments under the Barnett formula are somewhat lower than those in England as the Blair government seeks to move towards greater equity in resource allocation (Woods, 2004). Despite this, Scotland, Wales and Northern Ireland have benefited from the higher priority attached to the NHS by the government.

An assessment

In his analysis of devolution and health policy, Greer argues that policy divergence reflects the role of different policy coalitions and policy advocates, and he summarises the nature of divergence and its cause in the following way:

> Each system has taken a distinct path from the 1991 baseline of Margaret Thatcher's 'internal market'. England is the most market-based; the Labour government has pursued market-based service organisation and private participation and focused on service provision rather than new public health. Scotland is its near-opposite, rebuilding the unitary NHS with strong planning and service integration and a buyout of Scotland's most prominent private hospital as well as a small but meaningful commitment to new public health. Wales diverges not only in its reluctance to work with the private sector and its strong commitment to new public health but also in the way that commitment shapes its service organisation. Northern Ireland has changed little, retaining the 1991 internal market for want of a political structure able to change; it has thus combined a meaningful commitment to new public health and scepticism about the private sector with a market model derived from England. In each case the explanation has been the fit between the strongest advocacy coalitions in the country and the politicians' strategic positions; unless there is a good party reason not to, the politicians in charge tend to adopt the preferences of the strongest advocacy coalitions (Greer, 2003, pp. 198–9).

Alongside the limited degree of innovation in health policy in Scotland, Wales and Northern Ireland, reflecting underlying tendencies to policy maintenance discussed elsewhere in this book, there was a sense in some quarters that devolution had produced more negative than positive consequences. As a study of the impact of health policy and devolution observed:

> Some claim that the freedoms given to the devolved legislatures, and the greater responsiveness of the devolved executives, have produced both processes and outcomes which are actually worse than before devolution. The quality of debate in the legislatures has been described to us as unimpressive, while ministers' closeness to the public and to the arena in which decisions have to be implemented appears often to have had the effect of delaying necessary decisions, or of inhibiting the choice of potentially unpopular options. The cumulative effects of this militate against strategic thinking. (Jervis and Plowden, 2003, p. 54)

A more positive assessment is offered by Hazell who notes both the smooth introduction of devolution and the promising early results:

> Devolution has made a difference, in broadly the ways it was intended to. It has brought government closer to the people of Scotland, Wales and Northern Ireland; it has enabled the devolved governments to introduce policies more closely tailored to the needs of the local people; and it has introduced a new kind of politics to the United Kingdom (Hazell, 2003, 285).

One of the consequences of the lack of strategic thinking noted by Jervis and Plowden was the persistence of problems in the management of health services in the devolved administrations. These problems were starkly illustrated in the case of Wales by a review of health and social care carried out by a team advised by Derek Wanless (Wanless, 2003a). In his foreword to the report of the review, Wanless argued that the position in Wales was worse than in the United Kingdom as a whole. This was evident in long hospital waiting lists, and significant pressures on acute hospitals. The report noted that the configuration of services placed an insupportable burden on hospitals and their staff, and that Wales did not get as much out of its health spending as it should. In addressing these challenges, the report recommended a reorientation towards prevention and early intervention, and a greater emphasis on individuals' and communities' acceptance of responsibility for their health. It also suggested that the Assembly should stop funding hospital deficits and should provide stronger incentives to support performance improvements.

Regional government in England

The devolution of power to Scotland, Wales and Northern Ireland raises the issue of regional devolution in England and its potential impact on the NHS. Government offices of the regions have existed since 1994 and they bring together in one organisation the activities of a number of government departments. Since 2002 the Department of Health's regional public health teams have been located in the government offices and they work with colleagues in areas such as education and skills and transport in developing public health strategies and services in their regions. In parallel, regional development agencies were set up in 1999 and their main role is to coordinate regional economic regeneration and development and promote business efficiency and employment. In the case of London, the establishment of the Greater London Authority in 2000, including an elected mayor, indicated the government's interest in devolving power within England. The mayor has a duty to safeguard and promote Londoners' health and has worked closely with NHS bodies, particularly on public health issues.

Following a White Paper, *Your Region, Your Choice*, published in 2002, legislation was passed in 2003 to create powers to enable elected regional assemblies to be established where public support is expressed for them in a referendum. This opened up a debate that was resolved at the time of the inception of the NHS when the views of Aneurin Bevan that the NHS should be established as a national service under separate administrative agencies carried the day against Herbert Morrison's argument that local government control was the preferred option (see Chapter 1). At the time, Bevan acknowledged that putting the NHS under elected authorities was an option for the future, and the constitutional radicalism of the Blair government appeared to make this a real possibility, although health was not one of the services identified as a likely candidate for control by elected regional assemblies.

Conclusion

The developments described in this chapter underline the argument that a family of health services now exist in the United Kingdom, rather than a single national health service (Jervis and Plowden, 2003). In the first five years of devolution, there has been increasing divergence in NHS structures and the political processes impacting on health policy, with increased scrutiny by politicians in the devolved governments and greater accountability on the part of civil servants and managers. There have also been examples of policy divergence, through the Scottish approach to personal care for older people, the Welsh policy on user charges, and the English strategy of promoting greater plurality of provision and increased patient choice. It is too early to assess whether policy divergence will result in greater differences in policy outcomes, although the steady reductions in waiting times achieved in England compared with other parts of the United Kingdom suggested that this might indeed be the case. Policy divergence may well increase in the future, particularly if the dominance of the Labour party in three of the governments of the United Kingdom comes to an end. At that point, the scope for England to depart even more radically from arrangements in Scotland and Wales will be tested to the limits.

At the time of writing, policy makers seem more interested in pursuing their distinctive agendas than learning from the differences that have emerged. The natural experiments in the governance of health that have been stimulated by devolution have tended to reinforce national insularity rather than cross-systems comparisons. Yet with the public and the professions not constrained by national borders, and with information about differences in health and the performance of health systems increasingly available and transparent, the apparent lack of interest shown by politicians in what is happening outside their own jurisdictions may not be sufficient to stem the exchange of policy ideas. An early sign of this was the response of the Welsh Assembly Government to the Wanless report on Wales, including the decision to allow patients in Wales who had been waiting 18 months for an operation the choice of having their treatment at a different hospital. Echoing as it did the policies pursued in England to reduce waiting times and improve responsiveness to patients, this decision was an indication that initiatives developed in one country did not have to be rejected in others simply because they were not invented there.

A further counterweight to national insularity is the European Union. As we discuss in Chapter 11, in a number of areas the EU is having an impact on health policy, including the working time of staff and waiting times for patients. Although the jurisdiction of the EU in relation to health services is an uncertain and contested question, it seems likely that policy divergence within the United Kingdom will be constrained in some areas by policy convergence in Europe. The one safe prediction is that the sources of policy innovation and development will extend well beyond established centres of power as systems of government and governance multiply and fragment. In this pluralistic environment, the new governments of Scotland, Wales and Northern Ireland will co-exist with the Westminster government and the institutions of the EU. Health policy in the constituent parts of Britain will be forged out of the interplay of these different systems.

Chapter 6

The Policy-making Process in Central Government

The chapter begins with a definition of policy. The focus then shifts to the organisation of central government. At the core of the chapter is a description of the role of Parliament, the Prime Minister and Cabinet, Ministers and civil servants, and relationships between government departments. This is followed by an analysis of the role of outside interests and pressure groups. The increasing part played by these groups requires that we look beyond the formal institutions of government to the role of policy networks and policy communities. The final part of the chapter assesses whether central government is best described as pluralist or corporatist in character.

What is policy?

Although many writers have attempted to define policy, there is little agreement on the meaning of the word. It is therefore tempting to follow Cunningham and argue that 'policy is rather like the elephant – you recognise it when you see it but cannot easily define it' (quoted in Smith, 1976, p. 12). Attractive as this interpretation is, it may be worth spending a little time clarifying the meaning of policy, and the different ways in which it has been used.

A useful starting point is the work of David Easton, who has argued that political activity can be distinguished by its concern with 'the authoritative allocation of values' within society (Easton, 1953, p. 136). Easton uses values in a broad sense to encompass the whole range of rewards and sanctions that those in positions of authority are able to distribute. Values are allocated by means of policies, and for Easton 'A policy ... consists of a web of decisions and actions that allocate ... values' (Easton, 1953, p. 130). A number of points can be made about this definition.

First, Easton argues that the study of policy encompasses both formal decisions and actions. He points out that a decision by itself is not an action, but merely the selection among alternatives. What happens in practice may be different from what was intended by decision-makers, and it is important to focus on the processes that follow from a decision. Put another way, we need to consider how policy is implemented as well as how it is made.

A second point about Easton's definition is that it suggests that policy may involve a web of decisions rather than one decision. There are two aspects to this. First, the actors who make decisions are rarely the same people as those responsible for implementation. A decision network, often of considerable complexity, may therefore be involved in producing action, and a web of decisions may form part of the network. The second aspect is that even at the policy-making level, policy is not usually expressed in a single decision. It tends to be defined in terms of a series of decisions which, taken together, comprise a more or less common understanding of what policy is.

Third, policies invariably change over time. Yesterday's statements of intent may not be the same as today's, either because of incremental adjustments to earlier decisions, or more unusually because of major changes of direction. Also, experience of implementing a decision may feed back into the decision-making process, thereby leading to changes in the allocation of values. This is not to say that policies are always changing, but simply that the policy process is dynamic rather than static and that we need to be aware of shifting definitions of issues.

Fourth, the corollary of the last point is the need to recognise that the study of policy has as one of its main concerns the examination of non-decisions and inaction. Although not encompassed in Easton's definition, the concept of non-decision-making has become increasingly important in recent years, and a focus on decision-making has been criticised for ignoring more routine activities leading to policy maintenance and even inertia. Indeed, it has been argued that much political activity is concerned with maintaining the status quo and resisting challenges to the existing allocation of values. Analysis of this activity is a necessary part of the examination of the dynamics of the policy process (Bachrach and Baratz, 1970).

Fifth and finally, Easton's definition raises the question of whether policy can be seen as action without decisions. While Easton wishes to stress that policy is more than a formal, legal decision it is also appropriate to consider the view that there may be policies in the absence of decisions. Can it be said that a pattern of actions over a period of time constitutes a policy, even if these actions have not been formally sanctioned by a decision? In practice it would seem that a good deal of what happens in public agencies occurs because 'it has always been done this way', and cannot be attributed to any official pronouncement. Further, writers on policy have increasingly turned their attention to the actions of lower-level actors, sometimes called street-level bureaucrats, in order to gain a better understanding of policy-making and implementation. It would seem important to balance a decisional 'top-down' perspective on policy with an action-oriented, 'bottom-up' perspective (Barrett and Fudge, 1981). Actions as well as decisions may therefore be said to be the proper focus of policy analysis. Accordingly, in this and the subsequent chapter the main focus of attention is on the policy-making process in central government, while Chapter 8 examines the implementation of centrally determined policies and the local influences on health policy-making.

British central government

The organisation of British central government can be described simply. General elections, which must be held at least every five years, result in the election to the House of Commons of some 650 Members of Parliament (the precise number varies as constituency boundaries are redrawn). The leader of the largest single party in the Commons is asked by the monarch to form a government and the leader becomes the Prime Minister. The Prime Minister appoints from among his or her supporters around 100 people to take up ministerial appointments. The most senior of these, usually numbering around 20, comprise the Cabinet. The government is thus made up of Cabinet and non-Cabinet ministers, the majority of whom will be MPs. The remaining members of the government come from the House of Lords.

Ministers are responsible for the day-to-day running of the government's business through the departments of state. These departments include the Treasury, which is responsible for all matters to do with finance, and the Department of Health. Most of the work of the departments is in practice carried out by civil servants. Ministers are, however, individually responsible for the work done by civil servants in their name, and are held accountable by Parliament. Parliament also monitors the work of government departments through a system of select committees.

There is no written constitution in Britain and the relationship between the different institutions of government has evolved over the years. As one of the foremost students of the constitution has observed, the result is a 'curious compound of custom and precedent, law and convention, rigidity and malleability concealed beneath layers of opacity and mystery' (Hennessy, 1995, p. 7). In seeking to unravel the mystery of the unwritten constitution, much has been written about the role of the monarchy, the legislature and the executive. To summarise this literature briefly, the historical decline in the power of the monarchy and the House of Lords gave rise to the thesis that Britain had a system of 'Cabinet government'. In his book, *The English Constitution,* published in 1867, Walter Bagehot argued that the monarchy and the Lords had become 'dignified' elements in the constitution, compared with the Commons, the Cabinet and the Prime Minister which he described as the 'efficient' elements (Bagehot, 1963). Of these latter institutions, Bagehot saw the Cabinet as preeminent.

Almost 100 years later, Richard Crossman, writing an introduction to a new edition of Bagehot's book, contended that Prime Ministerial government had replaced Cabinet government. In Crossman's view, the extension of voting to all adults, the creation of mass political parties and the emergence of the civil service administering a large welfare state all contributed to the Prime Minister's power (Crossman, 1963). This interpretation was confirmed by Crossman's experience as a Cabinet Minister. In addition, he noted the important part played by official committees in Whitehall, a facet of government he had not observed while in opposition; and he encountered the power of civil servants to challenge and frustrate the wishes of ministers.

British central government has traditionally been seen as exemplifying a 'Westminster model' of politics characterised by free and fair elections, parliamentary sovereignty, control of the executive by the majority party, strong Cabinet government, a key role for government departments, ministerial responsibility for the actions of departments, and a neutral civil service. More recent research into the workings of government, however, has challenged the Westminster model.

Rhodes' 'differentiated polity' model (Rhodes, 1997) draws on trends such as the privatisation and contracting out of public services, the increasing role of international organisations like the European Union, and the establishment of agencies to take on some functions of government to question the key tenets of the Westminster model. Rhodes contends that the executive is weak and not strong and that the institutions of central government have been 'hollowed out' as a consequence of privatisation and the increasing role of international organisations and agencies operating at arm's length from government. The differentiated polity model argues that government is increasingly fragmented with networks replacing hierarchies and with institutions and organisations external to government playing a bigger part in governance. Rhodes' model has, in turn, been challenged by other researchers who maintain that power is more concentrated than this model suggests (Marsh, Richards and Smith, 2001). We explore these issues in the rest of this chapter by examining the role of different institutions and the relationship between them.

Parliament

It is important to distinguish the formal power of Parliament from its effective role. Although formally Parliament passes legislation, examines public expenditure and controls the government, effectively it carries out these functions within strictly defined limits. As long as there is a House of Commons majority to support the government, then Parliament has few significant powers within the system of central government. In Mackintosh's words, 'Parliament is one of the agencies through which the government operates and it is the place where the struggle for power continues in a restricted form between elections' (Mackintosh, 1974, p. 125).

The task of securing the government's majority in the House of Commons falls to the party whips. They ensure that MPs are present to vote, and that the government's legislative programme is passed safely. Most legislation originates from the government, and bills have to go through a number of stages before becoming law. Parliamentary debates on legislation provide an opportunity for party views to be reiterated, and occasionally the government will accept amendments put forward by opposition parties. On occasions, important legislation may be defeated or withdrawn. But the existence of a parliamentary majority coupled with strong party discipline ensures that these occasions will be rare.

Parliament provides opportunities for individual MPs to propose legislation in the form of private members' bills. The most important method of promoting a private member's bill is through the ballot of members which takes place every session. Usually, around 20 names are drawn in the ballot, but because of the pressure on parliamentary time only one-third to one-half of the MPs who are successful in the ballot stand a chance of having their bills enacted. Even in these cases, though, the MPs concerned are dependent on the government not being opposed to the legislation they propose. The Abortion Act of 1967, promoted by the Liberal MP David Steel, is an example of a private member's bill which became law.

Individual MPs are able to use Parliament in two other main ways. First, they can put down parliamentary questions, asking ministers about aspects of the work for which they are responsible. Some of these questions receive written replies, while others are answered orally, in which case there is an opportunity to ask a supplementary question. Second, MPs can raise adjournment debates, which are often on local or constituency issues. These debates provide a chance to air matters of concern to MPs and their constituents, and force ministers and departments to make a response. Also, although most of the parliamentary timetable is controlled by the government, certain days are available to the opposition to debate subjects of their choosing.

One of the key developments in Parliament in recent years has been the use of select committees. These are committees of MPs which investigate particular topics and publish reports on their findings. The aim of the committees is to provide MPs with a more effective means of controlling the executive, and to extract information about the government's policies. The establishment of the committees was in part a response to the perceived decline in the power of the Commons to control the government. It was the job of the Social Services Committee to monitor the work of the DHSS and it was superseded by the Health Committee when the department was divided in 1988.

During its lifetime, the Social Services Committee undertook a number of major inquiries, including investigations into perinatal and neonatal mortality, the Griffiths Inquiry into NHS Management, and community care. Also, the Committee regularly reviewed the expenditure plans and priorities of the DHSS. The reports from the Committee in this area and the replies by the DHSS provided a continuing dialogue on the issues involved in planning and monitoring the expenditure programmes within the control of the DHSS. The MPs on the Committee were supported by a House of Commons clerk and his staff, and by specialist advisers (Nixon and Nixon, 1983). As well as taking evidence from civil servants and ministers, the Committee called witnesses from outside the DHSS, including the officers and chairmen of a number of health authorities This practice has also been followed by the Health Committee whose recent investigations have covered issues such as NHS dentistry and the role of the private sector. Alongside the Health Committee, the Public Accounts Committee continues to examine the way in which government money has been spent, including spending on health services. The Public Accounts Committee has published a number of reports which have been critical of the management of the NHS, including analyses of the management of waiting lists, NHS emergency planning and the private finance initiative.

The actual impact of select committees on policy is largely determined by the government's willingness to accept their recommendations. Although it is expected that departments will respond to committee reports, this does not mean that the committees' findings will have an immediate influence on policy. Nevertheless, it can be suggested that committees create a more informed House of Commons, force departments to account for their actions, submit ministers to a level of questioning not possible on the floor of the House, and help to put issues on the agenda for discussion. Furthermore, at a time when the role and influence of individual MPs have come into question, the committees have given MPs useful and often satisfying work to do. They also enable outsiders to gain a better understanding of what is going on in Whitehall, and the information they extract provides ammunition for pressure groups to use in particular campaigns.

The development of the role of select committees is one of the factors which has led some writers to argue that the House of Commons is more powerful than often assumed. This is the view held by Norton (1981), who has drawn on evidence of a decline in the cohesion of political parties within Parliament and an increase in government defeats in division lobbies to suggest that the Commons can effectively scrutinise and influence government. As Norton points out, the key to government control of Parliament historically has been the existence of a single majority party with strong discipline being exercised by the whips, and any moves away from this system, such as the formation of minority or coalition governments, would further strengthen the position of those who wish to reassert the influence of the House of Commons. Norton himself summarises the role of Parliament in the following way:

> Parliament has never really been a law-making or policy-making body on any continuous basis. Its principal task in terms of proposals for public policy, as well as the conduct of government, has been one of scrutiny ... The fact that government needs Parliament to give assent to measures and its request for money means that Parliament has some leverage ... The impact of the British Parliament today, as in the past, might not be great, but it can and does have some effect on public policy. (Norton, 1997, p. 157)

The Prime Minister and Cabinet

The preeminence of the Prime Minister in the British system of government noted by Crossman and other commentators can be explained in a number of ways. First there is the Prime Minister's patronage. He or she has sole responsibility for appointing members of the government, and in addition has considerable discretion over the conferment of honours. Of course, the Prime Minister's power of patronage is not total, and is usually exercised with regard to the influence of other actors in the system. In appointing the Cabinet, for example, the Prime Minister will want to include people drawn from different parts of the majority party, possibly including former opponents. Nevertheless, it is ultimately the Prime Minister alone who decides, and who accepts responsibility for the appointments made.

Second, there is the Prime Minister's position as chairman of the Cabinet. This gives the Prime Minister control over the Cabinet agenda, and the power to appoint the members and chairmen of Cabinet committees. Much of the Cabinet's work is now done by committees whose activities were surrounded by secrecy until details of their work were published for the first time in 1992. This revealed that a subcommittee existed on health strategy and that this reported to a main committee on home and social affairs. Third, the Prime Minister may establish informal groupings of senior ministers to act as an inner Cabinet. The inner Cabinet may serve as a sounding board for the Prime Minister, and may help to incorporate potential rivals into the centre of government decision-making. The Prime Minister will also negotiate with individual ministers in order to gain influence over specific policies. This was very much Mrs Thatcher's style of government. Under Mrs Thatcher, the Cabinet and formal Cabinet committees continued to decline in importance, and greater use was made of *ad hoc* groups of ministers selected by the Prime Minister to deal with specific issues (Hennessy, 1986). The decline in the role of the Cabinet was confirmed by one of her most senior ministers, Nigel Lawson, who commented:

> When I was a minister I always looked forward to the Cabinet meeting immensely because it was, apart from the summer holidays, the only period of real rest that I got in what was a very heavy job. Cabinet meetings are ninety per cent of the time a dignified (rather than an efficient) part of Cabinet government. (quoted in Hennessy, 1995, p. 97)

Fourth, the Prime Minister's position is strengthened by the support of the Cabinet Office. Within the Cabinet Office the Cabinet Secretary is the key person, and he or she acts as the personal adviser to the Prime Minister. The Cabinet secretariat controls the distribution of minutes and papers in the Cabinet system and enables the Prime Minister to keep a close eye on what is taking place in Cabinet committees.

Fifth, since 1974, successive Prime Ministers have made use of their own Policy Unit located in 10 Downing Street. The Unit's principal purpose is to assist the Prime Minister in implementing the strategic goals of the government. One of its members during the 1980s has identified seven functions performed by the Unit. These are to serve as a think-tank, to act as an adviser, to follow up on the implementation of policy decisions, to raise important issues that might not otherwise have been passed to the Prime Minister, to lubricate relations between No. 10 and departments, to brief the Prime Minister directly on issues, and to help discover frustrated reformers and give their ideas another chance (Willetts, 1987).

As well as these sources of strength, the Prime Minister's powers are underpinned by his or her position as leader of the majority party and the politician with overall responsibility for the Civil Service. All of these factors give the Prime Minister a more powerful role than the traditional description, *primus inter pares*, suggests. Crossman's *Diaries* indicate that there were occasions when the Cabinet did engage in collective decision-making, but these tended to be when the Prime Minister had no definite view and was prepared to let the Cabinet decide. What seems clear is that the Prime Minister is rarely defeated in Cabinet, and an alliance between the Prime Minister and the Chancellor of the Exchequer, or the Prime Minister and the Foreign Secretary, is virtually unstoppable.

Yet before consigning the Cabinet to the dignified realm of the British constitution, the limits of prime ministerial power should be noted. For example, during the course of 1981 proposals for cuts in public expenditure put forward by the Chancellor of the Exchequer with support from the Prime Minister were defeated by the so-called 'wets' in the Conservative Cabinet (Young, 1989). Even more dramatically, Margaret Thatcher was forced to resign as Prime Minister in 1990 when she lost the confidence of her colleagues. Her successor, John Major, faced a similar challenge to his position in 1995 and chose to resign as leader of the Conservative Party in order to fight a leadership election with his critics. Major's victory in this contest reestablished his authority within the Party and as Prime Minister, although it weakened his standing in the country and contributed to the defeat of the government at the 1997 general election. In this case, the challenge to the Prime Minister arose not out of concerns about the diminution of the role of the Cabinet, which had become more significant following the departure of Mrs Thatcher, than through deep divisions within the Conservative Party in relation to Britain's role in Europe. In both of these examples, the challenge to serving Prime Ministers demonstrates the existence of a number of checks and balances in the British system of government, not in the form of codified rules of the kind found in the United States constitution but nonetheless effective.

The election to office of a Labour Government in 1997 marked a return to the centralisation of power around the Prime Minister and his close advisers. Indeed, Tony Blair adopted a presidential style and strengthened the Cabinet Office and the Policy Unit in 10 Downing Street to ensure that adequate support was available. Like Margaret Thatcher before him, Blair relied heavily on bilateral meetings with ministers rather than committees, and the Cabinet's position was further weakened (Hennessy, 2000). As one study noted, 'Blair's Cabinet meetings are too brief (usually less than an hour) to be effective decision-making forums' (Kavanagh and Seldon, 1999, p. 273). The same study observed:

> Blair's preferred method of work, as in opposition, is to hold one-to-one meetings with colleagues or to convene small ad hoc groups to tackle strategic issues. He holds bimonthly *stocktaking* bilaterals with Secretaries of State and their top officials in his key areas of education, health and crime ... Blair and his aides are not sympathetic to the committee style of policy-making. (Kavanagh and Seldon, 1999, p. 274)

Under Tony Blair, the Cabinet Office was strengthened to the point where, in the view of some commentators, it had become a Prime

Minister's Department (Hennessy, 2000; Riddell, 2001). Specific innovations included the establishment of a number of units within the Cabinet Office to support the Prime Minister and the government. These included the Performance and Innovation Unit and the Forward Strategy Unit, subsequently brought together in the Prime Minister's Strategy Unit; the Prime Minister's Delivery Unit; the Office of Public Services Reform; and the Social Exclusion Unit. As a consequence, 'The Cabinet Office must now be considered something of a corporate headquarters overseeing government strategy' (Kavanagh and Seldon, 1999, p. 303). After the 2001 general election, the Policy Unit was merged with the Prime Minister's private office to create the Policy Directorate. The significance of this change was that the special advisers who made up the majority of members of the Policy Unit were integrated with the civil servants in the private office with the aim of creating a more effective source of advice and support for the Prime Minister.

The position of the Prime Minister in British government is reinforced by the fact that on questions of government strategy or on broad economic policy departmental ministers are often reluctant to step outside their own areas of concern. Crossman bemoaned the absence of an overall strategy in the 1964–70 Labour government, and he explained it in terms of the entrenched departmentalism within Whitehall (Crossman, 1975, 1976, 1977). The Prime Minister, unencumbered by specific departmental responsibilities, is able to take the wider view, and so can set the direction of government policy as a whole. Only when the Prime Minister's leadership poses a threat to the government and its future electoral chances is the Prime Minister's dominance likely to be seriously challenged by Cabinet colleagues.

The principal exception to this generalisation is the Chancellor of the Exchequer whose overview of public finances and public spending enables the occupant of this office also to see the bigger picture and from time to time to emerge as a rival to the Prime Minister. The importance of the relationship between the Prime Minister and Chancellor was particularly apparent under the Blair Government, in which Gordon Brown as Chancellor exercised considerable influence over many aspects of policy. One of the mechanisms used by the Chancellor was the public service agreements negotiated with government departments setting out targets to be achieved with the resources agreed during spending reviews. Brown's influence under the person who was arguably the most powerful Prime Minister in the postwar era reinforces the thesis of those who caution against exaggerating the role of the Prime Minister in contemporary British politics (Kavanagh and Seldon, 1999). It also underlines the power of the Treasury in British central government (Marsh, Richards and Smith, 2001; Deakin and Parry, 2000). The influence of the Chancellor is acknowledged even by those who have emphasised the presidential nature of politics under Tony Blair: 'Brown is, in effect, overlord of the economic and domestic front. It is a bi-stellar administration with policy constellations revolving round the two stars in Downing Street' (Hennessy, 2000, p. 513).

In this context, the decision in 2003 to allow the Cabinet to debate British entry to the Euro should be seen not as a reassertion of the Cabinet's position but rather as a signal that on most major matters of government policy the Cabinet is not involved in decision-making. As Kavanagh and Seldon have noted, 'Blair's downplaying of Cabinet continues a trend towards it becoming, like the monarch before it, a 'dignified' rather than an efficient part of the constitution' (p. 315). At the time of writing, it is the power of the Prime Minister and the Chancellor, and the biltateral relations developed between each of these politicians and secretaries of state of government departments, that is more important in shaping policy outcomes than the formal machinery of the Cabinet and its committees. In these relations, ministers and civil servants in government departments themselves exercise considerable influence, notwithstanding the increasing power of the centre of government. We now examine their role in more detail.

Ministers and civil servants

The view encapsulated in the Westminster model that ministers decide policy and civil servants carry it out is no longer widely held. The memoirs of Crossman, Castle and other former ministers (RIPA, 1980) indicate that civil servants have considerably more influence over policy-making than suggested in conventional textbook accounts. At the DHSS, for example, Crossman had to overcome the reluctance of civil servants before he succeeded in establishing the Hospital Advisory Service in 1969 after the *Report of the Committee of Enquiry into Ely Hospital, Cardiff* (Crossman, 1977). What the Ely example demonstrates is that a minister with clear views and a strong commitment can achieve his goals. On other issues, though, ministers may have to bargain, cajole and compromise before they get their way. This is epitomised by the 'Yes, Minister' and 'Yes, Prime Minister' television series which offered a popular portrayal of life in government departments in which civil servants more often than ministers shaped the development of policy.

Civil servants influence policy-making in various ways. Their familiarity with the Whitehall machine, coupled with access to information and a repository of knowledge developed over a period of years, creates an expertise which is not easily challenged. Often, it is the strength of the departmental view on an issue, rather than any ideological antipathy, which politicians have to overcome (Young and Sloman, 1982). In many cases, ministers are not well-placed to challenge this view, if only because parties in opposition devote relatively little time to developing the policies they intend to carry out when in office. In addition, ministers may not always have the intelligence or skill to counter the weight of advice offered by civil servants. The debate about the relative influence of ministers and civil servants may therefore be more to do with weak ministers than conspiratorial civil servants. Ministers are not always appointed for their administrative ability or their analytical skills, and it is perhaps not surprising that they do not always carry through significant changes in policy (Hennessy, 1989).

Another reason why ministers may be less than fully effective is the variety of different jobs they are expected to do: run their department; participate in Cabinet and Cabinet committee discussions; take care of their constituents as MPs; and take part in the work of the House of Commons. With so many competing demands on their time, it may be easier for ministers to accept the advice they are given and to rely on their departmental briefs than to attempt to exercise an independent policy-making role. It is worth noting, though, that there have been attempts to bolster the position of ministers through the appointment of special advisers. These advisers were first appointed on a large scale in the 1960s by Labour ministers as a source of outside information and to provide an alternative form of briefing to that supplied by civil servants. A former Prime Minister, Harold Wilson, has identified seven functions for advisers:

> as a sieve, examining papers for politically sensitive or other important problems; as a deviller, chasing ministers' requests or instructions; as a thinker on medium and long term planning; as a policy contributor to departmental planning groups; as a party contact man, keeping in touch especially with the party's own research department; as a pressure group contact man; and as a speech writer. (Quoted in Blackstone, 1979)

Special advisers have been used by both Labour and Conservative governments, and they come and go with governments. Professor Brian Abel-Smith of the London School of Economics was used as a political adviser in the DHSS by Richard Crossman in the late 1960s, and by Barbara Castle and David Ennals in the mid-1970s. The more astute advisers are able to enhance their position by building up relationships directly with civil servants, senior and junior, rather than always working with or through ministers (Young and Sloman, 1982). In this way they seek to extend their influence over policy-making. A number of former ministers, including Shirley Williams, Barbara Castle and William Rodgers, have argued that special advisers perform a useful function

(RIPA, 1980; Castle, 1980) and their role increased markedly under the Blair Government.

The number of special advisers in government increased from 34 in 1994/95 to 83 in 2001/02. In most government departments, there are two special advisers who work alongside civil servants. One of these advisers is often involved in supporting ministers in communicating their views to the press and the public, while the other is usually engaged in the development of policy and maintaining links with the party and other important stakeholders. There is a much larger number of advisers in the Prime Minister's Office reflecting the growth in importance of this office discussed earlier. Twenty-seven of the 83 advisers in post in 2001/02 were based in 10 Downing Street and they were involved in supporting the Prime Minister in work on strategy and policy, strategic communications, and government and political relations. Within departments, special advisers are increasingly active in working with ministers and civil servants in the development of policy, including the area of health policy where advisers in both 10 Downing Street and the Department of Health have worked closely with ministers in the development of plans for the NHS. On many issues, this means that advisers may be more influential than civil servants. It also means that ministers have access to alternative sources of advice and are able to test the recommendations they receive from officials against the views of advisers and others. The increase in the number of special advisers working in government and their higher profile has raised questions about the boundaries between ministers, civil servants and advisers (Committee on Standards in Public Life, 2002). A report by the House of Commons Public Administration Committee in 2001 concluded that special advisers had a valuable contribution to make but argued that there should be greater transparency in their method of working and a clearer framework of accountability around their activities (Public Administration Committee, 2001).

Relationships between departments

In discussing the role of the Cabinet, we noted that attempts to develop overall government strategies were frustrated by the strength of individual departments. The importance of 'departmental pluralism' (Richardson and Jordan, 1979, p. 26) is nowhere more apparent than in the budgeting process of central government, which historically centred on the PESC cycle. PESC is the acronym for the Public Expenditure Survey Committee, the committee of officials which coordinated the preparation of the government's expenditure plans (Likierman, 1988). *The Castle Diaries 1974–76* provides fascinating insights into the PESC negotiations, particularly as they affected health services. During the later months of 1975 and early 1976 – a time of increasing control over public expenditure – Castle and her officials were in the position of defending the NHS budget against attempts by the Chancellor of the Exchequer and the Treasury to achieve significant reductions in planned spending levels. As Castle records in her diaries, the public expenditure White Paper 'demonstrated vividly how much more successful I have been than some of my colleagues in defending my programmes' (Castle, 1980, p. 641). And as she explained to a meeting of Regional Health Authority chairmen, the outcome was:

> no absolute cut; overall growth rate for health of 1½ per cent per annum; expansion of health centre programme; yearly growth of family practitioner services of 3½ per cent; no need to cut back services; capital programme levelling out at £250 million a year; joint financing to the tune of £20 million by 1978–79; enough elbow room to move towards the better system of regional allocation under the Resource Allocation Working Party criteria, based on deprivation; the greater flexibility in switching between revenue and capital which Dick Bourton [a Deputy Secretary in the DHSS] has won from the Treasury (I paid him a public tribute on this); last, but not least, greater flexibility in carrying over spending from one year to the next (1 per cent instead of the ¼ per cent we had won from them this year). Tough, but not catastrophic. (Castle, 1980, p. 654)

One of the aims of PESC was to develop a more corporate approach to public expenditure planning and policy-making. The need to encourage such an approach has been emphasised many times. The Central Policy Review Staff (CPRS), the government think-tank which started work in 1971 and was disbanded in 1983, had as one of its functions the examination of issues with implications for more than one department, but its resources were small compared with those of the departments. The CPRS, which worked for ministers as a whole under the supervision of the Prime Minister, carried out strategy reviews of government policy, prepared major studies on specific issues, and provided collective briefs for ministers. In a report published in 1975 the CPRS argued the case for a joint approach to social policies, stressing the importance of greater coordination between the various central government departments concerned with social policies.

From time to time government departments do publish joint circulars or joint White Papers, but most of their activity is concerned with single programmes or services, and the CPRS argued that 'a new and more coherent framework is required for the making and execution of social policies' (Central Policy Review Staff, 1975, p. 1). As at the local level, collaborative planning and policy-making is beset by such difficulties as different organisational and professional structures, a mismatch between planning systems and cycles, and competing definitions of social problems. Although the CPRS report resulted in the establishment of a coordinating committee of ministers, this had a short life and the initiative slowly fizzled out. The demise of the CPRS itself is a further indication of the difficulty of developing cross-departmental approaches within Whitehall.

Despite this, the Blair government elected in 1997 made renewed efforts to break down departmental barriers, setting up a Social Exclusion Unit in the Cabinet Office to coordinate the contribution of different departments to tackling social exclusion, and emphasising the need to develop 'joined up solutions' to complex policy problems. The Social Exclusion Unit was one of several units established by the government to strengthen the capacity of the Prime Minister through the Cabinet Office to take an overview of major policy issues and their implications (see above). In parallel, the Treasury under Gordon Brown was increasingly involved in using its position to move beyond discussions with individual departments to examine the connection between policy areas. The Treasury's efforts were focused particularly on the negotiations that took place in the comprehensive spending review.

Like PESC, the CSR centred on bilateral discussions between departments and the Treasury with negotiations between Ministers and the Chief Secretary to the Treasury following detailed discussions between officials. This process culminated in a report to the relevant Cabinet Committee and decisions on public spending covering a three-year period for most government departments. In practice, most of the key decisions were agreed between the Prime Minister and the Chancellor. As we noted in earlier chapters, unlike PESC the CSR sought to link expenditure plans with performance targets in the form of public service agreements. As the CSR evolved, it came to include a number of cross-cutting reviews of policy issues that affected more than one government department (Deakin and Parry, 2000). An example was the cross-cutting review of health inequalities that reported in 2002 and that led to the development of an action plan for tackling inequalities affecting a range of services (see Chapter 9). Other topics covered by cross-cutting reviews included children at risk, the role of the voluntary sector in delivering services, and the public sector labour market.

Despite attempts to strengthen the capacity for working across departments, individual departments retain considerable power within the framework of resources negotiated during the spending review. As a study of the Prime Minister has noted:

Compared with most departmental ministers, a Prime Minister has a tiny budget, a small staff and few formal powers. He has to work through Secretaries of State in whom statutory powers are vested. Viewed from Number Ten, Whitehall departments can look at times like a series of baronial fiefdoms, to which it can only react. Departmental ministers have large staffs, budgets, policy networks, information and expertise, and can draw up legislation in their areas of responsibility ... The strength of most departments is such that it requires enormous willpower, obstinacy, political authority and excellent briefing for the Prime Minister to prevail against them (Kavanagh and Seldon, 1999, p. 312).

This is a salutary reminder of the continuing role of departments in the policy-making process and the interdependence of institutions and people within central government. It also helps to explain why recent prime ministers have sought to strengthen their own capacity for policy-making and for reviewing the performance of government departments through the changes made to the Cabinet Office described earlier. There is little doubt that as a consequence the Prime Minister is now much better placed to challenge departments and to draw on the expertise of the Strategy Unit and Delivery Unit, as well as the Policy Directorate, in so doing.

Outside interests

So far we have discussed the process of decision-making itself and have focused on the institutions of government and the relationship between them. It is now necessary to examine inputs into the system from outside interests, in particular from pressure groups. In examining this issue, Richardson and Jordan suggest that the central policy-making machinery is divided into subsystems organised around central departments. They designate these subsystems as 'policy communities' (Richardson and Jordan, 1979, p. 44) and point to the close relationships which exist in these communities between departments and pressure groups. Indeed, the relationships may be so close that shared priorities develop between the inside and outside interests, amounting to 'clientelism' (Richardson and Jordan, 1979, p. 55). The boundaries between groups and government thereby become indistinct, with in some cases a high degree of interpenetration taking place. The increasing role of outside interests and pressure groups has given rise to the view that 'governance' rather than 'government' should be the focus of analysis in seeking to understand what happens in the core executive (Bevir and Rhodes, 2003).

The significant place occupied by pressure groups in the British political system exemplifies the growth of what Beer has called 'the collectivist theory of representation' (Beer, 1969, p. 70). This legitimises a much greater role for groups than earlier approaches such as the Westminster model. As Beer notes, as government sought to manage the economy it was led to bargain with organised groups of producers, in particular worker and employer associations. Governments of both parties sought the consent and cooperation of these associations, and needed their advice, acquiescence and approval. Similarly, the evolution of the welfare state provoked action by organised groups of consumers of services, such as tenants, parents and patients. The desire by governments to retain office led them to consult and bargain with these consumer groups, in an attempt to win support and votes.

Relationships between groups and governments vary, but it is the producer groups which tend to have the closest contacts and the greatest degree of influence. The extent to which some of these groups have been incorporated into the political system was illustrated by moves towards tripartism in the 1960s and 1970s, that is the three-sided talks between government, employers' organisations and trade unions which occupied a central place in the development of economic policy at that time. Likewise, a close relationship exists between the British Medical Association (BMA) and the DH. As Beer points out, producer groups and governments are brought together by the desire of groups to influence the authoritative allocation of values, and by the need of government departments for the information which groups are able to offer, the cooperation they provide in the implementation of policy, and the importance which group endorsement of policy brings. And as Stevens observed in her history of medical practice in England, the increasing involvement of the government in health services served to widen rather than diminish the influence of doctors (Stevens, 1966, p. 366).

Consumer groups tend to have somewhat less influence, partly because their cooperation is usually not as significant for policy-makers. It is mainly information and expertise they have to offer, and consumer groups have to operate through influence rather than through the use of sanctions. Traditionally, the consumers of services have been less well-organised than the producers. However, a variety of consumer groups are active in the central policy-making system, including generalist organisations like the National Council of Voluntary Organisations, and specialist associations such as Shelter, representing homeless people, Age Concern, campaigning on behalf of older people, and MIND, concerned with mental health. Many of these organisations are consulted on a regular basis by government, and indeed public money is spent supporting their activities. These groups also participate in the extensive network of advisory bodies which assist government departments in the development of their policies. It is important to add, though, that while some groups have close connections and good relationships with government, others have to attempt to exert pressure from a distance. Not all organisations are as well integrated into the decision-making system as the BMA, and attempts to influence policy indirectly through Parliament and the mass media are still an important part of pressure group behaviour.

Pluralism or corporatism?

The growth of pressure groups has been paralleled by work which has attempted to redefine democracy in a way which accommodates the part played by groups in the political system. Beer's (1969) analysis of the collectivist theory of representation was one of the first efforts in this direction, and Dahl's (1961) elaboration of pluralist theory was another. Pluralist theory argues that power in western industrialised societies is widely distributed among different groups. No group is without power to influence decision-making, and equally no group is dominant. Any group can ensure that its political preferences are adopted if it is sufficiently determined. The pluralist explanation of this is that the sources of power – like money, information, expertise and so on – are distributed non-cumulatively and no one source is dominant. Essentially, then, in a pluralist political system power is fragmented and diffused, and the basic picture presented by the pluralists is of a political marketplace where a group's achievements depend on its resources and its 'decibel rating'.

The importance of pluralist theory is demonstrated by the fact that. implicitly if not always explicitly, its assumptions and arguments now dominate much writing and research on politics and government in Britain. An example is Richardson and Jordan's analysis (1979) of post-parliamentary democracy, a study very much in the pluralist tradition. Yet, despite its influence, pluralism has come under increasing challenge in recent years from writers who have questioned whether the British political system is as open to group influence as the pluralists maintain. In particular, it has been suggested that pluralism has given way to a system of corporatism in which some groups are much stronger than others and are in a good position to influence the decisions of government agencies.

The political history of corporatism in Britain has been outlined most fully by Middlemas (1979). Middlemas argues that a process of corporate bias originated in British politics in the period 1916 to 1926 when trade unions and employer associations were brought into a close relationship with government for the first time. As a consequence, these groups came to share government power, and changed from mere interest groups to become part of the extended state. Effectively, argues Middlemas, unions and employers' groups became 'governing institutions' (Middlemas, 1979, p. 372) so closely were they incorporated into the governmental system. By incorporation, Middlemas means the inclusion of major pressure groups into the governing process and not their subordination to that process. The effect of incorporation is to maintain harmony and avoid conflict by allowing these groups to share power.

Middlemas' thesis finds echoes in Cawson's (1982) discussion of corporatism and welfare. Cawson argues that '[t]he pressure-group world is not fluid and competitive, but hierarchical, stratified and inegalitarian' (Cawson, 1982, p. 37). He maintains that groups are not all of the same kind, and that organisations such as the BMA are well-placed to bargain for favourable policy outcomes by virtue of their strategic location in society. According to this argument, corporatism is not confined to the field of economic policy-making but extends into the sphere of social policy. Indeed, for Cawson, the NHS provides one of the best examples of corporatist policy-making because government intervention in the provision of health services has necessitated close cooperation between the medical profession as the key producer group and government agencies. While some writers argue that corporatism has replaced pluralism, in Cawson's analysis corporatist policy-making coexists with pluralist or competitive policy-making. In the latter, consumer groups like MIND and Age Concern bargain with government agencies but lack the leverage available to producer groups.

In making these points, the dynamic nature of policy-making and power relationships must be acknowledged. As an example, the influence of trade unions and employer associations reached a peak in the 1970s and thereafter declined, particularly in the case of trade unions, as the Thatcher government departed from the corporatist tendencies of previous administrations and reasserted the role of government itself in policy-making. There were parallel developments in the field of health policy where again the Thatcher government unsettled established relationships between the DH and organisations like the BMA and implemented reforms such as the new contract for GPs and the internal market in the face of opposition from key producer groups (Lee-Potter, 1997).

Policy developments in the 1980s and 1990s marked a break with the postwar consensus that had bound together the Conservative and Labour parties in many areas of public policy and reflected the commitment of the Thatcher government to tackling the sclerosis that it diagnosed had invaded the body politic. As David Owen has commented on the handling of the dispute over private practice in the NHS in the 1970s:

we were in the last throes of the corporatist state. Leaders of the trade unions and the BMA expected to bargain directly with Ministers. It was the era of beer and sandwiches at No. 10 which ended with the Winter of Discontent in 1979 and with the defeat of the Labour Government. (Owen, 1991, p. 233)

In keeping with the Thatcher government's diagnosis, a series of reforms were introduced to the civil service involving significant reductions in the number of civil servants and the application of the new public management to the machinery of government. Among other things, this resulted in the establishment of over 120 executive agencies to take responsibility for the management of some public services at arm's length from government departments. Four executive agencies were set up under the Department of Health, namely the Medical Devices Agency, the Medicines Control Agency, the NHS Pensions Agency and NHS Estates, while the NHS Executive was created within the Department to oversee the management of the NHS.

The process of reform did not end with the election of the Blair government in 1997. Indeed, with its commitment to the devolution of power within the United Kingdom, including the establishment of the Scottish Parliament, the Welsh Assembly and the Northern Ireland Assembly, new Labour's policies were even more radical than those of its Conservative predecessors. Not least, they raised questions about the future of the United Kingdom as a unitary state and held out the prospect of increasing divergence in the organisation of the NHS and the development of health policy. The priority attached to devolution at a time when the European Union's influence on policy-making in Britain was increasing also implied a reduction in the role of the institutions of government in Whitehall and Westminster. This was underlined by the establishment of regional development agencies in England and elected mayors in major cities like London. With power moving up to Brussels in what became seen as an embryonic federal European state, and down to the territories and regions of the United Kingdom, the preeminence of central government appeared to be ending.

Within central government, recent research into the 'core executive' (Smith, 1999) has challenged both conventional accounts of the Westminster model and interpretations in the pluralist and corporatist traditions. As an example, Smith contends that arguments over whether Britain has a system of Prime Ministerial or Cabinet government are largely irrelevant when even powerful actors are dependent on others to achieve their goals. He also emphasises the extent of fragmentation at the centre and the difficulty of coordinating the work of different actors and institutions. Smith goes further in arguing that politicians and civil servants are themselves constrained by the structure and context in which they operate, a theme to which we return in Chapter 10. The main point in his analysis of relevance to this chapter is the interdependency of the policy communities and networks in and around Whitehall and the shifting pattern of power and influence.

In making these arguments, Smith is drawing on and developing the work of Rhodes, cited earlier in this chapter. Rhodes' research on policy networks and the core executive lay behind the subsequent development of the differentiated polity model (Rhodes, 1997; Bevir and Rhodes, 2003). This model is based in part on the argument that the institutions of central government have been hollowed out by privatisation, the increasing role of international organisations, and the use of agencies at arm's length from government. As we have noted, this process has been taken forward by the devolution of power to Northern Ireland, Scotland and Wales. Rhodes also argues that the executive is fragmented and weak, and that influence is increasingly exerted in policy networks in which government departments and pressure groups are interdependent. In putting forward these arguments, Rhodes is writing in an essentially pluralist tradition.

Rhodes' approach has been challenged by Marsh, Richards and Smith (2001) who draw on research into the operation of government departments to offer an alternative interpretation. At the heart of their argument is the view that the executive remains powerful, notwithstanding elements of hollowing out. Marsh and colleagues go further to note the influence of the Treasury within the executive as a whole and of Ministers and civil servants in government departments. By contrast, in the government departments they studied, outside interests and pressure groups were comparatively weak. From this perspective, exchange relationships, policy networks and interdependencies are acknowledged to be important, but even more significant is what happens in government itself. As Marsh and colleagues comment, 'the crucial actors in the policy process remain those located within departments, i.e. ministers and civil servants' (p. 179). Equally important, they argue that pluralist interpretations of the kind advanced by Rhodes do not adequately capture the inequalities in power in government, because '[i]n general, the Prime Minister has more resources than ministers, ministers have more resources than civil servants and departments more resources than interest groups' (p. 239). In challenging the pluralists, Marsh and colleagues are not embracing corporatism because their emphasis is on the power of government institutions rather than pressure groups. In this sense, their position is more closely aligned with that of elite theory (see Chapter 10), as indicated by the description 'asymmetric power model' attached to their approach.

Conclusion

It was stated earlier that it is possible to describe the organisation of the British political system in simple terms. It is more difficult to locate precisely the key points of power and decision-making within the system. Although Parliament retains formal, and in a few cases effective, powers over legislation, expenditure and administration, in Bagehot's language it is more of a dignified than an efficient element of the constitution. Much more significant are government departments, the Prime Minister and Chancellor, with an increasingly important part being played by outside interests. Within departments power is shared between ministers and civil servants, the exact balance depending to a considerable extent on the strength and personality of the minister. It is naive to assume that civil servants exercise no influence, and it is equally erroneous to argue that they have absolute control. Much depends on the weight of the departmental view on issues, the quality of the advice rendered by civil servants, and the commitment of the minister to a particular course of action. Increasingly important too are special advisers, whether located in departments or in 10 Downing Street.

We have noted that the strength of individual departments is a feature of central government, and this bears out the argument of researchers who emphasise the role of political institutions in the policy process (March and Olsen, 1989). Yet departmentalism, although a barrier to the development of corporate approaches, facilitates the establishment of policy communities between departments and their client pressure groups. And it is in these policy communities that a great deal of the more routine and less controversial aspects of policy are worked out in increasingly intricate systems of governance.

Our discussion of the dynamics of the policy process indicates the need for caution in drawing firm conclusions about the role and influence of the institutions of government. The changes introduced by the Thatcher government and those initiated by the Blair government have affected the machinery of government and relationships with outside interests. The impact of these changes will continue to be felt as policies on devolution are implemented and as the role of the European Union increases. The emphasis in this chapter on the power of a small group of actors at the core of central government will then need to be reassessed. In the future, it seems likely that power will be dispersed more widely, although in the case of the NHS in England it remains to be seen whether the rhetoric of devolution outweighs the tendency to recentralise power in Whitehall.

What are the implications of this discussion for the student of health policy? It should be clear that the starting point for gaining an understanding of the dynamics of health policy-making is to focus on the operation of the DH. An analysis of the workings of the Department, including its relationships with outside interests and its connections with other parts of Whitehall and Westminster, would seem to offer valuable insights into how health policies are made within central government. In turn, this analysis will form the basis of a discussion of the micro politics of health policy within the NHS.

Chapter 7

Making and Changing Health Policy

The aim of this chapter is to examine the policy-making process in the Department of Health. The chapter begins by describing the structure of the Department and the way in which this has evolved. This leads into a discussion of the health policy community and the influence of different organisations and interests in policy-making. The chapter concludes by reviewing attempts to strengthen the Department's capacity for policy analysis.

The Department of Health

Originally established as the Ministry of Health in 1919, the work of the Department of Health has evolved as a result of changes to the machinery of government and the structure of the NHS. The Ministry was merged with the Ministry of Social Security to form the Department of Health and Social Security in 1968, but 20 years later the Department was divided by Margaret Thatcher when it was perceived to be too large for any Cabinet minister to run effectively. Reforms to the civil service in the 1980s resulted in a reduction in the number of civil servants and the establishment of the NHS Executive (formerly the NHS Management Executive and Management Board) within the Department to oversee the implementation of policy and the performance of the NHS. In the 1990s, the functions and manpower review and the Banks review of the wider Department of Health strengthened the role of the NHS Executive and led to changes in the Department's structure and method of working (see below).

The Secretary of State for Health sits at the head of the Department and is a member of the Cabinet. He or she is supported by a number of ministers and in 2004 there were two Ministers of State and three Parliamentary Under Secretaries of State. The responsibilities of these ministers reflect the full range of the Department's responsibilities and encompass public health and social care as well as the NHS. The Secretary of State chairs the NHS Modernisation Board whose members include people drawn from professional organisations, patients' groups, and NHS management. The NHS Modernisation Board meets three or four times a year and is a forum in which the Secretary of State can discuss current issues of concern with stakeholder interests. On a day-to-day basis, the work of the DH is carried out by civil servants, and in 2003 there were around 3650 civil servants working in the Department, excluding those employed in executive agencies. The most senior of these civil servants is the Permanent Secretary who is also Chief Executive of the NHS. He (there has not yet been a woman in this post) works closely with the Chief Medical Officer and other senior colleagues in the Departmental Management Board.

The current structure of the Department is illustrated in Figure 7.1. As the figure shows, the staff of the Department are organised into three groups. The Health and Social Care Standards and Quality Group is led by the Chief Medical Officer. The Group includes directorates and divisions with responsibility for research and development, health improvement, health protection, care services and quality and standards. The Health and Social Care Services Delivery Group is headed by the Director of Delivery and includes directorates and divisions with responsibility for finance, workforce, access, and information management and technology. The Strategy and Business Development Group supports ministers and the Chief Executive in the effective running of the Department. It includes the Chief Executive's Office and directorates and divisions with responsibility for user experience, strategy and communications.

The current structure was agreed in 2003 following a review of the Department's role. This review was prompted by the devolution of some functions to the NHS and the transfer of other functions to bodies such as the Healthcare Commission. It was anticipated that the number of staff in the Department would be cut by one-third to 2250 as a result of these changes.

Figure 7.1 *The structure of the DH in 2004*

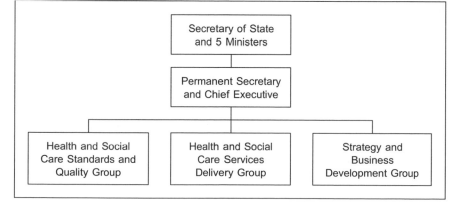

As these comments indicate, the work of the Department is organised into groups, directorates and divisions. The number and function of these groups changes from time to time in line with the developing role of the Department. For most of its life, the Department of Health and Social Security was divided into four main groups in relation to its responsibilities for health and personal social services. These were the NHS Personnel Group, which dealt with pay and conditions of service, and the recruitment and training of staff; the Finance Group, which handled all issues to do with finance, including negotiations with the Treasury; the Regional Group, which maintained contact with health authorities; and the Services Development Group, which was concerned with the development of policy. In addition, the Administration and Social Security Operations Group provided help across the Department on matters such as research and computers, and the Top of the Office helped the Secretary of State to provide central leadership and advised him on choices and priorities. Each group was led by a Deputy Secretary and divisions within groups were organised around Under Secretaries.

Just as government departments as a whole differ in that they have distinctive characteristics and working styles, so too groups, directorates and divisions within departments vary. In the case of the DHSS, the divisions and branches of the Services Development Group came to be identified to a certain extent with the client groups or services for which they had responsibility, such as older people and people with mental illness, and acted as a lobby for those groups or services. Similarly, the Regional Group, as well as communicating government policy to health authorities, at times acted as a pressure group for the NHS within the Department. These differences meant that policy-making in the DHSS tended to be fragmented.

The fragmentation at the centre was highlighted in an enquiry into the workings of the DHSS carried out by three regional health authority chairmen in 1976. The chairmen argued that many of the tasks performed by the Department should be devolved to health authorities, and they called for a sharper management focus for the NHS within the Department. These points were reiterated in the Griffiths Inquiry into NHS Management. The Griffiths Report pointed out that ministers and civil servants had demanding responsibilities other than the management of the NHS, with the result that the Department's capacity for overseeing the operation of the Service was underdeveloped. The Report argued for a significant shift in the stance and style of management in the Department involving the centre setting broad strategic objectives for the NHS and ensuring through appropriate planning and monitoring mechanisms that these objectives were achieved.

It was in response to the Griffiths Report that the Secretary of State established a Supervisory Board and a Management Board within the Department to provide the focus for the NHS that Griffiths argued was lacking (see Chapter 2). There was also a realignment of roles among groups. This involved the Services Development Group continuing to carry responsibility for policy. Those divisions concerned with the management of health authorities were brought together under the NHS Management Board, and a new group was formed to take responsibility for the family practitioner services and the pharmaceutical industries. The Services Development Group was later renamed the Policy Group and the key distinction that then emerged within the Department was that between formulating health policy and overseeing the management of the NHS. Following the establishment of the Department of Health in 1988, responsibility for policy came under the Health and Social Services Group (HSSG) and oversight of the NHS and implementation of policy fell to the renamed NHS Management Executive and its successor the NHS Executive.

One feature of continuing importance in the DH is the strong professional contribution to policy-making. As well as the generalist administrators who make up the bulk of the Department's senior staff, there are a wide range of civil servants from professional backgrounds. These include doctors, nurses, and social workers. Writing in the 1970s, Brown noted that the tradition in the Department is one of 'multi-disciplinary working in which questions are settled by agreement between the administrators and members of the appropriate professional hierarchy' (Brown, 1975, p. 58). An example from that time was policy development for older people which was organised around an assistant secretary working with a team consisting of a senior medical officer, a nursing officer, and a principal social work services officer (Kaye, 1977). More recently, there have been moves to establish integrated working within the Department by abolishing separate divisions in which civil servants from professional backgrounds report to their professional head.

Yet at the same time as these traditional divisions have become less significant, the increasing range of responsibilities taken on by the NHS Executive and the appointment of senior NHS managers to lead the work of the NHS Executive have opened up new tensions. The Banks review of the Department noted that 'the NHS Executive faces in two directions' and added:

As the top management of the NHS, the Executive must be 'of' the NHS, culturally close to it and credible if it is to lead and influence. That is why a distinct identity is so important. At the same time, the Executive is unequivocally a part of government, responsible for implementing the Government's policies for the NHS, holding health authorities to account on behalf of Ministers, and supporting and advising Ministers on health service matters. (Banks Review, 1994, p. 11)

The Janus-like character of the Department, in particular the NHS Executive, was dissected in a study of the two cultures of mandarins and managers (Day and Klein, 1997) and we shall return to explore this theme towards the end of the chapter.

It is also important to emphasise that the Department's responsibilities extend beyond the NHS to public health and social care. It has often been difficult to ensure that there is effective coordination of these responsibilities, although recent changes to the structure of the Department have sought to promote closer integration (see below). In reality, successive governments have seen the NHS as the highest priority and this has meant that neither public health nor social care have received the same attention. The coexistence of staff involved in NHS, public health and social care work adds to the complexity of the Department and reinforces the centrifugal tendencies that we now go on to discuss.

The policy community

In the previous chapter we introduced Richardson and Jordan's idea of the policy community to denote the extent to which policies are increasingly developed in consultation between government departments and the organisations concerned with their work. Consultation may take place through a variety of channels: through standing advisory committees or groups; through *ad hoc* enquiries or working groups set up to advise on particular issues; and through the more or less regular pattern of negotiation and discussion in which the DH engages with outside interests like the British Medical Association. In Richardson and Jordan's terms it may be misleading to use the word 'outside' to describe these interests. Their analysis emphasises the high degree of interpenetration which exists between pressure groups and government, and they point to the similarities which develop between departments and their client groups (Richardson and Jordan, 1979).

Valuable as this analysis is, it is necessary to recognise that not all groups are equally well-integrated into the national health policy community. Consumer groups, for example, are relatively weak and Brown, commenting on this in the 1970s, has noted that 'the machinery on the health and welfare side of the DHSS tends to be dominated by those who provide services rather than those for whom the services are intended'

(Brown, 1975, p. 193). Thus, although the health policy-making system appears to be pluralistic in that a wide range of interests is involved in the policy process, in practice this system may be skewed in favour of the well-organised groups who have a key role in the provision of health services. Producer groups are well able to promote and defend their interests, and this puts the DH in the position of appeasing these groups and resolving conflicts whenever they occur. As we argued in Chapter 6, corporatism may be a more accurate description than pluralism of a policy-making system in which producer groups are dominant.

One of the consequences of producer group dominance is that policy-making tends to be incremental, characterised by what Lindblom (1965) has termed 'partisan mutual adjustments'. Bargaining between the DH and pressure groups often results in small changes in the status quo, and this tends to be to the advantage of established interests. A great deal of the activity of the DH is not in fact concerned with policy-making as such. Rather, it is aimed at the continuation of existing services and policies and the maintenance of good relationships with key interests. Policy-making is a comparatively rare occurrence because:

> public resources for dealing with issues are relatively scarce. They are scarce in many terms – money and manpower obviously since public finance and public servants are finite quantities, but scarce also in terms of legislative time, media coverage, political will, public concern ... Political systems can only cope with a limited number of issues at once and these are always subject to displacement by new emerging issues of greater appeal and force. (Solesbury, 1976, p. 382)

Solesbury argues that issues must pass three tests if they are to survive the policy-making process. They have to command attention, claim legitimacy, and invoke action. It helps issues to command attention if they have particularity. Part of the reason why long-stay hospitals commanded attention is that they were associated with specific institutions, such as Ely Hospital, which came to symbolise the problems in this area of the NHS (see Chapter 4). Crises and scandals of this kind are often important in forcing an issue on to the agenda. Issues also need to become generalised. This helps them to claim legitimacy and attract the attention of existing political forces. Thus, a particular interest in Ely Hospital came to be generalised into a wider concern with social justice and humanitarian values, thereby bringing it within the dominant political culture and drawing the interest of established political groupings. An issue which has commanded attention and acquired legitimacy has passed two tests, but it must also invoke action. At this stage, issues run the risk of suppression, transformation into other issues, and token or partial responses.

Also relevant here is the notion of symbolic policy-making, a term developed by Edelman (1971) to refer to action intended to demonstrate that something is being done about a problem, rather than action which is a real attempt to tackle the problem. While there are undoubtedly difficulties in identifying the intentions and motives of policy-makers, in a number of areas it would appear that policies have significant symbolic elements. For instance, successive attempts to give greater priority to groups such as the mentally ill, people with learning disabilities and older people have not been accompanied by the allocation of significant amounts of additional resources, nor have ways been found of achieving a major shift towards these groups within existing budgets. In cases such as this, policies may act primarily as a way of maintaining political support and stability. Support is maintained in that the messages contained in policy statements may satisfy key political groups, thereby forestalling demands for more fundamental reforms. It is in this sense that words may succeed and policies fail (Edelman, 1977).

To return to Solesbury's discussion, what is valuable in his analysis is the examination of the hurdles which issues have to jump before they invoke action, the changing nature of issues, and the importance of subjective definitions in issue emergence. As Solesbury notes, in the policy process issues are:

> moving forward on many fronts, sometimes concerned with legitimacy, sometimes with attention, the issue itself changing its definition as it goes forward, linking with other issues, splitting from yet others, sometimes becoming totally transformed into a new issue altogether. The agenda metaphor provides the best indication of the nature of the process. (Solesbury, 1976, p. 396)

The agenda metaphor is developed at much greater length by Kingdon (1995) who contends that agendas are forged through the interaction of problems, politics and participants. In some cases, issues emerge onto the agenda because conditions are defined as problems. In other cases, changes in the political environment help shape the agenda. In yet other cases, participants may be important either in raising the salience of an issue or in framing the alternatives. These different streams come together into a 'policy primeval soup' (p. 200). The outcome is affected by the activities of policy entrepreneurs and by the opportunities offered by policy windows. There is a much greater chance of policy development occurring when problems, politics and participants are linked together, although this is not essential. Kingdon's framework allows for both random responses and predictable patterns of development, his key point being the complexity and messiness of the policy process and the lack of any simple explanations.

The sources of policy inputs

Pressure groups

There are many sources of inputs into the health policy-making system, several of which have already been mentioned. First, there are the inputs which come from pressure groups. As we noted in Chapter 6, the collectivist theory of representation legitimates a much greater role for groups than earlier theories of representation, and increasing state involvement in managing the economy and in the welfare state has led governments to negotiate and consult with pressure groups. A distinction has already been made between producer groups, which are often in a strong position to bargain for what they want, and consumer groups, which are relatively weak. There are also groups that exist to pursue a particular cause, an example being Action on Smoking and Health (ASH) which campaigns for control of smoking and limitations on advertising by tobacco companies. Yet ASH has backing from a key producer group, the Royal College of Physicians (RCP), demonstrating the difficulty of making clear distinctions in the pressure group world surrounding the DH (Popham, 1981).

Both the British Medical Association (BMA) and the medical Royal Colleges expect to be consulted over the development of policy and Eckstein (1960) has shown how often it is negotiation rather than consultation which characterises the relationship between these groups and the government. Occasionally relationships become strained, as in the dispute over pay beds in the 1970s and the NHS reforms in the 1980s, but on many issues there is a partnership between the medical profession and the DH, equivalent to those that exist in the educational and agricultural policy communities between the relevant departments and their client groups. The position of consumer groups within the health policy community is not as strong (Ham, 1977). Consumer groups are heavily dependent on the advice, information and expertise they have to offer, and cannot threaten sanctions in the same way as producer groups. Because their cooperation is usually not vital to the implementation of policy, consumer groups are dependent on the quality of their arguments and the willingness of ministers and civil servants to listen to what they have to say. In most cases, too, they have to supplement the pressure they exert on the DH by operating through Parliament and mass media.

The pressure exerted by producer and consumer groups may be welcomed by Ministers as it may help them in their negotiations with Cabinet colleagues. This explains why some groups receive financial support from government. In her diaries, Barbara Castle indicates that in her time as Secretary of State she encouraged the National Association of

Health Authorities 'to become a pressure group for the NHS' (Castle, 1980, p. 459). She also notes that during the dispute with the medical profession over pay beds, Ministers stimulated trade union activity to persuade the BMA to accept limitations on private practice within the NHS. Similarly, civil servants with responsibility for policy for particular client groups, such as the mentally ill, may welcome pressure from organisations like MIND as it may strengthen their hand in the competition for resources and priority within the DH. It is important to remember, then, that demands may not always arise autonomously in the community, and that pressure may sometimes be welcomed and encouraged by policy-makers.

Pressure groups make demands on a wide range of issues. These demands may require a change in legislation, a decision by a civil servant, or intervention by ministers. Occasionally, they may involve the Prime Minister, the Cabinet and other government departments. The effectiveness of groups in pressing their demands will depend on a variety of factors: the information they possess, their contacts with policy-makers, their expertise, and the sanctions they have at their disposal. In responding to groups, policy-makers will weigh their own preferences against those of the groups. They will also be alert to the need to secure the compliance of key interests, and to the electoral consequences of their decisions. The exact process of decision-making is difficult to define because, as Solesbury notes, it is at this stage that 'one passes into the relatively closed world of the executive departments of state, and to a lesser extent interdepartmental and Cabinet committees, where the consideration given to issues and possible responses by politicians and officials is largely shielded from the public gaze' (Solesbury, 1976, p. 392).

Despite the difficulties of penetrating the intricacies of decision-making within central government, it can be suggested that the national health policy community is itself fragmented into a series of sub-communities concerned with specific aspects of policy. These sub-communities are organised around issues such as policies for older people, primary care, health inequalities, and so on. As we noted earlier in the chapter, different parts of the DH have different characteristics, and in one sense the Department itself can be seen to be made up of pressure groups for particular functions, services and client groups. Outside pressure groups are drawn towards those parts of the Department which have responsibility for the policies which the groups are interested in, and sub-communities are formed from the relationships which develop between these groups and civil servants.

In an attempt to analyse these relationships, one study of policies for older people suggested that these policies were worked out in an 'iron triangle' rather than an 'issue network' (Haywood and Hunter, 1982). The terminology is that of Heclo, who has argued, in the context of American federal government, that decision-making has moved away from iron triangles involving a small number of participants in a stable relationship with one another, to issue networks comprising a large number of participants in a less stable relationship (Heclo, 1978). In their examination of policies for older people, Haywood and Hunter found that the process was well-represented by the iron triangle image. The key participants were Departmental officials, leading medical and nursing professionals, and two key producer groups: the Royal College of Nursing and the British Geriatrics Society. Although the consultative process was later widened to encompass a range of other groups, the crucial decisions at an early stage were arrived at by this small set of interests. However, Haywood and Hunter warn that on other issues, such as pay beds and health service organisation, issue networks may be a more appropriate metaphor.

Parliament and the mass media

Not all the demands made by pressure groups will invoke action and groups which are unsuccessful in their attempt to influence civil servants and ministers will often turn their attention to Parliament and the mass media. Here, then, are two further sources of inputs into the health policy-making system, and not just as vehicles for pressure group demands, but as originators of demands themselves. In recent years the mass media have played an active role in publicising the low standards of care that exist in the so-called 'Cinderella' services. Ever since the appearance of newspaper reports of cruelty to patients in the mid-1960s, the media have been prominent in the campaign to improve conditions for groups such as the mentally ill and people with learning disabilities. Television programmes on Rampton Special Hospital and on hospital services for disabled people have maintained public attention on this area of the NHS to the extent that journalists and television producers have taken on the appearance of pressure groups for underprivileged sections of the community.

The role of Parliament was discussed in Chapter 6. It will be recalled that parliamentary inputs to health policy-making take the form of MPs' questions, issues raised during debates, private members' bills, and reports from select committees. Some indication of the volume of Parliamentary business is given by the fact that in a parliamentary session there are around 11 000 parliamentary questions and approximately 60 000 letters are received, of which 20 000 are from MPs. The significance of these mechanisms is that they are important centralising influences in the NHS. The accountability to Parliament of the Secretary of State for Health requires a considerable amount of detailed information about health services to be fed up to the DH by NHS bodies. Equally, demands raised in

Parliament may have an influence on health policy-making and on the local operation of health services. An obvious example would be legislation resulting from a private members' bill, such as the Abortion Act. On other occasions, government-sponsored legislation may be amended in the course of its passage through Parliament. An example was the legislation that established NHS Foundation Trusts on which the government accepted a series of changes as a result of debate on the Health and Social Care Bill in the House of Commons and the House of Lords. These changes included the creation of a board structure for the independent regulator of NHS Foundation Trusts instead of a single office holder, and a requirement that Trusts should ensure that their membership was representative of those eligible to become members.

Increasingly, too, the House of Commons Health Committee and the Public Accounts Committee have provided an informed contribution to the policy-making process. The Health Committee has produced a variety of reports on health service issues. The MPs on the Committee are supported by a small group of full-time staff and specialist advisers appointed for particular inquiries. Select committees tend to have greatest impact when they present unanimous reports and in this respect the choice of topics for investigation is important. In its work, the Health Committee has chosen to examine issues which in the main are non-controversial in party political terms and this has helped the Committee to present a united front. Recent inquiries have included examination of delayed discharges in the NHS, the National Institute for Clinical Excellence, NHS dentistry and the role of the private sector. The work of select committees rarely leads directly to changes in policy but they have strengthened parliamentary scrutiny of government departments and over a period of time their reports may influence the work of these departments. As a study of the former Social Services Committee noted of the Committee's investigations into the expenditure plans of the DHSS, 'their cumulative effect has been to make the Department improve its own procedures for reviewing and coordinating its policies, as well as preparing and presenting expenditure plans' (Nixon and Nixon, 1983, p. 352).

The Public Accounts Committee scrutinises government spending as a whole and in recent years has examined a number of different aspects of the NHS, including the private finance initiative, NHS emergency planning, NHS Direct, and the management of surplus property by NHS trusts. A report published in 1981 which criticised the lack of control exercised by the DHSS over the management of the NHS was one of the factors which led to the introduction of the review process in the NHS in 1982. Nairne has referred to the Public Accounts Committee as 'the premier committee of Parliament' (Nairne, 1983, p. 254) and has described the pressures placed by the Committee on the Permanent Secretary in his capacity as Accounting Officer. This has been confirmed by Stowe, another former Permanent Secretary, who has described his relationship with the Committee as:

> a powerful reinforcement of the Permanent Secretary's authority and an even more powerful incentive for him or her to take very seriously his obligation to ensure that publicly financed programmes of expenditure are managed with integrity and efficiency. (Stowe, 1989, p. 57)

As Stowe notes, the power of the Committee derives in large part from the support it receives from the Comptroller and Auditor General and the National Audit Office. Staff of the National Audit Office have continuous access to the Department's files and the reports they produce provide the basis for investigations by the Committee. Stowe has observed that the relationship between the Department and the National Audit Office 'is anything but cosy: a mutual admiration society it is not. Some of the most fractious dogfights in my experience occurred in this quarter' (*ibid.*). Certainly, ministers and civil servants have faced some rigorous questioning from the MPs on the Committee and the Committee has had a demonstrable impact on such issues as premature retirement among NHS staff, manpower control within the Service and policy on maternity services.

NHS bodies

NHS bodies (the collective term for health authorities and trusts) represent a fourth source of inputs into the DH policy-making system. Indeed, these bodies do not simply carry out nationally-determined policies, but have important policy-making responsibilities in their own right. In many cases, policies are developed jointly by civil servants and NHS managers, an example being the performance indicators for the NHS published in 1983 which were the result of work done by staff from the Department and the Northern RHA. There are many other examples of policy proposals developed jointly by the centre and the periphery. The DH is dependent on NHS bodies for information about the local development of services and for actually providing the services, while these bodies are dependent on the DH for the resources required to carry out their functions. This mutual dependence helps to explain why it is that national policies are often shaped and influenced by NHS bodies.

The establishment of the NHS Management Board and its successors the NHS Management Executive and the NHS Executive within the Department served to strengthen the links between the centre and the NHS. Senior health service managers played an important part in the work of both bodies. This was first evident in the appointment of Duncan

Nichol, a regional general manager, as Chief Executive of the NHS in 1988 followed by Alan Langlands in 1994, and Nigel Crisp in 2000. Other staff have been seconded to work in the Department, and a number of civil servants have spent time in the NHS. Ministers as well as civil servants draw on advice from within the NHS in developing their policies and at the highest level this found expression in regular meetings between the Secretary of State and regional chairmen. Norman Fowler, Secretary of State in the mid-1980s, explained that regional chairmen 'operate as a health cabinet as far as I am concerned' (Social Services Committee, 1984, p. 165). Meetings with regional chairmen were two-way affairs in which ministers explained their thinking and priorities and regional chairmen reported on developments within the NHS.

A further source of advice is the NHS Confederation. This has gone through a number of guises and it exists to represent the views of NHS bodies to government. Membership of the NHS Confederation comprises a high proportion of health authorities and trusts and the staff and officers of the Confederation meet regularly with Ministers and civil servants to discuss issues in health policy and the NHS. As we noted earlier, Barbara Castle encouraged the forerunner of the NHS Confederation to be a pressure group for the NHS and it publishes a number of reports on current developments and lobbies to ensure actively that the opinions of NHS bodies are heard. Alongside the Confederation, the views of primary care groups are articulated by organisations like the NHS Alliance and the National Association of Primary Care and these organisations and their predecessors have been particularly vocal on behalf of GPs and other staff working in primary care.

The consultative machinery

A fifth input to policy-making comes from the consultative machinery attached to the DH. This machinery is made up of standing advisory groups, like the Standing Medical Advisory Committee, and *ad hoc* working groups and inquiries. The latter include royal commissions which tend to be used relatively sparingly and inquiries which are set up more frequently to advise on specific topics. In recent times these inquiries have examined issues such as inequalities in health, NHS management, community care and paediatric heart surgery at the Bristol Royal Infirmary. The reports that emanate from royal commissions and inquiries provide an almost continuous flow of demands into the DH. As with other inputs into the political system, demands coming from these sources have to compete for the time and attention of policy-makers. Some may be rejected out of hand, others may be subjected to further discussions, while others may be adopted immediately.

It is not unusual for the DH response to advisory bodies to be ambiguous or unclear. This applied to the Court Report on Child Health Services, where the Department accepted the report's demand for an integrated child health service, but rejected many of the more specific proposals put forward. Similarly, the government agreed in principle with the model of care for people with learning disabilities set out in the Report of the Jay Committee, but called for further consideration of various aspects of the Report. In this case, the opposition of powerful, established interests in the nursing profession to the Jay Committee's recommendations was one of the factors the Department had to consider.

As well as advice provided by standing or *ad hoc* groups such as the Jay Committee, there are the regular rounds of formal consultation with NHS bodies and pressure groups which have already been referred to. Formal consultation typically occurs when a consultative document on a particular issue is published. The extent to which these documents are really open to influence varies: in many cases there may be little scope for groups to influence what is decided, but on some occasions a well-organised group can have a significant impact. Whether groups are able to exercise influence may depend on the stage during the consultative process that they become involved. Haywood and Hunter (1982) point out that formal consultation is often preceded by informal consultation on draft documents. In some cases informal consultation may itself be foreshadowed by discussions among a small number of key participants, as in the iron triangle which develops policies for older people. As a rule of thumb, the earlier a group becomes involved, the more likely it is to influence what is decided.

Ministers and civil servants

Sixth, and most important, there are demands which come from ministers and civil servants within the DH. A new Secretary of State is likely to have a number of issues he or she wants to pursue while in office. Many will have been developed in Opposition, and may have been included in an election manifesto. Both Banting (1979) and Kingdon (1995) suggest that politicians are particularly important in making certain issues salient, and in defining the agenda for discussion. In the case of health policy, Webster has noted on the basis of his historical analysis of the NHS many examples of politicians influencing the agenda (Webster, 1996). Examples cited by Webster include Kenneth Robinson's involvement with the Doctors' Charter in the 1960s, Richard Crossman's emphasis on improving conditions in long-stay hospitals, and Keith Joseph's reorganisation of the NHS in the 1970s. Another area in which politicians made a difference was private health care which for many years was not a salient issue. Only in 1974, when Barbara Castle attempted to reduce the number of pay beds in NHS hospitals and limit the growth of private hospitals, did the issue become prominent. Private medicine remained a salient issue when the Conservative government elected in 1979 reversed Castle's policy and sought to encourage the growth of the private health care sector.

Having made this point, it should also be noted that ministers have to work with and through civil servants to take forward policy. In the case of pay beds referred to above, Barbara Castle notes in her diary that the permanent secretary at the time, Sir Philip Rogers, had submitted a paper stating that DHSS officials 'feel they would be failing in their duty if they did not let me know how opposed they all were to the phasing of private practice out of NHS hospitals' (Castle, 1980, p. 170). Castle's account is confirmed by the memoirs of one of her junior ministers at the time:

> In the summer of 1974 Sir Philip Rogers came to see Barbara Castle and myself to discuss privately our controversial manifesto commitment to phase pay beds out of NHS hospitals. Sir Philip deployed a strong case against our taking any action. He warned us that the mood of the medical profession was very brittle and said that the considered judgement of himself, the Chief Medical Officer and all the top officials was that, in the best interests of the NHS, we should avoid a confrontation with the doctors on this issue. Rather movingly, he insisted that if the Secretary of State, having heard him out, came to a different conclusion then that was the last that she would hear of it and everyone in the Department would carry out her policy faithfully and to the best of their abilities...
>
> Sir Philip kept his promise and from then on defended our decisions and refused to let the British Medical Association get away with the attempt to present officials as not being fully behind our policy. It was a fine example of the best of the civil service tradition of serving governments irrespective of party. (Owen, 1991, p. 232)

Of course, civil servants are not a homogeneous group, and Castle herself notes that 'the department is split into two different worlds: the conventional, change-nothing world of the top Establishment; the challenging irreverent world of the press office and some of the younger officials' (Castle, 1980, p. 209). Of particular interest in this context is the role of doctors in government. As we noted at the beginning of the chapter, there is strong medical involvement in decision-making in the DH, and a former Chief Medical Officer, Sir George Godber, has observed that 'the doctor in Government has to be facing two ways: he is a Civil Servant and his Minister must be able to rely on his complete loyalty: but he is also a member of his profession, which must be able to trust him too' (Godber,

1981, p. 2). These dual loyalties create the possibility that conflicts may arise in which professional ties will emerge the stronger. Godber notes that such a possibility arose during Crossman's tenure as Secretary of State but did not reach the point where the Chief Medical Officer would have resigned. On another occasion Godber states that 'The Permanent Secretary and I once declined to accept our Civil Service increases so long as the doctors' incomes were frozen' (Godber, 1981, p. 3). Clearly, then, civil servants have their own loyalties and views, and these views have an influence on policy-making. Further evidence of this point comes from Pater's study of the creation of the NHS. Pater argues that the credit for the establishment of the NHS should be widely shared, but he contends:

> There is no doubt, however, that the main credit for the emergence of a viable and, indeed, successful service must rest with two ... officers of the ministry: Sir William Jameson, chief medical officer from 1940 to 1950, and Sir John Hawton, deputy secretary from 1947 to 1951 and permanent secretary thereafter until his retirement through ill-health in 1960. (Pater, 1981, p. 178)

In different ways both Godber and Pater, writing as former civil servants, confirm the thesis to be found in the memoirs of ex-ministers, that the civil service has a significant impact on the development of policy. This need not mean that civil servants pursue their own policy preferences against the wishes of ministers. Nairne acknowledges that civil servants are influential, but maintains that the influence of officials derives from a partnership between ministers and civil servants rather than conflict. In Nairne's view, it is misleading to analyse what happens within government departments in terms of whether ministers or civil servants have power because the reality is that senior civil servants have to share responsibility with ministers for formulating policy (Nairne, 1983; Young and Sloman, 1982). One of the implications of partnership is that there will be occasions when civil servants themselves put forward initiatives to ministers. These initiatives will in many cases stem from a review of existing policies and will take the form of suggestions for improving those policies. *The Crossman Diaries* provide an example of this in relation to resource allocation which emerged onto the agenda in the late 1960s following a review initiated by civil servants (Crossman, 1977, p. 569)

Another example of a policy where internal factors were important is the Hospital Plan of 1962. This was prepared by hospital boards and committees under the guidance of the Ministry of Health. Although outside interests were pressing for increased spending on hospital buildings, the origins of the Plan owed a great deal to the Minister at the time, Enoch Powell, his Permanent Secretary, Sir Bruce Fraser, and the Deputy Chief Medical Officer, Sir George Godber. These three men effectively transformed a vague idea about the need for an expanded building programme into a detailed plan. The coincidence of interests between the Minister and senior civil servants helped to account for the promotion of this development in policy. What is also relevant is that here was a policy which had to be agreed between the Ministry of Health and the Treasury because of the major expenditure implications. Fraser, who had previously been a Treasury official, played a key role in these negotiations (Allen, 1979).

A recent study of the Secretaries of State who held office between 1988 and 1997 offers further insights into the world of ministers and the influences on policy-making (Ham, 2000). This study drew on interviews with the ministers concerned to note the importance of the views and experience of ministers themselves and their reliance on civil service advice and support. The latter included the advice provided by the civil servants working in the Secretary of State's private office and not just the most senior officials at the Top of the Office. In passing, it is relevant to note that an analysis of the role of the Prime Minister has also drawn attention to the influence of the civil servants in his private office on policy-making (Kavanagh and Seldon, 1999). Secretaries of State for Health were influenced too by pressure groups and outside interests. Of particular importance were producer groups like the BMA whose role in the implementation of policy acted as a constraint on the radicalism of politicians. As comparative analysis of policy networks in the United Kingdom and the United States has shown (Smith, 1993), health policy in Britain involves a relatively stable and cohesive policy community and this tends to result in incremental change. To be sure, stability and incrementalism may be challenged when politicians like Mrs Thatcher seek to promote fundamental reforms to the NHS, but the evidence suggests that these periods are relatively unusual and short lived. As the study of Secretaries of State for Health concluded:

> it is the influence of individuals working within established structures that shapes health policy. The interdepedency of these individuals and their interaction with key organisations leads to bargaining and negotiation out of which policy evolves. Politicians are important in shaping the agenda and in working with civil servants to identify and choose between policy options. Outside organisations and interests are involved in this process to a greater or lesser degree, with some like the BMA particularly well placed to influence the direction of policy. Periods of relative stability and continuity are interrupted by periods of innovation and change, most obviously when politicians external to policy communities seek to question the established consensus. (Ham, 2000, p. 72)

Special advisers did not figure prominently in the recollections of Secretaries of State when they were asked about the influences on policy-making in the 1990s. As we noted in the previous chapter, the number of advisers and their influence have grown under the Blair government, both in 10 Downing Street and the Department of Health. The involvement of special advisers in health policy is not new, as the use of Brian Abel-Smith by the Labour Government in the 1970s illustrates. Nevertheless, advisers played a significant part in the development of health policy after 1997, working closely with ministers in the development of major policy documents like *The New NHS*, *The NHS Plan* and *Delivering the NHS Plan*. One of the most influential of these advisers was Simon Stevens who worked with Frank Dobson and then Alan Milburn in the Department of Health before moving to work as a health policy adviser in 10 Downing Street in 2002.

An examination of the processes of policy-making and the various inputs into those processes creates, rightly, the impression of a complex policy system in which those responsible for making policy are subject to numerous competing demands. In the last part of the discussion we have drawn attention to examples of policy change, but it is worth remembering the earlier point that change is the exception rather than the rule. A considerable part of the activity of the DH is devoted to the maintenance of existing policies and to the continuation of established routines. Although change is possible, it is difficult to achieve because of the operation of demand regulation mechanisms which limit the number of issues on the agenda at any one time. And even in relation to these issues, incremental changes to the status quo are more probable than major shifts in direction. This has been clearly demonstrated in a study of government policy on smoking, where it has been argued that decisions were:

> the outcome of a process in which groups have played a major role ... For many years tobacco interests had no difficulty in keeping the subject off the political agenda; their power took a non-decision-making form. Forerunners of ASH, such as the National Society of Non-Smokers, encountered indifferent or hostile attitudes from Government ... It took the prestige and evidence of elite medical groups, such as the BMA and the RCP, to break the agenda barrier. Even then Government response was cautious because possible adverse electoral consequences were feared by some Ministers if too rigorous a policy of discouragement was pursued. (Popham, 1981, p. 345)

Inertia in policy-making is reinforced by the existence of stable relationships in the health policy community. The power of the medical profession in these relationships derives in no small part from the need of government for the support of doctors and their representatives in the implementation of policy. As we discuss in the next chapter, the medical profession exerts a strong influence on implementation and is itself often a source of service change and innovation.

Industrial and commercial interests

The example of smoking draws attention to the role of industrial and commercial interests in the health policy community. At least three sets of interests need to be considered. First, there are those interests which are involved in the provision of private sector health care services. Private providers include both the provident associations such as BUPA and the private hospital groups. A second set of interests consists of those companies supplying goods, equipment and services to the NHS. These include firms seeking to obtain contracts for the provision of services such as catering and laundry; the manufacturers of medical equipment and supplies; and the drugs industry. The last of these is particularly significant in view of the fact that the drugs bill makes up over 10 per cent of total NHS expenditure. Although the industry contributes significantly to employment and exports there has been concern at the level of profits earned. Regulation occurs through the Pharmaceutical Price Regulation Scheme, a voluntary scheme in which the DH attempts to control prices and profits in the industry. Despite this, the House of Commons Public Accounts Committee has criticised the Department for not doing more to limit profits, and in response to the Committee's criticism action was taken to introduce tighter controls.

A third set of interests is represented by companies producing goods which may be harmful to health. The tobacco, alcohol and food-processing industries are included in this category. The influence of the food industry has been examined by Cannon (1984) in an analysis of the response to a report on nutritional guidelines for health produced by the National Advisory Committee on Nutrition Education. The report, which recommended reduced consumption of sugar, salt and fat, and increased intake of dietary fibre, was opposed by the food industry. Cannon demonstrates how government is divided between ministers principally concerned with issues of public health and ministers concerned with economic and employment issues. Changes in eating habits which pose a threat to jobs and profits in the food industry are likely to be resisted not only by the industry but also by politicians and civil servants involved in spheres such as trade, industry and agriculture.

Similar issues arise in the case of tobacco. In a thorough analysis, Taylor (1984) has investigated why governments have historically done so little to regulate the tobacco industry in the face of overwhelming medical evidence about the harmful effects of cigarette smoking. As Taylor points out, the tobacco industry is composed of a relatively small number of large and wealthy multinational companies whose power derives not so much from their activity as pressure groups – although this may be important – as from their position in the economy. The industry is significant as an employer and as a source of tax revenues, and while DH ministers may want to control the industry on health grounds, ministers in the Treasury are inclined to oppose regulations on economic grounds. As Taylor comments:

> In principle, as guardians of the public health, governments ought to be the tobacco industry's fierce opponents, but in practice they are often its firm ally. Cigarettes provide governments with one of their biggest and most reliable sources of revenue; they create tens of thousands of jobs in hard economic times; they present a healthy surplus on the balance of payments; they help development in Third World Countries where tobacco is grown. In purely economic terms, the political benefits of cigarettes far outweigh their social cost. (Taylor, 1984, p. xix)

For this reason, the introduction of health warnings and changes in advertising practices have been brought about largely on a voluntary basis until recently.

The development of alcohol policy exhibits many of the same features. As Baggott (1986) has shown, successive governments have been slow to develop policies to control the misuse of alcohol. He attributes this to the power of commercial interests, the relatively weak and diffuse nature of the groups pressing for reforms, the hostility of voters and public opinion, and opposition by government departments who stand to benefit from a strong alcohol industry. The examples of food, tobacco and alcohol lend support to Lindblom's (1977) thesis about the power of business corporations in contemporary politics, and it is this power which helps to account for the predominance of policy maintenance and incremental changes. These examples also illustrate the importance of what Moran (1999) refers to as 'production politics' in the health care state, by which he means the process of negotiation and bargaining between commercial interests involved in health and health care and government.

The role of ideas

The policy process is not, however, entirely a matter of responding to political demands. An increasingly important part of the process is the attempt to examine a wider range of options, and to subject existing policies to a more thorough analysis. There are two aspects to this. First, there is the contribution which academics and researchers make to policy-making. As Banting (1979) points out echoing the work of Heclo (1974), policy-making is both an intellectual activity and a political process. Thus, as well as examining the impact of pressure groups, politicians and other key actors, it is necessary to look at the role of ideas and information in shaping policy. One of the areas of health policy where ideas have had an influence is the organisation of the NHS. The administrative structure introduced in 1974, for example, derived from theories of management and organisational behaviour developed by organisational sociologists at Brunel University and management consultants at McKinsey & Co Ltd.

A second area where ideas had an impact was in the thinking behind the Black Report on inequalities and health. The Report was the outcome of the deliberations of an expert working group whose most influential member was Peter Townsend, then Professor of Sociology at Essex University. Townsend's previous work on the nature and causes of poverty and deprivation clearly contributed much to the analysis and recommendations of the Black Report. What is interesting is that Townsend's work is very much in the LSE social administration tradition which Banting found to have had a strong influence in other areas of social policy (Banting, 1979). It is apparent, though, that this tradition, of which Brian Abel-Smith, a special adviser to a number of Secretaries of State, was also a part, has had a greater impact on Labour governments than Conservative governments. Special advisers are often a channel through which ideas find their way into the policy process as studies of the history of the NHS have noted (Webster 1996).

A third example of ideas contributing to policy formulation was the influence of the American economist, Alain Enthoven, during the Ministerial Review of the NHS. In 1985 Enthoven published a monograph entitled *Reflections on the Management of the NHS* (Enthoven, 1985) in which he proposed the establishment of an internal market in health care. These ideas were picked up and developed during the Ministerial Review and had an appreciable influence on the White Paper, *Working for Patients*. The government's debt to Enthoven was acknowledged by the Secretary of State at the time of the Review, Kenneth Clarke. In an interview about the NHS reforms, Clarke referred to Enthoven's advocacy of internal markets, arguing 'I liked it because it tried to inject into a state owned system some of the qualities of competition, choice, and measurement of quality that you get in a well run private enterprise' (Roberts, 1990, p. 1385).

Academics and researchers apart, there have been a number of attempts within the DH to develop a more 'rational' approach to policy-making. In varying degrees, these mechanisms have sought to introduce a greater measure of analysis into the policy process, and in the penultimate part of this chapter we review the recent experience of policy analysis in the Department.

Policy analysis in the Department

In 1970 the Conservative government published a White Paper setting out proposals for increasing the policy analysis capabilities of central government. Among the innovations to follow from the White Paper were the Central Policy Review Staff, established to provide advice on government policies independent of that offered by existing departments, and Programme Analysis and Review, involving an in-depth study of specific topics within departments. Both innovations affected central government as a whole. At around the same time, and reflecting the spirit of the White Paper, a number of specific developments were taking place in the DHSS designed to improve the Department's capacity for reviewing its policies and priorities. Two developments in particular merit consideration: the introduction of programme budgeting, and the creation of a planning system for the Department.

Programme budgeting was developed in the United States in the 1960s, and its use was first considered within the DHSS in 1971. Its aim is to provide a framework for linking policies with resources, thus enabling priority decisions to be made within an overall strategy. The programme budget originally developed within the DHSS covered both health and personal social services and grouped these services under seven main headings: primary care; general and acute hospital and maternity services; services mainly for the elderly and the physically handicapped; services for the mentally handicapped; services for the mentally ill; services for children; and other services, for example social work. Expenditure on each of these services can be compared through the programme budget, enabling a comprehensive analysis to be undertaken (Banks, 1979).

Alongside the programme budget was developed the DHSS planning system. The intentions behind the system were to link policy development with resource availability, to provide the Department with information on objectives which could be used in the PESC negotiations (see Chapter 6), and to form the basis of national guidance to health authorities and local authorities. The system was based on planning statements prepared by branches within the DHSS which were then grouped under a number of main headings such as primary care, the mentally handicapped, children and manpower. The results of the planning system eventually found their way into the consultative document on *Priorities*, providing guidance to field authorities on the local development of services (Razell, 1980).

Within central government as a whole, the spirit of the 1970 White Paper gave way to a particular concern to increase management efficiency and cut down on bureaucracy after the election of the Thatcher government in 1979. Programme Analysis and Review and the Central Policy Review Staff were terminated, to be replaced by Rayner Scrutinies, reductions in manpower, and an initiative on financial management (Cmnd 9058, 1983). In the DHSS, the planning system was wound down – a victim, like its NHS counterpart, of exaggerated expectations. The programme budget, split into separate programmes for hospital and community health services and personal social services, continued to be used, but more as a tool for monitoring past trends in expenditure than as a mechanism for projecting future growth rates. Consistent with the spirit of the times, the number of civil servants in the Department was reduced by 20 per cent between 1979 and 1984 (Social Services Committee, 1984, p. 163) and Nairne has described how the Rayner regime and the drive for efficiency and effectiveness in the civil service forced the pace of Departmental management (Nairne, 1983).

Alongside the emphasis on efficiency, there was a continuing concern to improve the Department's capacity for strategic policy-making. An important influence in this respect was the House of Commons Social Services Committee whose reports on the public expenditure programmes covered by the DHSS stimulated ministers and civil servants to review the effectiveness of the Department's policy-making procedures. In response to the Committee's criticisms of an 'apparent lack of strategy policy-making at the DHSS' (Social Services Committee, 1980), the Department gave details of a number of committees and groups which existed to undertake strategic policy analysis (DHSS, 1980d). These included the Health and Personal Social Services Strategy Committee, chaired by the Permanent Secretary and meeting quarterly to review overall policy developments; and the Cross-Sector Policy Review Group, established in 1979 to look at issues of cross-sector policy and wider social policy. The DHSS added in its reply that ministers were considering how to strengthen arrangements for policy-thinking across administrative boundaries. By the time of the Social Services Committee's second investigation into public expenditure in 1981, the Department was able to point to the Policy Strategy Unit, set up to replace the Policy and Planning Unit, as a further example of a group concerned with policy in the round. Issues examined by the Unit included ophthalmic services, prescription charges, strategy for the elderly, unemployment and health and the role of voluntary bodies in the field of alcohol misuse (Social Services Committee, 1981). In some ways, the Policy Strategy Unit was similar to the Central Policy Review Staff, except that it worked only within the DHSS. In the end, the Unit met the same fate as the CPRS, being superseded in 1984.

Back to management

As the 1980s progressed, the concern to strengthen the Department's capacity for managing the NHS gained momentum. The most visible manifestation of this was the establishment of the NHS Management Board following the Griffiths Report of 1983. As Griffiths argued, there was a need for the Secretary of State to be supported at the centre by:

> a small, strong, professional management group, able to devote considerable time to running the NHS. This is in no way intended to derogate from your strategic role of Chairman and Chief Executive, but in fact to allow that role to be given expression through a General Manager seen to be vested with your authority and to be acting on your behalf and as your right hand man, in ensuring that the statutorily appointed authorities manage the NHS effectively. (Griffiths Report, 1983, p. 15)

Griffiths went on to propose that the Department should no longer concern itself with detailed management issues. Instead, it should set the overall direction of the NHS and hold authorities accountable for their performance. This would enable the Department to 'rigorously prune many of its existing activities' (*ibid.*). To signal a clear break with the past, Griffiths proposed that the chairman of the Management Board should come from outside the NHS and the civil service

These recommendations were accepted and Victor Paige was appointed as the Board's first chairman. Almost immediately, difficulties emerged. In the words of the then Permanent Secretary, Sir Kenneth Stowe, 'it was nearly a disaster' (Stowe, 1989, p. 52). One of the reasons for this was the limit imposed on the Board's activities by politicians. As Paige has written:

> because of Ministers' accountability to Parliament, the high political pressures and sensitivity associated with virtually every central management decision within present policies, then the reality is that ministers take all the important decisions, political, strategic and managerial. (Paige, 1987, p. 7)

This meant that it was impossible to devolve executive authority to the Board. Unable to operate within political constraints, Paige resigned in 1986. Reflecting on what happened, Stowe has maintained that government will never be able to operate like a commercial business. He stated that:

> [i]nevitably tensions will arise between, on the one hand, Ministers (and those officials supporting them) who must always be accountable to Parliament, and on the other, officials (irrespective of their nomenclature) who have been charged by those same ministers with the task of achieving an efficient delivery of services within prescribed policies and predetermined resources. (Stowe, 1989, p. 54)

In an attempt to tackle these tensions more effectively, membership of the Board was changed after Paige's resignation, with the Minister of State for Health taking the chair, and Len Peach (from IBM) being appointed as Chief Executive. This was deliberately projected as an interim arrangement and it was superseded in 1988 when the NHS Management Executive (ME) was created. The NHS Management Executive was chaired by a Chief Executive drawn from the NHS and it operated under the strategic direction of the Policy Board.

The ME put considerable effort into creating a separate identity for itself within the Department and in working closely with NHS bodies. This was reflected in its operating style which often involved NHS managers joining civil servants in working parties and project groups to produce reports and guidance on specific aspects of the reforms. As a consequence, the ME was perceived less as part of the Department and more as a 'head office' for the NHS. Although in formal terms it remained firmly within the Department and accountable to the Policy Board, the ME began to take on the appearance of an agency at arm's length from political control and able to operate semi-autonomously. This impression was reinforced by the relocation of the ME to offices in Leeds in 1992. The functions and manpower review which reported in 1993 examined the possibility of the Management Executive becoming an executive agency but ministers concluded that this option should not be pursued. This was mainly because of the intense public and political interest in the NHS and the need to ensure effective accountability in a service spending over £30 billion a year at that time.

Implementation of the Banks Review (1994) enabled the work of the Department to be streamlined with further reductions in the number of civil servants and a shift in the balance of work and power to the NHS Executive as it came to be known. The decision to place responsibility for policy in the hands of the NHS Executive meant that the wider Department focused mainly on public health and social care. As a consequence of the Banks Review, the recommendations of the Griffiths Report were finally implemented over a decade after its publication, although it should be emphasised that the Permanent Secretary remained the head of the Department and retained oversight of all its responsibilities. This was reflected in the wording of the Statement of Responsibilities and Accountabilities prepared after the Banks Review which noted that the Permanent Secretary had the task of 'advising the Secretary of State on the discharge of all the duties of his or her office' while the Chief Executive of the NHS Executive was 'the Secretary of State's principal policy adviser on all matters relating to the NHS' (DH, 1997, paras 1.7 and 1.8).

The tensions in this arrangement came to a head in 2000 when a decision was made to create a single post of Permanent Secretary and NHS Chief Executive. This post was filled by Nigel Crisp who had pursued a career as an NHS manager before becoming a regional director of the NHS Executive. In the jockeying for power between the mandarins and managers, to borrow the language of Day and Klein (1997), managers therefore emerged as the more powerful, and this reflected the increasing emphasis within the civil service under the Blair government of management expertise and the delivery of government targets. The creation of the post of Permanent Secretary and NHS Chief Executive was followed by the integration of the NHS Executive into the Department in 2001 as part of an effort to achieve more effective coordination of the full range of the Department's responsibilities. This included an attempt to achieve better links between those parts of the Department dealing with the NHS, public health and social care.

To close the circle, the end of the 1990s also witnessed a renewed interest within the Department in policy analysis and strategy. This was indicated by the establishment of a Strategy Unit in 2000 to report directly to the Secretary of State and subsequently the creation of a Strategy Directorate as part of the changes to the Department introduced in 2004. The latter development reflected wider reforms to the civil service in which the size of departments was reduced and their strategic capability increased. These changes stemmed from an initiative led by the Prime Minister and Cabinet Secretary and were an attempt to achieve a better balance between management expertise and strategic capability in central government.

Conclusion

As this chapter has illustrated, the DH is not a monolith. The existence of a variety of professions, divisions and groups gives rise to a high degree of pluralism within the Department and this is complicated by the interplay with outside interests. The landscape of the Department is continuously being reshaped in response to changing needs and fashions and the struggle for power between different interests. In the 1980s and 1990s the main distinction was between those responsible for policy and those overseeing the NHS and the implementation of policy. This was eventually resolved when the NHS Executive took charge of both functions after the Banks Review. The role and influence of the NHS Executive within the Department was progressively extended and it came to occupy a pivotal position between ministers and the wider Department on the one hand and the NHS on the other. The recent integration of the NHS Executive into the Department has strengthened the position of managers at a time when management expertise is highly valued in the civil service.

The health policy community that surrounds the Department contains a large number of organisations and interests. Pressure groups are drawn towards those parts of the Department that deal with issues of concern to them and sub-communities emerge around these issues. In these policy communities, producer groups have greater influence than consumer groups and are often involved in negotiation with ministers and civil servants rather than consultation. Other inputs to the policy process come from Parliament and the mass media, NHS bodies, standing advisory groups and *ad hoc* inquiries, industrial and commercial interests, and academics and researchers. Ministers and civil servants themselves are particularly important in policy formulation, as are special advisers. One of the consequences of the diversity of interests in the policy community is that policy maintenance is more common than policy initiation, and this is reinforced by stability within the health policy community and the need on the part of government for the support of the medical profession and its representatives in the implementation of policy.

There have been a number of attempts to strengthen the Department's policy analysis and strategic functions. Nevertheless, bargaining, negotiation and accommodation between different interests are the principal forces that shape the development of policy. Also important is the way in which policy is adapted and amended as it is implemented, and it is to a consideration of policy implementation that we now turn.

Chapter 8

Implementing Health Policy

The aim of this chapter is to examine the implementation of health policy and the micro politics of the NHS. The chapter begins with a description of the management of the NHS and the role of NHS bodies such as health authorities, and trusts. This leads into a discussion of the relationship between the Department of Health and the NHS and of policy-making within the NHS. The influence of the medical profession is reviewed and the chapter concludes by summarising the various factors relevant to an understanding of health policy implementation

The management of the NHS

The Secretary of State for Health has overall responsibility for health services, and he or she is also responsible for overseeing social care. Different arrangements exist for the administration of these services outside Whitehall, and it is interesting to compare these arrangements. Social care comes under the control of local authorities and they have considerable autonomy from central government. Local elections give local authorities an independent power base, while the existence of council tax as a source of revenue provides the means by which authorities can determine spending levels. In practice, central government involvement in local affairs has increased in recent years, but local authorities retain some freedom to decide on the range and mixture of services to be provided in their areas. As would be expected, local autonomy also means local variation, and there are wide differences in spending levels and types of services provided.

The Secretary of State discharges his or her responsibility for providing health services through NHS bodies whose boards are appointed to oversee the commissioning and provision of services at a local level. These bodies comprise health authorities, NHS trusts, primary care trusts and special health authorities. While the main function of NHS bodies is to ensure that health services are delivered in a way that is consistent with national policies and priorities, they have policy-making responsibilities in their own right and do not simply carry out the Secretary of State's wishes.

On the other hand, unlike local authorities they lack the legitimacy derived from elections and have no significant independent sources of revenue. To explore these issues in more detail, we now examine the operation of NHS bodies and their functions and responsibilities.

The regional tier

The need for a regional agency in the NHS has been recognised ever since the establishment of the Service in 1948. In the first phase of the NHS, regional hospital boards played a crucial role in turning a disparate collection of hospitals into a planned and coordinated service. In 1974 their functions were extended and their name changed to regional health authorities. After 1992 regional health authorities coexisted with regional outposts of the NHS Management Executive, set up to oversee the performance of NHS trusts. The functions of regional health authorities and regional outposts were combined when regional offices of the NHS Executive were established in 1996. The decision to retain a regional presence reflected the difficulty of managing the performance of a large number of health authorities and trusts from the centre and also the value of having a buffer between the DH and the NHS.

The establishment of regional offices was associated with a reduction in the number of staff working at a regional level. This reduction was partly the result of eight regional offices replacing what until 1994 had been 14 regional health authorities, and partly the consequence of tight controls being exercised over the staffing of regional offices. Whereas regional health authorities and regional hospital boards had each been significant NHS bodies in their own right, regional offices as arms of the civil service and with far fewer staff worked much more in the background. Not only this, but also regional directors were accountable directly to the Chief Executive of the NHS Executive and sat alongside him as members of the NHS Executive Board. The effect was to strengthen the grip of the centre over local management by moving towards the single chain of command for the NHS proposed in *Working for Patients*. In this respect, they built on the system of accountability reviews introduced in the 1980s and developed into a means of setting targets and monitoring performance within the NHS (see below).

Subsequently, regional offices were abolished and replaced by four new regional directorates of health and social care in the DH. This change in the regional tier was part of the programme of reforms to the structure of the NHS announced in *Shifting the Balance of Power* in 2001 (DH, 2001a). The stated purpose of these reforms was to devolve as much responsibility as possible to a local level, in particular by giving primary care trusts more control over budgets and decision-making. As well as announcing the abolition of regional offices, *Shifting the Balance of Power* included proposals to reduce the number of health authorities. In the event, 28 strategic health authorities were established in April 2002 in place of the previous 95 health authorities, and one of their core functions was to manage the performance of NHS trusts and primary care trusts. Changes to the organisation of the DH introduced in 2003 led to the abolition of regional directorates of health and social care and meant that strategic health authorities became, in effect, the regional tier of the NHS, albeit covering smaller populations than their predecessor bodies. In parallel, regional public health groups, based in the nine government offices of the regions, were responsible for taking forward the wider public health agenda. The current structure of the NHS in England is illustrated in Figure 3.2 (p. 66).

Health authorities

Health authorities were established at the time of the 1974 reorganisation of the NHS (see Chapter 1) and their boundaries and names have changed at regular intervals since then. The decision to merge district health authorities and family health services authorities in 1996 had the effect of creating a single body to oversee the full range of services at a local level for the first time and was intended to promote the more effective integration of services. One of the main responsibilities of health authorities at that time was the commissioning of services from NHS trusts and other providers. The creation of 28 strategic health authorities (SHAs) in 2002 was designed to distance health authorities from service planning and commissioning in order to enable them to lead the strategic development of the local health service.

The three main functions of SHAs are to create a coherent strategic framework, agree annual performance agreements and performance management, and build capacity and support performance improvement. Each health authority has a board of executive and non-executive directors led by a chairman. The NHS Appointments Commission appoints the chairman and non-executive directors, and they are responsible for appointing the chief executive and working with him or her to appoint the other executive directors. Health authorities are accountable to the DH and are responsible for managing the NHS locally on behalf of the Department. In so doing, they are expected to work closely with local authorities and other agencies to improve the performance of health services and to tackle the determinants of health and health inequalities.

The DH assesses the performance of health authorities against the objectives set out in their franchise plans. These objectives in turn derive from guidance on planning and priorities published by the Department. The accountability review process introduced in the 1980s formalised what had previously been *ad hoc* arrangements for performance management in the NHS and the current system centres on progress in implementing the franchise plan and the local delivery plan. These plans identify the priorities and targets to which health authorities are working with NHS trusts and primary care trusts and progress is reviewed with the Department. Health authority chief executives meet regularly with the Permanent Secretary and Chief Executive and there are numerous links between senior staff of SHAs and their counterparts in the Department.

Extensive as these links are, there is no certainty that national policies will be implemented locally. The existence of health authorities made up of appointed chairmen and non-executives as well as senior managers creates the possibility that national policies will be modified during the course of implementation as the members of authorities put their own interpretation on these policies and adapt them in the light of local knowledge and circumstances. Not only this, but also health authorities themselves are not always in a position to carry through the intentions of Ministers even when they agree with the direction that has been set. As Malone-Lee has commented on the basis of his experience in the NHS:

> It is unusual for a health authority or its senior officers to be in a position to take a decision on an important matter and to have effective executive control over its implementation. The organisation is diffuse, loyalties centrifugal. To be effective most important decisions require at least the acquiescence of a large number of individuals or interest groups whose first loyalty is not to the health authority or its senior officers. (Malone-Lee, 1981, p. 1448)

Malone-Lee was writing at a time when health authorities directly managed hospitals and other health services but his observations are echoed by McDonald in a study of NHS decision-making in the 1990s. As McDonald noted:

> Although they were accountable for health services provided for their populations, HAs did not have direct control over the organisations and individuals supplying those services. Getting things done through other organisations was a key feature of HA business but HAs often lacked the leverage to do this. Pressure to contain 'management costs' at HAs meant that a small number of staff were responsible for commissioning a

wide range of health services with the result that they were placed at a disadvantage when dealing with hospital consultants who are expert in their field. (McDonald, 2002, p. 45)

These comments highlight the fact that there may be an implementation problem within health authorities, particularly when policy is directed at changing the actions of professional groups. We explore this issue more fully later in the chapter.

NHS trusts

NHS trusts were first established in 1991 under the changes set out in the White Paper, *Working for Patients*. Each trust is run by a board of directors comprising a chairman and up to five non-executive directors appointed by the NHS Appointments Commission, and an equal number of executive directors. The latter are appointed by the chairman and non-executives and usually include the chief executive, finance director, medical director and nursing director. Like health authorities, NHS trusts work as corporate bodies and are collectively responsible for their actions. In 2004 there were around 280 NHS trusts in England.

The main function of NHS trusts is to manage the services for which they are responsible. The configuration of services for which NHS trusts are responsible varies with some trusts running acute hospitals, others managing mental health services or learning disability services, and yet others combining some of these responsibilities. There are also trusts responsible for ambulance services. Prior to the establishment of NHS trusts, health authorities directly managed all of these services. The income of trusts derives from the service agreements negotiated with primary care trusts and other commissioners and they are expected to deliver care to the specifications contained within those agreements. They also have a duty to put and keep in place arrangements for monitoring and improving the quality of care. This duty is a core element in the drive to improve standards and to promote clinical governance within the NHS.

NHS trusts were set up as self-governing organisations and the intention was that within the framework of the NHS they should have considerable freedom to run their own affairs. To this end, *Working for Patients* included plans to enable trusts to borrow money, hire and fire staff on their own terms, and take decisions without having to seek permission up the management line. In practice, the freedoms of NHS trusts were constrained by Treasury rules and by the reluctance of the Major government to follow through the logic of its reform programme (Ham,

2003). NHS trusts were further constrained by the changes introduced by the Blair government during its first term and the emphasis placed by the government on partnership working in the NHS rather than organisational independence. The decision to make NHS trusts accountable to health authorities and to give SHAs responsibility for the performance management of trusts was consistent with these changes. Only with the emergence of proposals to create NHS Foundation Trusts did policy-makers show any interest in genuinely devolving responsibility for decision-making, though again the intervention of the Treasury seemed likely to limit the extent of devolution.

Primary care trusts

Around 300 primary care trusts (PCTs) were formed in 2002 and they have taken over functions previously undertaken by health authorities (for example, the commissioning of services) and NHS trusts (for example, managing community health services in many parts of the country). PCTs emerged out of the primary care groups established by the Blair government in 1999 and they have three main functions. These are to improve the health of the community, develop primary and community health services, and commission secondary care services. Each PCT is run by a board comprising a lay chairman and non-executive directors and a minority of executive directors, including the chief executive, the finance director and the director of public health. The NHS Appointments Commission is responsible for appointing the chairman and non-executives and they in turn appoint the chief executive and work with him or her to appoint the other executive directors. The day-to-day running of the PCT is the responsibility of the professional executive committee made up of a majority of professional members such as GPs and nurses.

PCTs build on the experience of fundholding and GP commissioning and provide a means of involving all GPs in the commissioning of services and their provision. To this extent, they mirror changes to the management of hospital and community health services instituted in the 1980s, centring on moves to integrate clinicians more closely in the management of services. The challenge for PCTs is to seek to involve doctors in management in a context in which GPs consider their first loyalty to be to patients. For many family doctors, participation in the management of budgets and services is not a high priority, and as we discuss later the independent contractor status of GPs epitomises the value attached to professional autonomy. The aspiration to manage primary care and to achieve closer integration with community health services that lies behind the establishment of PCTs is an attempt to move general practice into the mainstream of the NHS and to ensure greater consistency in standards and services across the country. As such, primary care trusts represent a challenge to the continuing independence of the medical profession and are designed to facilitate the implementation of national policies, particularly those concerned with the quality of care.

Studies of primary care groups and trusts during their establishment found that a major preoccupation when they were set up was the appointment of staff and their development as organisations. Subsequently, more attention was given to the strengthening of primary care, improving the quality of primary care services, and health improvement. Commissioning of services was slower to develop, particularly the commissioning of acute services. The transition from primary care groups (PCGs) to PCTs had the effect of diverting staff time away from service developments in some places as organisational change took priority (Regen *et al.*, 2001). The option for PCTs to become Care Trusts held out the prospect of greater integration of health and social care services, although initially the number of PCTs choosing this option was small. Early experience also indicated that it was not proving easy to involve GPs in the work of PCGs and PCTs (Regen, 2002). Differences in perception between managers, GP leaders and frontline GPs (NHS Alliance, 2003) on the working of PCTs indicated that securing effective engagement by GPs remained a challenge.

Special health authorities and other bodies

A number of services are organised and delivered through special health authorities. Examples include the National Blood Authority, the Health Development Agency, the NHS Litigation Authority, the National Patient Safety Agency, and the National Institute for Clinical Excellence (NICE). Each authority is run by a board whose chairman and non-executive members were appointed by the Secretary of State until this function was taken over by the NHS Appointments Commission, which is itself a special health authority. The Commission not only makes appointments to NHS boards but also ensures that there is a system of annual appraisals in place and that training and development is provided for board members.

As well as special health authorities, a number of functions are performed by executive agencies of the Department of Health. In 2003 these included NHS Estates, the NHS Pensions Agency, and the NHS Purchasing and Supply Agency. In addition, there are a number of non-departmental public bodies, such as the Human Fertilisation and Embryology Authority and the Healthcare Commission. The existence of these arm's length bodies symbolises both the 'hollowing out' of the state referred to in Chapter 6 and the growth of audit and inspection arrangements discussed in the next chapter. They can also be seen as further evidence of a shift from a managed to a regulated health care system. In 2003 a review of the number and function of arm's length bodies was set up and it was expected that some bodies would be merged and others abolished as a result of the review.

The role of the DH

It is apparent, then, that a large number of bodies are involved in the management and regulation of health services. The intentions of the DH have to be filtered down through health authorities and trusts before they have an impact on service provision. These bodies do not simply carry out the Department's wishes. NHS bodies are the Secretary of State's agents, but the agency role does not involve merely implementing instructions received from above. These bodies are semi-autonomous organisations who themselves engage in policy-making, and as such exercise some influence over the implementation of central policies.

Having stressed the point that NHS bodies are not simply a means of translating central policy into local action, it is important to note that the health service is a national service for which the Secretary of State is accountable to Parliament. The basis of parliamentary accountability lies in the voting by Parliament of funds for the NHS, and the statutory responsibility of the Secretary of State for the way in which these funds are spent. The existence of parliamentary accountability is a centralising influence, and requires that the Secretary of State is kept informed of local developments. As we noted in earlier chapters, MPs are able to ask questions and raise issues in debates about the operation of the NHS, and the Secretary of State is expected to be in a position to respond to these questions. Also, the investigations carried out in the NHS by the Public Accounts Committee and the Health Committee require that ministers and civil servants have available relevant facts about the local organisation of health services. NHS bodies therefore have to provide the DH with detailed information about specific aspects of service provision, as well as routine statistical returns, to enable the Secretary of State to answer MPs' enquiries.

The influence of the DH is most apparent in the case of the budget for the NHS and its allocation. These matters are determined centrally and there are no significant independent sources of revenue available within the NHS. Not only that, but also NHS bodies have a statutory duty to balance their budgets and this acts as an overriding constraint on their freedom of manoeuvre. DH gives guidance on the use of resources in a number of forms. First, circulars are issued on a range of topics setting out national policy which NHS bodies are expected to follow. Some of these circulars are prescriptive and identify procedures that have to be implemented but much of the guidance issued in this form is advisory, allowing scope for local interpretation. Circulars are often discussed in draft form with NHS staff and this enables local influence to be brought to bear on national guidance. In theory, this increases the likelihood of local compliance, although research indicates that historically circulars were of doubtful effectiveness as a means of central control (Ham, 1981).

Second, the DH publishes White Papers and consultative documents (also known as Green Papers) proposing developments in specific areas of service provision. This form of guidance is often used to make a major statement of government policy and is intended to reach a wider audience than health circulars. Consultative documents usually prepare the ground for White Papers, and enable NHS bodies and other interests to influence the more definitive statements incorporated in White Papers. White Papers set out general directions in which the government wishes policy to develop, and may represent a departure from previous intentions. They may also prepare the ground for legislation. Examples include the White Papers *Working for Patients* and *The New NHS* which contained the proposals of the Thatcher Government and the Blair Government respectively for the reform of the NHS. A different example was the White Paper on the future of primary care, which formed the basis of the 1997 Primary Care Act.

Third, the DH issues regular guidance on priorities for service development. This process started in 1976 with the consultative document on *Priorities* (DHSS, 1976b), and was followed by publication of *The Way Forward* in 1977 (DHSS, 1977b) and *Care in Action* in 1981 (DHSS, 1981c). Circulars have elaborated on these guidelines. The aim of these documents has been to inform NHS bodies of priorities for the development of health and personal social services. National guidance on priorities has varied in the degree to which it has prescribed what should be done, the advisory nature of *Care in Action* in 1981 – 'We want to give you as much freedom as possible to decide how to pursue these policies and priorities in your own localities. Local initiatives, local decisions, and local responsibility are what we want to encourage' – giving way to a more prescriptive approach in recent years. The greater use of prescription is connected with the earmarking of NHS resources for particular purposes.

The priorities and planning framework for 2003 to 2006, issued in 2002, brought together guidance from a number of sources. The framework was based on the public service agreement negotiated between the DH and the Treasury. The priorities set out in the framework were to improve access to services, improve services and outcomes in areas of clinical priority such as cancer and coronary heart disease, improve the overall experience of patients, reduce health inequalities, and contribute to the cross-government drive to reduce drug misuse. These priorities drew heavily on the national service frameworks that had been developed by expert groups in the main areas of clinical care as well as on the guidance published by NICE on the appropriate use of drugs and other technologies in the NHS. As we noted in Chapter 3, taken together, national service frameworks and NICE guidance constitute a concerted effort to reduce variations in the availability and quality of services between areas.

DH guidance on priorities is part of the more general attempt by central government to influence local patterns of service provision. The NHS Planning System, introduced in the 1970s (DHSS, 1975b), was intended to reveal cases where health authorities were deviating from national guidelines, and until 1984 it was the Regional Group within the DHSS, which was responsible for receiving RHAs' plans. Within the Regional Group, the regional liaison (RL) divisions had the task of discussing plans with RHAs. One of the civil servants involved in this process has indicated that when there was a disparity between the plan of a region and national policies, 'the RL division goes back to the authority and says, look, you've got this completely wrong. But there won't be many of those instances where the problems are sufficiently clear' (Clode, 1977, p. 1315).

There were also discussions between ministers and regional chairmen. This was indicated by a former Permanent Secretary, Sir Patrick Nairne, in evidence to the Public Accounts Committee. When asked what the DHSS would do about a recalcitrant region, Nairne stated, 'In my experience the Secretary of State has sometimes had to directly approach a regional chairman and say, "I have been looking at your plans and I really do not feel happy that you are making enough progress: for example, in the direction of the mentally handicapped"' (Public Accounts Committee, 1981, p. 86). After hearing this evidence, and after considering the range of mechanisms available to the DHSS, the Public Accounts Committee concluded that the Department should be in a position to control more effectively what was happening in the NHS. This view was shared by the Social Services Committee. Both committees argued that the Department should pay more attention to issues such as manpower control, hospital building and variations in costs.

Partly in response to the Public Accounts Committee's report, and partly as a result of changes among ministers and senior officials in the DHSS, the accountability review process was established. The review process superseded the NHS Planning System and involved a scrutiny of plans and performance leading to annual regional and district review meetings.

The purpose of the meetings was to review the long-term plans, objectives, efficiency and effectiveness of the region, and to provide a means of holding the RHA to account. Following the regional review, the RHA held a series of review meetings with each of its health authorities. The procedure was similar to that followed at regional reviews and an action plan was agreed at the end of the meeting. The review process was described by the Griffiths Inquiry into NHS Management as 'a good, recent development which provides a powerful management tool' (Griffiths Report, 1983, p. 12).

The system of accountability reviews has developed and been adapted in line with the changing structure of the NHS. Under the Blair government, the DH has become increasingly involved in managing the performance of the NHS, and there are regular reviews of performance between each health authority and the Department. Health authorities that deviate significantly from the policies set out nationally are expected to explain the reasons to the Department and take remedial action. This may include the chairmen and chief executives of health authorities being called to see ministers to explain variations from national targets. The increasing scrutiny of the Department's own performance by the Treasury and the Prime Minister's Delivery Unit has reinforced the Department's management of NHS performance. In major areas of significance to the government, this means that there is much closer alignment between local performance and the goals set out by ministers than has traditionally been the case, but in other areas there may be a gap between policy intent and what happens on the ground.

The difficulty of achieving local compliance with national policies was demonstrated in a study of the impact of *The Health of the Nation* during the 1990s. This study found a significant gap between the objectives of the national health strategy and its implementation (DH, 1998a). As the study noted, one of the reasons for this was the large number of policies and priorities being pursued by the government at the time. In a situation of priority overload and initiative conflict, some policies did not receive particular attention and management effort was directed to other areas. Specifically, *The Health of the Nation* was seen as a low priority in the accountability review process and the signal this sent out meant that neither regional offices nor health authorities saw it as a priority issue. It was therefore not surprising that the strategy failed to make a major impact, indicating that the ability of those at the centre of the NHS to influence decisions at a local level depended at least in part on the commitment put behind national initiatives. The more directive approach to performance management adopted by the Blair government was in part a response to the failure to achieve effective implementation of policies like *The Health of the Nation*.

The other instrument of control, and potentially the most significant of all, is the Secretary of State's power of direction. This power enables the Secretary of State to direct NHS bodies to comply with his wishes in relation to any aspect of their work. Also, the Health Services Act 1980 gave the Secretary of State specific powers to direct authorities to keep expenditure within income. In addition, the Secretary of State is able to suspend health authorities and NHS trusts, and to set up inquiries into their work. In practice, these powers are used sparingly. As Brown explains, they are used:

> only when a Minister decides to use them – in other words when he feels that the political or administrative need to wield the big stick outweighs the political and administrative cost that will be incurred. The more drastic powers are about as usable in practice as nuclear weapons. None can be used as an instrument of day-to-day control. (Brown, 1979, pp. 10–11)

There is some overstatement here, as the suspension of the Lambeth, Southwark and Lewisham AHA in 1979 indicates. The AHA was suspended by the Secretary of State for threatening to overspend its budget, and a team of commissioners was appointed in its place. Twenty years later the Secretary of State removed the non-executive directors of the Guild Community Health Care NHS trust in Lancashire because of concerns about the management of the trust. Nevertheless, Brown's underlying point is valid, and the reason why these powers are used so rarely is that only very occasionally do they need to be invoked. The DH is able to maintain oversight of the NHS through the other instruments already described, and through bargaining and negotiation rather than legal sanctions. This includes persuading chairmen and non-executive directors of NHS bodies to resign should this be necessary, rather than using legal powers to remove them from office.

The balance of power between the centre and the periphery in the NHS has been viewed in various ways. Enoch Powell, Minister of Health from 1960 to 1963, argued that the centre had almost total control (Powell, 1966). Richard Crossman, Secretary of State from 1968 to 1970, maintained that the centre was weak and the periphery strong (Crossman, 1972); and Barbara Castle, Secretary of State from 1974 to 1976, likened Regional Health Authorities to:

> a fifth wheel on the coach. They neither speak as elected representatives nor do they have the expertise of their own officials. And their attitude to the Secretary of State and department is necessarily pretty subservient – they want to keep their jobs! (Castle, 1980, p. 315)

The subservience noted by Castle was not much in evidence in a report on the workings of the DHSS prepared by three Regional Health Authority chairmen in 1976 (Regional Chairmen's Enquiry, 1976). The report was highly critical of the DHSS, and argued, perhaps not surprisingly, that more powers should be delegated to health authorities. In the chairmen's view too much control, and too many detailed decisions, were vested in the DHSS. These points were echoed in the Griffiths Inquiry into NHS Management. Griffiths argued that '[t]he centre is still too much involved in too many of the wrong things and too little involved in some that really matter' (Griffiths Report, 1983, p. 12). The establishment of the Health Services Supervisory Board and the NHS Management Board in the DHSS were an attempt to meet these criticisms.

One point made in the regional chairmen's enquiry was that there should be a greater interchange of staff between the NHS and the DHSS as a way of improving understanding and communication. In fact, this has happened on an increasing scale in recent years, with a number of civil servants undertaking secondments in the NHS, and a number of health service managers and other staff being seconded into the Department. The process was taken a stage further in 1988 with the appointment of a regional general manager as Chief Executive of the NHS Management Executive. As we noted in Chapter 7, the Department of Health often works through joint groups of civil servants and NHS staff. In addition, the Permanent Secretary and Chief Executive uses meetings of health authority chief executives as a key mechanism for explaining national policies and receiving feedback on the impact of these policies in practice.

It is apparent from this discussion that neither the DH nor NHS bodies can act independently of one another. The reason for this is that underlying the relationship between the different tiers of management in the NHS is the dependence of one tier on the other for resources of various kinds: finance, manpower, information and so on. As a result of this dependence, a process of exchange develops through which policies are implemented (Rhodes, 1979). An alternative way of viewing the interaction between management tiers is not as a system of exchange, but rather as a negotiating process in which policy is evolved as it is implemented (Barrett and Fudge, 1981). Whichever conceptualisation is adopted, a key factor in the implementation of health policy is the link between members of the same profession at different levels. Of particular importance is the position of the medical profession, and we now turn to an examination of its influence on the implementation of health policy.

Professional influences on policy implementation

The medical profession is involved in the management of the NHS at all levels. In the DH, doctors are represented at the very top of the Department through the Chief Medical Officer and his senior colleagues.

Also, under the Blair government, a number of NHS doctors have been appointed as national clinical directors within the Department to lead the development of services in areas of major clinical priority such as cancer and coronary heart disease. At the regional level, directors of public health are responsible for taking forward the public health strategy, and they do so by working both through the NHS and other government departments and agencies. Within the NHS, the boards of health authorities and trusts almost invariably include at least one senior manager from a medical background. Their contributions are supplemented by advice received from medical advisory committees and from individual clinicians whose views will often carry considerable weight in the policy-making process. The establishment of primary care trusts exemplifies the influence of doctors in the new NHS with GPs strongly represented on the professional executive committees of trusts and therefore in a position to exert considerable influence over resource allocation.

As well as having access to the DH, health authorities and trusts, the medical profession is in an influential position because of the role of doctors as the direct providers of services. In the case of GPs, this is reflected in their status as independent contractors within the NHS. Family doctors have for a long time resisted political or managerial interference in their work and have preferred to contract with the NHS to provide a service to patients rather than to be employed by health authorities. As independent contractors, GPs have been able to deliver care in the way they consider appropriate and only since the late 1980s have governments sought to monitor standards in general practice and give health authorities more influence over primary care. This has entailed the use of funds to improve premises and staffing levels and the employment of professional advisers to review prescribing patterns. There have also been moves to encourage GPs to take part in clinical audit. The introduction of personal medical services contracts under the 1997 Primary Care Act was particularly significant in this context as it entailed health authorities negotiating contracts for the provision of primary care directly with GPs. While GPs retain a good deal of freedom to organise their work and determine how services should be provided, the effect of these developments has been to strengthen arrangements for accountability.

Hospital doctors are salaried employees of the NHS, but again their actions cannot be directly controlled by managers and NHS trusts. The reason for this, as the DHSS has explained, is that:

> At the inception of the NHS, the Government made clear that its intention was to provide a framework within which the health professions could provide treatment and care for patients according to their own independent professional judgement of the patient's needs.

This independence has continued to be a central feature of the organisation and management of health services. Thus hospital consultants have clinical autonomy and are fully responsible for the treatment they prescribe for their patients. They are required to act within broad limits of acceptable medical practice and within policy for the use of resources, but they are not held accountable to NHS authorities for their clinical judgements. (Normansfield Report, 1978, pp. 424–5)

Consequently, hospital doctors determine what is best for their patients, including the place and length of treatment, and the kinds of investigation to be carried out. Medicine is one of the clearest examples of an occupation that has achieved the status of a profession, and a key feature of professions is the autonomy of their members to determine the content of their work. A central issue in the implementation of health policy is therefore how to persuade doctors to organise their work in a way that is consistent with central and local policies. Because doctors have a major influence on the use of resources in the NHS, it is ultimately their behaviour that determines patterns of resource allocation and service development. And because they have considerable clinical autonomy, there is no guarantee that policies will be carried out.

Nevertheless, attempts are made to influence medical practices, as in the consultative document on *Priorities* (DHSS, 1976b), which contained a bibliography of reports concerned with alternative ways of providing services. The reports drew the attention of doctors to innovations in clinical practices, including methods of treating patients on an outpatient basis rather than as inpatients, and ways of reducing the number of unnecessary x-rays carried out. As the consultative document noted, 'decisions on clinical practice concerning individual patients are and must continue to be the responsibility of the clinicians concerned. But it is hoped that this document would encourage further scrutiny by the profession of the resources used by different treatment regimes' (DHSS, 1976b, p. 28). This attempt to influence professional behaviour suggested that more attention might be given to the important part played by doctors in determining the use of resources. In fact, the successors to the consultative document on *Priorities* placed less emphasis on this issue, and *Care in Action,* published in 1981, stressed instead the scope for improving the efficiency of non-medical services (DHSS, 1981c). In practice, most attempts to change professional practices originate within the profession, and indeed one of the characteristics of professions generally is that control is exercised through self-regulation from within. Thus publications in medical journals, conferences organised by professional associations, and discussion with peers are the main means by which change is facilitated. In this context, the role of the DH has traditionally been, wherever possible, to put the profession in the position of moving in the direction desired by both central and local agencies.

This has begun to change as resources have become constrained and attention has focused on the efficiency with which these resources are used. Particular attention has been paid to the involvement of doctors in management. In the past, the main vehicle for achieving greater medical participation in management was the so-called 'cogwheel' system. This system derived its name from three reports on the organisation of medical work in hospitals which were published between 1967 and 1974 with a cogwheel design on their covers (see Ministry of Health, 1967). The cogwheel system involved clinicians in associated specialities coming together in divisions and these divisions forming a medical executive committee to examine hospital services as a whole. The Griffiths Report into NHS management suggested that the cogwheel system provided a basis for clinicians to participate in decisions about priorities in the use of resources. More specifically, Griffiths proposed that a system of management budgeting should be developed involving clinicians and relating workload and service objectives to financial and manpower allocations.

In 1986, management budgeting was superseded by the resource management initiative. Resource management seeks to improve patient care by giving doctors and nurses a bigger role in the management of resources. This usually involves the appointment of doctors as clinical directors to run services with support from a nurse manager and a business manager. Initially, resource management operated at six acute hospital sites established as pilot projects. Evidence from these sites indicated that the costs of implementing resource management were underestimated, and that the process of involving doctors in management was more complex and time-consuming than had been assumed. Research also suggested that there were few tangible benefits in terms of better services for patients and improved value for money. Nevertheless, doctors and nurses remained positive about resource management (Packwood, Keen and Buxton, 1991) and government policy throughout the 1990s continued to support moves to involve doctors in management in both hospitals and general practice. By the end of that decade, the principles of resource management had become widely established throughout the NHS, albeit with continuing variation in the detailed arrangements that were adopted.

In parallel, successive governments promoted the use of clinical audit in the hospital and community health services. Until 1998 this was done on a voluntary basis with resources being earmarked by the DH to provide the support needed to introduce audit arrangements and to encourage doctors and other health care professionals to participate. Participation in clinical audit became compulsory following a series of cases that identified failures in clinical performance within the NHS (Kennedy Report, 2001). The action taken by the Blair government to improve the quality of care, including the establishment of the National Institute for Clinical Excellence and the Commission for Health Improvement and the introduction of clinical governance, heralded the beginnings of a new era in medical accountability. Not least, these initiatives sent out a clear signal that self-regulation was no longer seen as sufficient to safeguard standards and patients. The adoption of these policies was possible because of the accumulation of evidence that existing arrangements for ensuring quality were inadequate and this created a policy window (Kingdon, 1995) for politicians to push through changes that had previously been ruled off the agenda because of anticipated opposition from the medical profession.

The continuing influence of doctors over the development of services has been confirmed by research into the impact of quality improvement programmes in the NHS. Studies of the application of total quality management (Joss and Kogan, 1995) and business process reengineering (McNulty and Ferlie, 2002) have found that hospital consultants often resist changes imposed by others. Partly in response to this evidence, the programmes taken forward by the Modernisation Agency (and its predecessor, the National Patients Access Team) have made use of quality collaborative methods in which consultants work with their peers to bring about change with the assistance of outside experts. The same methods have been applied in primary care to improve access to GP services. Evaluations of quality collaboratives indicate some success in improving performance while underlining the importance of consultants and GPs being fully engaged in bringing about change (Ham, Kipping and McLeod, 2003). These evaluations have also highlighted the time needed to achieve improvements in a service in which frontline professionals shape how services are delivered and developed.

Policy-making in NHS bodies

From the point of view of the DH and NHS bodies, clinical freedom may appear to be entirely negative, an obstacle to the implementation of national policies. However, the definition of policy adopted in Chapter 6, emphasising the idea that policy involves actions and decisions, drew attention to what might be called a bottom-up as well as a top-down perspective on policy. From a bottom-up perspective, the local autonomy of both NHS bodies and the medical profession is a positive feature in that it permits the development of policies that are appropriate to local circumstances, or at least local preferences. Indeed, local autonomy may lead to innovations that might not occur in a highly centralised system. In the final part of the chapter we therefore examine the local sources of policy change and development, and the micro politics of the NHS.

We have argued that, subject to broad guidance on policy from the DH, NHS bodies have some freedom to determine what policies to pursue in their areas. However, it is important to recognise that NHS bodies, like the DH, are not wholly or even mainly concerned with making new policies or initiating developments. As studies of policy-making in health bodies have shown, policy maintenance is more prevalent than policy-making, and any changes that do occur are likely to involve marginal adjustments to the status quo. The reason for this is that within the NHS various interests are competing for scarce resources, and in the absence of any one dominant group, bargaining between these interests tends to result in incremental change. As the author has argued elsewhere:

> In policy systems where there are many different interests and where power is not concentrated in any individual or group, it is easier to prevent change than to achieve it. Successful policy promotion in such systems is dependent on the winning of a coalition of support by an active individual or 'interest' (Ham, 1981, p. 153)

With this in mind, what interests contribute to health policy-making at the local level? Hunter, in a study of resource allocation in two Scottish health boards in the 1970s, suggests that decisions were influenced by a policy triad, comprising health board members, managers, and professional and lay advisory bodies (Hunter, 1980). Hunter argues that the influence of health board members on resource allocation was minimal. This confirms evidence from other sources indicating that the appointed members of health authorities experience difficulties with their role (Haywood, 1983; Ham 1984). Hunter goes on to note that health board managers, although active and visible in the resource allocation process, were not themselves dominant. Like their counterparts in DHAs, managers appeared to be in control of the business of their authorities, but were constrained by inherited commitments and established patterns of service provision. Managers were able to exert some influence but their freedom of manoeuvre was limited by history and, more particularly, by the power of the medical profession. As we noted earlier in the chapter, this power derives as much from the profession's key position as the direct provider of services, as from its involvement in advisory committees. Hunter expresses the point in the following way:

> allocations ... did not always reflect directly the wishes and wants of doctors; nor did they arise from some conspiracy on the part of the medical profession to win for itself the biggest share of available

resources, so depriving other groups in need of them. The process was altogether more subtle ... in their present established position as leaders of the health care team and as the primary decision-makers, doctors' decisions to treat patients commit resources ... and impose additional pressures on administrators charged with allocating resources. (Hunter, 1980, p. 195)

The author's own work on policy-making in the Leeds Regional Hospital Board (RHB) came to similar conclusions. Through a variety of channels, medical interests were able to influence what was decided, and overall 'the distribution of power was weighted heavily in favour of the professional monopolists' (Ham, 1981, p. 198). The terminology used here is derived from the work of Alford, who argues that health politics are characterised by three sets of structural interests: professional monopolists, who are the dominant interests; corporate rationalisers, who are the challenging interests; and the community population, who are repressed interests (Alford, 1975a). Applying these concepts to the Leeds RHB suggested that 'the history of hospital planning between 1948 and 1974 can be seen as the history of corporate rationalisers, represented by regional board planners, trying to challenge the established interests of the medical profession, with the community hardly in earshot' (Ham, 1981, p. 75). A key point to appreciate is that because the medical profession is in an established position, small changes do not seriously threaten professional dominance. In other words, policy maintenance benefits medical interests by preserving the existing pattern of services within which the profession is predominant.

Further light is shed on local health policy-making by a study of two DHAs carried out between 1981 and 1985 (Ham, 1986). The study examined how a number of issues were handled in the two authorities. In the case of issues which were initiated at a national level, the Griffiths Report on general management and policy on competitive tendering, the study showed that the most influential interests were DHSS ministers supported by RHA chairmen. Within the constraints imposed from above, DHA chairmen and managers had some influence over how the issues were taken forward, but authority members were only marginally involved. In the case of issues that were initiated at a local level, the decision to acquire a CT scanner in one authority and the siting of orthopaedic services in the other, no one group or interest emerged as most influential. The medical profession was actively involved and undoubtedly exerted influence but this was mediated by the views of DHA managers and chairmen. Also significant were the RHAs, particularly in shaping the financial context within which local issues were debated and resolved. DHA members played some part in policy-making but were important mainly in lending support to chairmen and managers.

Although the configuration of interests involved in policy-making and the individuals, groups or organisations who held power varied between issues, the overall picture to emerge from this study is of DHAs faced with pressure from above in the shape of national and regional policies, and pressure from below in the form of demands from hospital medical staff. DHA chairmen and senior managers played the major part in responding to these pressures and in articulating their own views in the policy process. This does not mean to say that managers have replaced doctors as the dominant interest in the NHS, even though the Griffiths Report undoubtedly served to consolidate and strengthen the position of managers. In neither of the two DHAs was the dominant value system seriously questioned and doctors were therefore able to maintain their influence.

As Hunter found in his study, the power of the medical profession was manifested not so much through formal bids for development considered by health authorities as through the continual process of innovation that preempted resources for development. This was well illustrated by the way in which growth money was taken up by creeping development resulting from doctors deciding to use particular drugs and introduce new methods of treatment with significant implications for supplies and equipment. Put another way, the influence of doctors was exercised through decisionless decisions (Bachrach and Baratz, 1970). The clinical freedom of doctors to do the best for their patients, and the consequent power of clinicians over resource allocation, was thus an important factor limiting the role of health authorities. This was reinforced by the influence of the medical profession at other levels, as in the requirements imposed by the medical royal colleges on the training and staffing of hospitals. These requirements define the parameters within which policies are formulated at a local level and constrain NHS bodies in the planning of specialist services by forcing compliance with professionally determined standards.

Studies of policy-making in NHS bodies since the implementation of general management and the White Paper, *Working for Patients*, have sought to analyse whether established relationships have been altered by the reforms initiated by the Thatcher government. These studies point to some evidence of change with the members of NHS boards appearing to have increased their influence in certain cases and the balance of power within the medical profession shifting away from hospital doctors towards GPs. In parallel, hospital doctors who took on management responsibilities as a consequence of resource management became more prominent and there was evidence of managers gaining some influence in relation to the medical profession (Ferlie *et al.*, 1996). Researchers who in an earlier study had found strategic change taking place in some areas but not others (Pettigrew, Ferlie and McKee, 1992), concluded in their later analysis that there was evidence of transformational changes in the NHS, while adding that many of these changes were not well-embedded (Ferlie *et al.*, 1996). Notwithstanding this, the same analysis contended that the dominance of the medical profession remained largely intact.

A similar conclusion was reached by McDonald in her study of decision making in a health authority in the 1990s. McDonald's analysis of decision making in relation to coronary heart disease services emphasised in particular the influence of hospital consultants and GPs and the limited power of health authorities. As she commented:

> HAs charged with assessing need and commissioning care to meet that need have little control over the supply and demand of care. Their staff engage in the production of policy documents, but the extent to which these impact on patients is questionable. They disseminate guidelines, but have no control over the prescribing practices of local GPs. They contract for additional elective activity at the margins, but often this is dictated by the length of waiting lists and they have no choice in the matter. They have little or no control over demand for services, particularly in the context of emergency care (McDonald, 2002, pp. 164–5).

These comments are reinforced by the analysis undertaken by the Kennedy Inquiry. In a comprehensive review of the events leading up to the failures in paediatric heart surgery that occurred at Bristol, the Inquiry found that there were neither external nor internal mechanisms in place to monitor the quality of care provided by hospital consultants. The chairman and non-executive directors of the NHS trust were not closely involved in overseeing the services provided and the chief executive delegated a large measure of responsibility to individual consultants and clinical directors. The culture of the hospital emphasised the importance of clinical autonomy and did not encourage scrutiny of clinical standards and performance by managers or external bodies like health authorities. Clinical audit was not an effective mechanism for monitoring and reviewing standards, and as a consequence problems in the provision of children's heart surgery persisted (Kennedy Report, 2001).

The important conclusion this suggests is that while the decline of corporatism may have weakened the influence of the medical profession in negotiations over *national* policy, the power of doctors within the NHS remains significant. In Alford's terms, the medical profession continues to be dominant and the challenge of corporate rationalisers, especially politicians and managers, has not seriously threatened this dominance at the micro level. Furthermore, the exclusion of the medical profession from national policy developments like *Working for Patients* was followed by the reincorporation of doctors into policy-making when the influence of the profession in policy-implementation led to a realisation that it was better to involve doctors and their representatives throughout the policy process (Ham, 2000). The reincorporation of the medical profession has continued under the Blair government through the appointment of senior doctors as national clinical directors in the Department of Health, and the establishment of primary care groups and trusts in which GPs and other professionals control around 75 per cent of NHS resources. To date, there have been no studies of policy-making in primary care groups and trusts of the kind that have been conducted in relation to health authorities, although the evaluations of primary care groups that have been carried out indicate that GP board members tend to dominate discussion and the contribution of other interests is more limited (Regen *et al.*, 2001).

Writing in 1966, Rosemary Stevens noted that:

> by accepting increased participation in the provision of medical services – even in this case by accepting direct employment by the state – the medical profession does not necessarily endanger its autonomy, and its span of influence is almost inevitably widened. (Stevens, 1966, p. 366)

Although much has changed in the intervening 40 years, the clinical autonomy of doctors and their influence over health policy have continued to shape the development of the NHS in important ways.

Conclusion

Policy-making in NHS bodies involves a range of interests each seeking to influence what is decided. In assessing the strength of these agencies and interests, the powerful position occupied by the medical profession is again apparent. DH policies that challenge the interests of key groups within the profession are likely to be resisted. An example was Richard Crossman's attempt to shift resources from acute hospital services to the long-stay sector after the Ely Report. Crossman failed in his attempt because of opposition from the medical profession, and he was forced to earmark additional funds in order to give greater priority to long-stay services (Crossman, 1977). Thirty years later, the Blair government was able to introduce changes to the regulation of the medical profession because of the accumulation of evidence about failures in clinical performance, although the time taken to make clinical audit compulsory and to introduce a greater measure of independent scrutiny into the assessment of quality and standards speaks volumes about the ability of the profession to delay or resist policies that threaten clinical autonomy.

While it is difficult to overemphasise the strength of medical interests, it should be noted that in some areas of service provision other interests may also be important. For example, policies for mentally-ill people and people with learning disabilities may be more open to lay and community influences than policies for other client groups. It is, of course, particularly in these areas that the medical contribution is at its weakest. Again, for similar reasons innovations in community health services and prevention may arise among consumer groups and may develop through non-medical interests. Increasingly, too, managers and board chairmen are playing a bigger part in policy-making. Granted these qualifications, the general conclusion of this discussion is that nationally determined health policies are mediated by a range of interests at the local level, among which the medical profession is the most influential.

The picture that emerges, then, is of a complex series of interactions between the centre and periphery, through which each attempts to influence the other. While the existence of parliamentary accountability gives the appearance of centralisation in the NHS, the reality is rather different. Recognising that the stance taken by the centre tends to change over time, it can be said that the DH is able to exercise control over total health service spending and its distribution, but has less control over the uses to which funds are put. Circulars, consultative documents and White Papers, and guidelines on priorities are the main instruments the Department uses to attempt to influence the decisions of NHS bodies, but the advisory nature of these documents, and often their ambiguity, leaves scope for local interpretation of national policy. The accountability review process was a significant innovation and led to greater central involvement and in some cases central control over policy-making. The review process has been reinforced by the strengthening of performance management and the oversight of health authorities exercised by the Department. Overall, though, as a mechanism for influencing NHS bodies, persuasion is more important than are statutory controls, necessarily so perhaps in a Service where considerable discretion is accorded to those who provide services.

Chapter 9

Auditing and Evaluating Health Policy

The aim of this chapter is to examine how health policy is audited and evaluated and the way in which the results of audit feed back into policy-making. The chapter begins by tracing the evolution of interest in audit and evaluation and it describes the variety of audit arrangements that currently exist. The discussion then moves on to the performance of the NHS in relation to health improvement and access to health care.

The context

Auditing the implementation of policy and evaluating impact and outcome are continuing activities. Both the Department of Health and NHS bodies play a part in audit and evaluation, and their work is supplemented by *ad hoc* inquiries and investigations and reviews undertaken by parliamentary committees and bodies like the Audit Commission and the Healthcare Commission. Increasingly, too, researchers are contributing to this process through studies commissioned both by government and independent foundations. A wide variety of audit arrangements are currently in place but this has not always been the case. Historically, the capacity for audit and evaluation was not well-developed, and the current emphasis placed on audit and performance management needs to be located in its historical context.

As far as the DH is concerned, for many years the Department lacked the means to undertake a sustained review and analysis of health policies. Brown has noted that part of the reason for this was that 'until 1956 the Ministry had no statistician, no economists and no research staff or management experts apart from a small group of work study officers' (Brown, 1979, p. 12). Although there were moves to make greater use of statistical information and economic analysis during the 1960s, the most significant changes did not occur until the reorganisation of the DHSS in 1972 and the parallel development of the Department's policy analysis capability. A number of innovations resulted from these developments, including the use of programme budgeting to analyse expenditure on health and personal social services, and the publication of studies of policies on the acute hospital sector (DHSS, 1981e), community care (DHSS, 1981a and 1981d), and the respective role of the general acute and geriatric sectors in the care of elderly hospital patients (DHSS, 1981f). In addition, reports were prepared on the progress made in implementing policies for mentally-handicapped people (DHSS, 1980c), and on NHS capital and buildings (DHSS, 1979b). The DHSS also published a review of the performance of the NHS over the decade to 1981 (DHSS, 1983a). These were all indications that the Department's monitoring role was being given greater priority.

Yet it remains the case that audit and evaluation are difficult tasks to perform within the NHS. This was noted in a memorandum submitted by the DHSS to the House of Commons Expenditure Committee in 1972 on services for older people. The Department argued that general aims could be formulated for services, such as 'to enable the elderly to maintain their independence and self respect', but measuring the extent to which these aims were achieved was problematic (Expenditure Committee, 1972, p. 3). Nevertheless, the Department noted that:

> this is not to say that the problems are wholly insoluble. It may, for instance, be possible in time to devise means of measuring the condition of individuals against agreed scales of, for example, mobility or social participation and correlating changes in different areas over time with the pattern of services provided; or to establish indicators of the health and social wellbeing of the elderly in particular communities or areas and to undertake similar correlations ... But it will take many years to develop and test agreed measures, to establish a methodology for applying and interpreting them and to collect the necessary information. (Expenditure Committee, 1972, p. 4)

Many of these points apply to other areas of the NHS. The objectives of service provision are often stated only in general terms, and they may not be entirely consistent with one another. Devising measures in order to assess whether objectives have been met is beset with difficulties, and as a result many of the indicators used concern either inputs into health care, for example expenditure and staffing levels, or activity levels, such as the number of beds occupied or patients treated. Outcome indicators, for example on mortality or morbidity rates, are rarely employed, and it is therefore difficult to judge whether policy is having an impact on the health of the population.

The area of service provision in which performance indicators have been applied most consistently in the past is that of hospital services for the mentally ill and people with learning disabilities. A series of reports published by the DHSS in the 1960s and early 1970s identified those hospitals falling within the lowest tenth of all hospitals for these patients for certain grades of staff and services (see for example DHSS, 1972). Thereafter, the reports measured progress made in achieving minimum standards of staffing and patients' amenities (see for example DHSS, 1974). Subsequently, considerable effort went into the production of a set of performance indicators covering the core services provided by DHAs. The indicators covered clinical activity, finance, manpower and estate management functions. They drew on routinely available statistical information and enabled health authorities to examine performance in areas such as the length of stay of patients in hospital, the costs per case of treating patients, the costs of providing services such as laundry and catering, and the number of staff employed. The published reports on performance indicators were not intended to be league tables. Rather, they provided a starting point for analysis, and it was expected that exceptional performance as revealed by performance indicators would lead to further investigation. As well as providing a tool for use by local managers, performance indicators were examined during the accountability review process and enabled the DH to question RHAs, and RHAs to question DHAs on the provision of their services.

Performance indicators formed one part of a series of initiatives promulgated by the DHSS in the search for greater efficiency in the NHS (see Chapter 2). The indicators published in 1983 were seen as experimental and a Joint NHS/DHSS Group was established to advise on future developments. Subsequently, performance indicators were renamed health service indicators and greater emphasis was placed on their publication in a user-friendly form. The importance attached to the indicators by ministers was indicated in a speech made by the Secretary of State to accompany publication of the 1986/7 indicators. The Secretary of State highlighted the fact that there were:

> considerable variations in performance between districts. For example, some districts treat only 25 patients a year in each surgical bed whilst others manage 53. Even when adjusted to take into account differences between the patients treated, some districts are still treating 14 per cent fewer patients than would be expected, whilst others are treating 27 per cent more.
>
> Similarly there are districts with an average length of stay 13 per cent longer than expected, whilst others manage a length of stay almost 22 per cent less than expected.
>
> And if we turn to costs we again find large variations. Costs within any one group of similar districts can vary by as much as 50 per cent. Even when adjusted for different types of patients, some districts are 15 per cent more costly than expected, others 15 per cent less. In other

words, £1 spent on health care in one place might buy £1.15 worth of product, whereas somewhere else it might buy only 85 pence worth.

So despite the Health Service's unquestionable achievements in boosting efficiency, I am convinced there is room for yet more improvements in performance. (Moore, 1988)

The importance of performance monitoring, as it was referred to, was emphasised by the House of Commons Social Services Committee as well as the Public Accounts Committee. As the Social Services Committee commented, 'the DHSS should continue to seek to develop ways of assessing quality independently of the input of resources; this is already the role of the Health Advisory Service and could usefully become a responsibility of any new Management Advisory Service' (Social Services Committee, 1981, p. xiii). The view of the DHSS at that time was that there were two kinds of performance monitoring: strategic monitoring, which examined whether services were developing in line with agreed policies and strategies; and efficiency monitoring, which assessed whether resources were being used to the best advantage (DHSS, 1980d). Both types of monitoring were the responsibility of the Management Advisory Service (MAS), described by Sir Patrick Nairne, a former Permanent Secretary at the DHSS, as 'an external, critical inspectorial eye translated into the NHS' (Public Accounts Committee, 1981, p. 69). The MAS was taken forward in two regional initiatives between 1982 and 1985 and was an indication that monitoring and audit were receiving greater attention. Even more significant was the introduction of the accountability review process as a mechanism for reviewing the performance of health authorities throughout the NHS on a routine basis (see Chapter 8). The accountability review process was the forerunner of current arrangements for performance management within the NHS, and was the first systematic attempt since the establishment of the NHS to manage the implementation of policy.

Notwithstanding the MAS, the development of performance indicators and the accountability review process, the Griffiths Report commented in 1983:

> The NHS ... still lacks any real continuous evaluation of its performance ... Rarely are precise management objectives set; there is little measurement of health output; clinical evaluation of particular practices is by no means common and economic evaluation of these practices extremely rare. Nor can the NHS display a ready assessment of the effectiveness with which it is meeting the needs and expectations of the people it serves. (Griffiths Report, 1983, p. 19)

Some of the reasons why audit and evaluation are underdeveloped in the NHS have been identified by Klein, a former specialist adviser to the Social

Services Committee. As Klein (1982) has noted, the health policy arena is characterised by complexity, heterogeneity, uncertainty and ambiguity. Complexity is evident in the wide range of occupations involved in providing services; heterogeneity in the variety of services provided; uncertainty in the absence of a clear relationship between inputs and outputs; and ambiguity in the meaning of the information which is available. Given these factors, Klein concluded that performance evaluation is most usefully seen as a process of argument rather than a mechanism for rewarding or penalising organisations.

If this is the case, what territory should the argument cover? Most attempts to audit performance in the NHS have made use of measures of the input of resources and activity levels. Doll (1974) has suggested that these measures of economic efficiency need to be considered alongside indicators of medical outcome and social acceptability. Doll's analysis was developed by Maxwell (1984) who identified six dimensions of the quality of health care: access to services, relevance to need, effectiveness, equality, social acceptability, and efficiency and economy. There is considerable overlap between Maxwell's dimensions of quality and the performance assessment framework (PAF) developed by the Blair government which we now go on to discuss.

The audit explosion

Like Maxwell's approach, the Blair government's framework also contained six areas of assessment and these are displayed in Table 9.1 (Secretary of State for Health, 1998b). In outlining this framework, the government announced that an annual survey of patient and user experience was being established to collect data about the social acceptability of services. In taking this line, the government was extending the approach initiated under the Major government through publication of

Table 9.1 *NHS performance assessment framework domains, 1998*

1	Health improvement
2	Fair access
3	Effective delivery of appropriate healthcare
4	Efficiency
5	Patient/carer experience
6	Health outcomes of NHS care

the *Patient's Charter* in 1991 and performance tables analysing the achievement of NHS trusts in terms of the standards included in the *Charter*. A key component of the Blair government's approach was a commitment to go beyond the indicators of access and convenience contained in the *Patient's Charter* to assess clinical performance and the outcome of treatment. This approach took forward work that had been started by the Major government and was given added impetus by evidence of failures of clinical performance within the NHS that came to light after the 1997 general election, such as the inquiry into paediatric heart surgery at the Bristol Royal Infirmary (Kennedy Report, 2001).

Subsequently, performance indicators for health authorities and NHS trusts were published and effort focused on the development of a system of star ratings (originally referred to as performance ratings) for NHS trusts and primary care trusts. Star ratings for NHS trusts providing acute hospital services were first published in 2001 and in later years they were followed by ratings for specialist trusts, ambulance trusts, mental health trusts and primary care trusts. The ratings were based on the performance of trusts as measured by their success in achieving key government targets. The ratings also took into account the performance of trusts in relation to a broader range of performance indicators, and the clinical governance reviews undertaken by the Commission for Health Improvement. Taken together, these measures resulted in trusts being placed in one of four categories: three stars were awarded to trusts with the highest levels of performance; two stars were awarded to trusts performing well overall; one star was awarded to trusts where there was some cause for concern; and trusts with the poorest levels of performance were awarded a zero star.

The operation of the star rating system can be illustrated by the approach taken to NHS acute trusts in 2002. The performance of these trusts was assessed in relation to the following key targets: no patients waiting more than 18 months for inpatient treatment, fewer patients waiting more than 15 months for inpatient treatment, no patients waiting more than 26 weeks for outpatient treatment, fewer patients waiting on trolleys for more than 12 hours, less than 1 per cent of operations cancelled on the day, no patients with suspected cancer waiting more than two weeks to be seen in hospital, improvement to the working lives of staff, hospital cleanliness, and a satisfactory financial position. The broader range of indicators used to assess the performance of acute trusts covered clinical issues, such as deaths within 30 days of surgery and emergency readmissions following discharge; patient issues, such as waiting times and patient survey results; and issues concerned with capacity and capability, such as staff satisfaction and the sickness and absence rate for staff. On this basis, 45 acute trusts were awarded three stars, 77 received two stars, 34 received one star and 10 were awarded a zero star. The same four categories of performance were used for other trusts, although the targets and indicators against which performance was assessed were modified to reflect the services delivered by these trusts.

Star ratings were given extensive publicity and were intended in part as a guide for the public on the performance of their local health services. The ratings were also used by the DH to reward NHS trusts that were performing well and to intervene in trusts that were performing poorly. In the case of trusts awarded three stars, extra resources were made available, and these trusts were also given additional management freedoms. With the advent of NHS Foundation Trusts, only NHS trusts that achieved three stars were initially eligible to apply to become Foundation Trusts. Trusts that received zero stars were expected to produce a plan to demonstrate how they intended to improve performance and if these plans were not satisfactory then the DH required a new chief executive to be appointed. In some cases this entailed the so-called 'franchising' of management with the chief executives of high performing NHS trusts being appointed to help poorly performing trusts to improve. As time went on, franchising was extended to allow private sector companies the opportunity to take on the management of zero star trusts. Zero star trusts also received support from the Modernisation Agency.

In commenting on the development of the ratings, Smith has noted that 'the measures used in the first set of performance ratings show a preoccupation with waiting times, with only a tangential reference to clinical quality' (Smith, 2002, p. 110). Given that star ratings had a greater impact on NHS bodies than the PAF, in terms of the allocation of funds and the implications for chief executives, this meant that the focus on access and convenience that had been so much a feature of health policy in the 1990s was maintained under the Blair government. In so far as clinical performance and quality did receive somewhat greater attention, this was mainly through the introduction of clinical governance and the work done to develop measures of clinical outcome in areas such as cardiac surgery. Also, the experience of patients was given higher priority through the work on patient surveys instituted by the Blair government. The first of these surveys was conducted in 1998 and covered general practice patients. This was followed by surveys of patients with heart disease and cancer and patients treated in acute hospitals, as well as a second survey of primary care services. Publication of the results of these surveys added to the interest in NHS performance generated by star ratings. As a consequence, work on performance indicators and performance ratings moved decisively out of the committee room and into the public domain.

Alongside work done in the DH and the NHS to assess and improve performance, a number of other organisations are involved in audit activity. The National Audit Office (NAO) is the longest established of these organisations and it is involved in assessing on behalf of parliament the use of public funds, including value for money in the NHS. The reports of the NAO cover a wide range of issues and in recent times these have included the procurement of vaccines by DH, NHS emergency planning, tackling obesity, and the acquisition of the London Heart Hospital. These reports are often used as a basis for enquiries by the Public Accounts Committee (PAC) which calls ministers and civil servants to give evidence and to be questioned on their stewardship of public funds.

The work of the NAO and the PAC is complemented by that of the Audit Commission whose remit was extended to the NHS in 1990. The Audit Commission has a role in both financial audit and performance audit or value for money studies. The national studies carried out by the Audit Commission have included the use of operating theatres, primary care prescribing, the education, training and development of health care staff, and mental health services for older people. An analysis of the work of the Audit Commission noted that these national studies 'have directed a powerful searchlight on the activities of the service' (Day and Klein, 2001). Whereas the NAO supports parliament in auditing the use of NHS funds, the Audit Commission's work is directed towards improving performance in the NHS, although this distinction has become less clear cut in recent years. Also, as an independent body, the Audit Commission contributes to public debates and understanding of the performance of public services, including the NHS. Recognising the difficulties in distinguishing the impact of the Audit Commission from that of other influences on NHS performance, the evidence suggests that managers in the NHS do perceive its work to be influential, especially when local auditors carry credibility (Day and Klein, 2001). At a national level, the Audit Commission has played an increasing part in assessing the overall performance of the NHS, as indicated by its analyses of progress in implementing *The NHS Plan* and government targets for the NHS (see, for example, Audit Commission, 2003).

The role of the Audit Commission is changing as a result of the establishment of the Commission for Health Improvement and its successor, the Healthcare Commission. The Commission for Health Improvement (CHI) was set up by the Blair government as a statutory body at arm's length from government to:

- provide national leadership to develop and disseminate clinical governance principles;
- independently scrutinise local clinical governance arrangements to support, promote and deliver high-quality services, through a rolling programme of local reviews of service providers;

- undertake a programme of service reviews to monitor national implementation of National Service Frameworks, and review progress locally on implementation of these frameworks and NICE guidance;
- help identify and tackle serious or persistent clinical problems. The Commission will have the capacity for rapid investigation and intervention to help put these right; and
- over time, increasingly take on responsibility for overseeing and assisting with external incident inquiries.

(Secretary of State for Health, 1998b, p. 52)

CHI built on the experience of the Health Advisory Service and its predecessor, the Hospital Advisory Service, established by Richard Crossman following the Ely Report of 1969 to visit long-stay hospitals and advise on how standards could be raised (see p. 209). The particular significance of CHI was that its remit covered all NHS trusts and primary care trusts, and its powers to monitor quality and act on its findings were considerably greater than those of the Health Advisory Service. By 2003, CHI had carried out reviews of over 250 NHS organisations in England and Wales, published a major report on services for people with cancer, and conducted a number of investigations of serious failures in NHS services. It had also published a review of the progress made by the NHS in implementing *The NHS Plan* and improving performance (CHI, 2003). The increasing significance of CHI was indicated by the decision of the government to transfer responsibility for star ratings of NHS organisations from the DH to CHI in 2003.

As part of the changes included in *Delivering the NHS Plan*, the government announced that a new Commission for Healthcare Audit and Inspection (CHAI) was to be established and this is known as the Healthcare Commission. It encompasses the work of CHI, the Mental Health Act Commission, the national value for money work of the Audit Commission, and the work on independent health care providers undertaken by the National Care Standards Commission. The Commission worked in shadow form alongside CHI in 2003 before taking over its responsibilities in 2004. The creation of the Commission was intended to streamline arrangements for audit and inspection and it means that a single body now oversees both public and private providers of care. Not only this, but also the Commission has a greater measure of independence from government than CHI and it reports to parliament annually on the state of health care. The role of the Audit Commission in relation to the NHS will change as a consequence and will focus on financial audit and the local implementation of value for money studies.

Another national institution involved in auditing the performance of the NHS is the Health Services Commissioner or Ombudsman. The

Ombudsman is particularly involved in investigating complaints and publishes an annual report identifying trends and issues arising in his or her work as well as reports into selected investigations. The Ombudsman has also published reports on issues of wider significance. An example of the latter which was particularly influential in shaping policy was the report published in 1994 into the failure of the NHS in Leeds to fund the continuing care of a patient. More recently, the Ombudsman produced a report on the funding of long term care of older and disabled people that highlighted the failures of the NHS to adopt the correct policies and procedures in relation to charging people for the use of long term care (Health Services Commissioner, 2003). In the case of both reports, the DH acted to issue revised guidance requiring health authorities and local authorities to review local policies and services to ensure that statutory obligations were being fulfilled.

As these comments indicate, there has been a considerable expansion of audit activity both within the NHS and by statutory bodies and related organisations. This reflects the 'audit explosion' (Power, 1994) across government as a whole in the 1980s and 1990s, and the particular concern in the case of health services to strengthen existing forms of regulation, including the regulation of medical work (Allsop and Mulcahy, 1996). Reviewing the history of regulation in the NHS, Walshe has argued that the election of the Blair government was a watershed:

> The real growth in healthcare regulation in the UK has occurred since 1997. The present Labour government has moved away from relying on the market as a primary mechanism for managing and improving performance in the NHS for both ideological and pragmatic reasons, but has been unwilling to rely on the traditional bureaucratic mechanisms for controlling the NHS through the line of accountability from the Department of Health downwards to NHS trusts and primary care trusts. Instead it has turned increasingly to regulation (Walshe, 2003, p. 113)

Under the Blair government, the growth of regulation was part of the attempt to develop a third way in health policy, different from traditional bureaucratic mechanisms and the internal market of the 1990s (see Chapter 3). The extension of audit into the quality of medical care marks a further stage in the development of audit within the NHS, building on self-regulation and peer review by clinicians and introducing new mechanisms for promoting high standards of care. As the Kennedy Report noted, in the 1980s and early 1990s neither external organisations nor NHS bodies saw it as their role to review clinical standards, and it was left to hospital consultants to ensure that the care provided to patients was of the appropriate quality. The failure of some doctors in Bristol to audit and review their practices meant that children undergoing heart surgery died unnecessarily. The Kennedy Report concluded that more effective safeguards were needed for patients and it endorsed steps already taken by the Blair government to improve the quality of care, such as the establishment of CHI and the introduction of clinical governance. In addition, the report made a series of recommendations for improving performance, including the regulation of health care professionals to ensure that they maintained their professional competence, and the validation of NHS trusts to ensure that they met generic standards. The report also endorsed the government's proposal to set up a National Patient Safety Agency (NPSA), and this came into existence in 2001. The role of the Agency is to run a mandatory reporting system for logging all failures, mistakes and errors and to introduce an approach for dealing with errors and learning the lessons.

In its response to the Kennedy Report, the government accepted both the analysis of why things had gone wrong at Bristol and many of the recommendations for reform. Specifically, it acknowledged the need to establish a Council for the Quality of Health Care to coordinate the work of the various NHS organisations involved in standard setting, regulation, monitoring and inspection. As well as the Healthcare Commission, NICE and the NPSA, these organisations included the National Clinical Assessment Authority, established in 2001 to provide a fast response to concerns about doctors' performance. The government's response also accepted the need for a Council for the Regulation of Health Care Professionals to strengthen and coordinate systems for self-regulation of the professions. Beyond these proposals, the government placed particular emphasis on the need to make better use of information to audit and improve performance. In this area, it announced plans to publish over time data on the clinical performance of consultants, and to undertake national audits of each of the clinical priority areas of *The NHS Plan*. The aim was to start publication of data on the clinical performance of consultants by making available data on death rates within 30 days of surgery of patients undergoing heart operations.

One of the effects of the Kennedy Report was to accelerate moves to strengthen the role of the General Medical Council (GMC) by streamlining its membership and speeding up its procedures. As we noted in Chapter 1, the GMC was set up in the nineteenth century, and it represents a good example of state sanctioned self-regulation. Concerns about the role and functioning of the GMC began to emerge in the 1970s and 1980s and some limited reforms were made following the Merrison Inquiry (Stacey, 1992). Criticisms of the GMC centred on the dominance of doctors in its membership and proceedings, its cumbersome and lengthy procedures for disciplining doctors, and the limited protection offered to patients. Donald Irvine, a past president of the GMC, has traced the history of attempts to reform the GMC in the last decade, and the changes that resulted (Irvine, 2003). These changes were precipitated by events at Bristol and elsewhere, events that made it difficult for doctors who were opposed to reform to win the argument. As a consequence, the number of members of the GMC was reduced to 35, and new systems for appraising doctors and revalidation were introduced. The aim of these changes was to strengthen self-regulation and to restore public and professional confidence in the GMC.

The audit explosion of recent years has not been confined to the establishment of new organisations to regulate and inspect health services and the work of external inquiries. There has also been increasing involvement by independent organisations and by government itself. The work of independent organisations is exemplified by the research carried out by the King's Fund, a charity involved in health policy analysis whose studies have included a review of health policy in the first five years of the Blair government (Appleby and Coote, 2002). Of increasing importance too have been the publications of Dr Foster, an organisation that uses NHS data to produce consumer guides to the quality of health services. The topics covered by these guides include hospitals, maternity services and cancer services. The most comprehensive independent evaluation of government policy was the Nuffield Trust's analysis of the Blair government's quality agenda (Leatherman and Sutherland, 2003). This analysis reported progress towards the objectives set by the government while also noting a number of weaknesses and risks for the future. These weaknesses included inadequate data collection and analysis, limited engagement of the clinical professions, and limitations in the proposed inspection strategy. The Nuffield Trust put forward a series of proposals for overcoming these weaknesses to enable the progress made between 2000 and 2003 to be consolidated and extended.

Partly in response to the growth of external audit and scrutiny, government has strengthened its own capacity for monitoring and review. Within government, this takes the form of regular reviews between the Treasury and the DH on progress towards the public service agreement targets (see Chapter 3), and between the Prime Minister's Delivery Unit and the DH on progress in delivering the priorities set out in *The NHS Plan*. These reviews involve detailed assessments of NHS performance and may lead to action to strengthen implementation in areas where there is a risk that targets will not be achieved. For its part, the DH has published a series of reports on the implementation of the national service frameworks (see, for example, DH, 2003d), and it has offered a number of assessments of overall progress towards *The NHS Plan* targets (see, for example, DH, 2002, and 2003e). Although, by definition, these reports and assessments are less independent than those conducted by bodies such as CHI and the Audit Commission, they are further evidence of the importance attached to audit and delivery, to use a phrase in currency in the second term of the Blair government

Alongside the expansion of audit, there has also been an increasing interest in the evaluation of health policy. Of particular importance in this context has been the establishment of the NHS research and development programme and the DH's policy research programme, both of which have provided funding and support not only for the evaluation of clinical interventions, but also for studies of the implementation and impact of policy. Recent examples of policy evaluations commissioned by the DH include studies of the introduction of total purchasing within the NHS (Mays *et al.*, 1998), the implementation of *The Health of the Nation* (DH, 1998a), the introduction of primary care groups and trusts (Regen *et al.*, 2001; Wilkin *et al.*, 2002), the implementation of health action zones (Bauld and Judge, 2002), and the impact of quality improvement programmes (Joss and Kogan, 1995; McNulty and Ferlie, 2002; Ham, Kipping and McLeod, 2003). Indeed, after a period at the beginning of the 1990s when ministers were reluctant to evaluate health policy, many major initiatives are now launched in association with independent assessments funded by government. In parallel, there are examples of evaluations conducted by researchers with the support of research councils and independent foundations. There is, of course, no certainty that the results of evaluations will be acted upon, and initiatives ostensibly launched as trials to be assessed before being implemented nationally are often taken forward before the findings of evaluations are known. Nevertheless, there is some evidence to suggest that the contribution of ideas and research to policy-making, one of the themes addressed in Chapter 7, is increasing as a result of the emphasis placed on evaluation.

Audit and evaluation are important in providing feedback on the impact of health policy and in so doing may influence policy-making. As we have emphasised throughout this book, the policy process is complex and is subject to a range of political and other influences. Those involved in audit and evaluation, whether within the NHS or outside, are only one set of actors in this process. In Kingdon's terms, the influence of audit and evaluation depends on the coming together of problems, politics and participants at a time when there are opportunities to influence policy (Kingdon, 1995). The results of audit and evaluation contribute to the development of policy by identifying problems that demand attention, and linking these problems with participants in a position to influence the outcome.

Against this background, we now turn to an examination of the performance of the NHS. This is a large topic and it is one that may be approached in a number of ways. For the purposes of this chapter, and given the space available, the focus is on health improvement and access to health care. In Chapter 11 we examine the performance of the NHS in the context of the experience of other countries.

Health improvement

The available evidence indicates that the health of the population has improved steadily not just in the lifetime of the NHS but over the last 150 years. This is most apparent from a major review of trends in mortality in Britain undertaken by the Office of National Statistics (Charlton and Murphy, 1997). In the period from 1841 to 1991, the expectation of life increased at all ages and was particularly pronounced in the younger age groups. A boy born in 1841 could expect to live until 41 years and a girl until 43 years; by 1991 the comparable figures were 73 years for boys and 79 years for girls. More recent data show that expectation of life at birth increased to 76 years for boys and 81 years for girls in the United Kingdom by 2002.

Another way of examining improvements in health is to look at trends in death rates by age. These trends illustrate declining death rates at all ages with the decline again being greatest in the younger age groups. Charlton's analysis has shown that improvements in survival in the nineteenth century were in fact confined to children and young adults (Charlton, 1997). These improvements extended to other age groups in the twentieth century, although life expectancy for people aged 75 and over only increased from around 1950. Analysis shows that by 2000, 83 per cent of deaths in England and Wales occurred at age 65 and over compared with less than 25 per cent a century earlier (Griffiths and Brock, 2003). Between 1984 and 1994 the greatest improvement in health occurred among adults aged 15–19 and 45–64, and the least improvement among adults aged 20–44 (Dunnell, 1997).

In the case of infants, there was a marked acceleration in the decline of infant deaths after the Second World War. For boys born in England and Wales in 1950, 96.6 per cent survived to the age of 1 compared with 99.1 per cent of those born in 1990. For girls the figures were 97.4 per cent in 1950 and 99.3 per cent in 1990 (Botting, 1995). Infant mortality rates continued to fall during the 1990s and for boys and girls combined had declined to 5.3 deaths per 1000 births in England and Wales by 2002. Data from the national birth cohort studies illustrate trends in health in the second half of the twentieth century and show improvements in childhood health as measured by growth in height and survival of low weight at birth (Ferri, Bynner and Wadsworth, 2003).

Long-term improvements in health have been associated with changes in the causes of death. As we noted in Chapter 1, public health measures taken in the nineteenth century played a major part in tackling infectious diseases which at that time accounted for one death in every three. In place of infectious diseases there have been marked increases in mortality from cancers, heart attacks and stroke, although death rates from many of these causes have started to fall recently. At the end of the twentieth century, heart disease and stroke accounted for 30 per cent of deaths in England and Wales, and cancers accounted for 25 per cent of deaths. There is evidence that the decline in premature mortality has been accompanied by an increase in morbidity as measured by patient consultations with GPs and self-reported illness (Dunnell, 1997). Data from the General Household Survey show that the prevalence of self-reported longstanding illness increased from 21 per cent in 1972 to 32 per cent in 2001 and the prevalence of limiting longstanding conditions increased from 15 per cent to 19 per cent over the same period (Office of National Statistics, 2002). Research has also shown that the number of years of healthy life has increased but not at the same rate as overall increases in life expectancy (Bebbington and Darton, 1996; Kelly and Baker, 2000). This means that people are living more years in poor health or with a limiting longstanding illness.

The increase in morbidity may reflect rising expectations on the part of patients as well as increased survival time following initial diagnosis. In relation to the latter, if medical science has contributed to the decline in premature mortality, then it has done so at least in part by turning fatal conditions into treatable (or at least containable) illnesses. Examples include cancer and heart disease where medical advances have resulted in a range of effective interventions, encompassing surgery, drugs and radio-therapy, that enable many people with these conditions to be treated with increasing likelihood that death will be postponed and quality of life improved. There is also evidence of an increase in the prevalence of chronic medical conditions like diabetes and arthritis. Many of these conditions are not life threatening, but nor can they be cured. The changing pattern of health identified in the national birth cohort studies, including rising levels of obesity and depression, help to explain why chronic conditions have become more important (Ferri, Bynner and Wadsworth, 2003). With more people surviving into older age, the challenge facing the NHS is increasingly how to prevent and treat these conditions, particularly when many people have more than one illness.

To make these points is to put into perspective the contribution of the NHS to health improvement. The gains in health made in the last 50 years may have been associated with the introduction of health services available free at the point of use to patients, but this is not the same as demonstrating that they have been caused by the NHS. Just as in the nineteenth century when public health legislation and the provision of pure water supplies and better housing were instrumental in the fight against infectious diseases, so too in the twentieth century factors outside the NHS exert an important influence on the health of the population. As Ferri and colleagues note in commenting on long-term trends in childhood health:

> The improvements are likely to be the outcome of a combination of improvements in education, housing and nutrition, and in the reduction of poverty, as well as the result of improved preventive care and the treatment of disease (Ferri, Bynner and Wadsworth, 2003, p. 305)

The existence of inequalities in health between social groups underlines the importance of non-medical influences on health. The extent of health inequalities was documented in the 1980 Black Report and the findings of this report have been updated and confirmed by later analyses. Social class inequalities are traditionally analysed using the classification of occupations employed by the Registrar-General. This divides occupations into five main groupings varying from social class I, which contains professional occupations such as accountants and doctors, to social class V, which contains unskilled manual occupations like labourers and office cleaners. An analysis of death rates reveals evidence of social class differences in all age groups (Drever and Bunting, 1997). Class differences in morbidity have been reported in the General Household Survey in relation to self-reported longstanding illness (Bunting, 1997) and in the Health Survey for England in relation to the prevalence of disability (Bajckal and Prescott, 2003). The national birth cohort studies have also demonstrated socio-economic inequalities in health and have emphasised the origins of inequalities in childhood (Ferri, Bynner and Wadsworth, 2003).

Of particular concern in recent times has been the long-term trend in class differences in health. Analysis shows that the gap in mortality between professional and unskilled manual men increased almost two-and-a-half times between 1930–32 and 1991–93 (DH, 2003b). More recent data indicate a widening in inequality between the 1970s and 1990s in the adult population, and a narrowing of differences among infants (Drever and Whitehead, 1997). In the case of life expectancy at birth and at age 65, inequalities widened between the 1970s and the 1990s as illustrated in Figure 9.1. A boy born into social class I in 1997–99 could expect to live to age 79 whereas a boy born into social class V could expect to live to age 71. For girls, the comparable figures were 83 years for social class I and 77 years for social class V. There are also class differences in self-reported illness and disability. Figure 9.2 illustrates these differences in relation to reported disability for men and women.

Figure 9.1   *Changes in life expectancy at birth by social class between 1972–76 and 1997–99 in England and Wales*

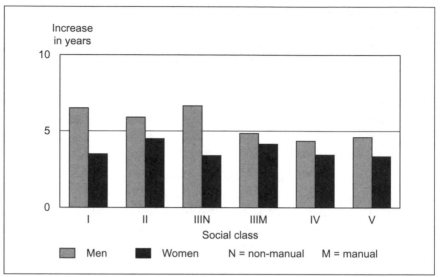

Figure 9.2   *Prevalence and severity of disability (age-standardised), by social class*

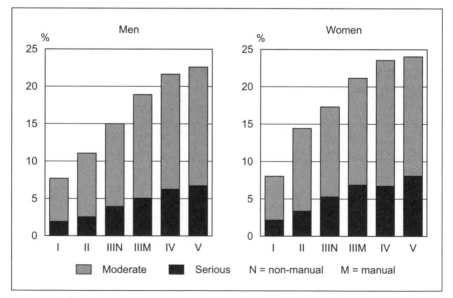

Source: Bajekal and Prescott (2003).

The argument of the Black Report was that 'differences in the material conditions of life' (Black Report, 1980, p. 357) were mainly responsible for health inequalities, although the Report acknowledged that the causes were complex and multiple. The implication that followed was that steps to reduce inequalities needed to focus on tackling these material conditions. This entailed action in a range of areas of public policy, including, in the view of the Black Report, increases in child benefit, the introduction of a childcare allowance, improvements to housing conditions, and free school meals for children. These proposals were rejected by the Thatcher government which disputed both the explanation of health inequalities offered in the Black Report, and the proposal that additional public expenditure was required to address these inequalities. This meant that the issues raised in the Report were largely ignored in central government despite evidence that inequalities in the 1980s not only persisted but also increased (Whitehead, 1987).

It took the election of the Blair government in 1997 to refocus attention on health inequalities. The Acheson Report (1998) was commissioned by the government to update the findings of the Black Report and particularly to advise on priorities for policy development. In so doing, the Acheson Report emphasised the importance of measures to reduce poverty, improve education, increase work opportunities, and strengthen access to housing. It also noted that action in the NHS should be concentrated on the prevention of ill-health and premature mortality. In this area, the proposals of the Acheson Report included ensuring equitable access to effective health care and the development of partnerships between the NHS and other agencies. Like the Black Report, the Acheson Report stressed the need to improve the health of families and children, drawing on the findings of the national birth cohort studies (Ferri, Bynner and Wadsworth, 2003) and the emphasis placed by those studies on the origins of inequalities in childhood. Other research has confirmed the importance of early life influences on health while also noting that for some medical conditions deprivation during adulthood appears to be a more significant factor (Davey Smith, Gunnell and Ben-Shlomo, 2001). The Acheson Report also examined inequalities between the genders and those affecting minority ethnic groups.

The Blair government accepted the Acheson Report and argued that a wide range of policies were in place to tackle inequalities. The agenda for action set out by the government encompassed raising living standards and tackling low income, initiatives relating to education and early years, and measures within the NHS to help people in the poorest health. Subsequently, national targets were set for reducing health inequalities, and a cross-cutting review was set up to assess progress and agree the priorities for future action. The cross-cutting review was important in bringing together Ministers and officials from across government departments and from local government to make recommendations for further work to tackle inequalities. In a wide-ranging analysis, the report of the review emphasised the need to break the cycle of health inequalities through education, parental employment, tackling smoking in pregnancy, and reducing teenage births. The report also reiterated the importance of tackling the major killers such as heart disease and cancer, and it identified smoking as 'the single most significant causal factor for the socio-economic differences in the incidence of cancer and heart disease' (Cross-Cutting Review, 2002). The report noted too the importance of nutrition and physical activity. In the case of public services, the report argued that access to services, including the NHS, by disadvantaged groups needed to be improved, and it highlighted the role of area-based initiatives in strengthening communities. These initiatives included the government's Neighbourhood Renewal strategy. Finally, the need for targeted interventions for specific groups such as rough sleepers and prisoners was emphasised. The report of the cross-cutting review was followed by publication of a programme of action to be taken forward across government (DH, 2003b). An analysis of European experiences of tackling inequalities in health compared the approach taken in different countries and concluded that 'the UK, after a period of lagging behind other European countries, now is ahead of continental Europe in development and implementation of policies to reduce socio-economic inequalities in health' (Mackenbach and Bakker, 2003).

What does the evidence about improvements in health and the persistence of inequalities tell us about the performance of the NHS? It would be simplistic to give credit to the NHS for all the improvements in health that have occurred since the Second World War, in the same way that it would be wrong to blame the NHS for the persistence and widening of health inequalities. Recognising that the role of medicine in improving the population's health has been more significant in the twentieth century than the nineteenth century, but is less important than the influence of other factors, it can be suggested that by making available medical advances to the population the NHS has contributed to the long-term trends we identified at the beginning of this section. The main gains have occurred from the prevention of ill-health, for example through vaccination, and also through the extension of life made available by new forms of treatment for cancer and heart disease. The contribution of improved treatments has been analysed in a study of changing patterns of heart disease, demonstrating a strong association between improved outcomes and the use of treatments like clot-busting drugs and cardiac surgery (Tunstall-Pedoe *et al.*, 2000). A further contribution has been in relation to the quality of life where medical advances have contributed to

Table 9.2 *Comparison of mortality rates per million population in England and Wales in 1950 and 1994*

Cause of death	1950	1994	Percentage fall
Eight 'avoidable' causes (all ages)*	513	102	80
All other	12 451	7 669	38

Note: * Tuberculosis, hypertensive disease, cerebrovascular disease, chronic rheumatic heart disease, appendicitis, cholelithiasis and cholecystitis, cervical cancer, Hodgkin's disease.

Source: Charlton, Fraser and Murphy (1997).

the relief of pain and suffering, for example through surgery for joint replacements.

By comparing trends in mortality from avoidable causes and other causes between 1950 and 1994, Charlton and colleagues suggest that the application of medical advances has had a beneficial effect. This is illustrated in Table 9.2 which shows that the decline in mortality from conditions where effective treatments are available is around twice that for other conditions (Charlton, Fraser and Murphy, 1997). It has been argued that medical care will have a much bigger influence in health improvement in the future, both in increasing life expectancy and improving quality of life (Bunker, 2001), especially in view of evidence that the benefits of spending in areas such as treatment of heart attacks exceed the costs (Cutler and McClellan, 2001). It follows that ensuring that the population has access to cost effective care will be an increasingly important objective of health policy, and we now turn to an examination of the record of the NHS in relation to access.

Access to health care

The Bill that established the NHS stated:

> All the Service or any part of it, is to be available to everyone in England and Wales. The Bill imposes no limitations on availability – e.g. limitations based on financial means, age, sex, employment or vocation, area of residence, or insurance qualification. (Ministry of Health, 1946, p. 3)

Over 50 years later, the NHS can claim considerable success in meeting this objective. Notwithstanding the introduction of charges for some services, the Royal Commission on the NHS argued in 1979 that 'one of the most significant achievements of the NHS has been to free people from fear of being unable to afford treatment for acute or chronic illness' (Royal Commission on the NHS, 1979, pp. 10–11). For a generation brought up on a health service largely free at the point of use, it is easy to overlook this achievement. Yet at a time when some other developed countries, such as the United States, have still to ensure access to health care for all citizens, it is salutary to remember that the United Kingdom takes this for granted and the population does not live in fear of bankruptcy in the event of contracting serious medical conditions. More positively, international comparisons indicate that funding health services through general taxation, as in the United Kingdom, is more equitable than other methods (van Doorslaer, Rutten and Wagstaff, 1993; Wagstaff *et al.*, 1999).

Despite this achievement, there remain a variety of inequities in health and health care, including between the English regions (defined here as government office regions). For example, in 2002 the infant mortality rate in England stood at 5.3, and within England the rate varied from 4.4 in the South West to 6.5 in the West Midlands. In the same year the perinatal mortality rate for England was 8.4, and within England the rate varied from 7.5 in the East to 10.1 in the West Midlands. These differences between regions mask even bigger variations in health within regions (Griffiths and Fitzpatrick, 2001). Variations in the provision of services also exist. These illustrate that in 2000/01 the number of general and acute beds per 100 000 population varied from 315 in the North West to 222 in the South East. Similarly, the number of hospital medical staff per 100 000 population varied from 112 in the East to 200 in London (Office of Health Economics, 2002). Variations in service provision are related to differences in the allocation of NHS resources to the English regions.

These differences have been recognised since the early 1970s. An internal DHSS review led to the introduction of a new method of allocating revenue in 1971–72, and in 1975 the Resource Allocation Working Party (RAWP) was established to produce a formula:

> To reduce progressively, and as far as is feasible, the disparities between the different parts of the country in terms of opportunity for access to health care for people at equal risk; taking into account measures of health needs, and social and environmental factors which may affect the need for health care. (DHSS, 1975c)

The RAWP report recommended a formula based on the size of each region's population, weighted for age, sex and morbidity, with standardised mortality ratios being used as a proxy for morbidity (DHSS, 1976a). Using this weighted capitation approach, the Working Party found that some regions had allocations around 10 per cent below their target share of resources, and others had allocations more than 10 per cent above. In accepting the recommendations put forward, the Secretary of State recognised that they would have to be implemented in stages, and the result was a progressive reduction in inequities in resource allocation. The slow pace of implementation was, however, a source of frustration to health authorities below their weighted capitation target and was one of the reasons the Acheson Report recommended that there should be more rapid movement towards target allocations. The principles of the RAWP approach have been maintained even though the detail of its application have changed, sometimes quite significantly, in the light of research into the indicators that best reflect variations in need and alterations to the structure of the NHS. Currently, most primary care trusts are within 10 per cent of their target allocations, and there are plans to reduce variations from target through differential allocations to trusts (DH 2003a, p. 69).

Alongside regional differences there are social class differences in access to health care. The significance of these was recognised by Titmuss writing in 1968:

> We have learnt from 15 years' experience of the Health Service that the higher income groups know how to make better use of the Service; they tend to receive more specialist attention; occupy more of the beds in better equipped and staffed hospitals; receive more elective surgery; have better maternity care; and are more likely to get psychiatric help and psychotherapy than low income groups – particularly the unskilled. (Titmuss, 1968, p. 196)

Support for Titmuss's analysis came from Alderson's examination of a number of mainly preventative services. This found underuse of services in relation to need, and Alderson commented:

> The data presented are compatible with the hypothesis that there is a group in the community who are aware of the provisions of the health service and who obtain a higher proportion of the resources of the health service than would be expected by chance and a much higher proportion in relation to their needs when compared with others in the community. (Alderson, 1970, p. 52)

One of the explanations of variations in the utilisation of services by social class is that these services may not be equally available in different parts of the country. It is this observation that lies behind the inverse care law formulated by Julian Tudor-Hart which states that 'the availability of good medical care tends to vary inversely with the need of the population served' (Tudor-Hart, 1971, p. 412). Tudor-Hart's thesis is that areas of social deprivation containing high proportions of people from the lower social groups tend to have access to less good health services even though their need for these services is greater than that of higher social groups. This argument is reinforced by the work of Le Grand who combined data on the utilisation of services and need to demonstrate that higher social groups benefited more from the NHS than lower social groups (Le Grand, 1978). In other words, Le Grand contended that in terms of utilisation the NHS was pro-rich.

Later evidence has been reviewed and summarised by Propper (1998). Her analysis of data on utilisation and need reported much less systematic variation in the use of services in relation to need than was evident from Le Grand's study. On the other hand, research into the provision of specific interventions do demonstrate variation. For example, the use of GP services was related to social class, with people in the lower social groups making greater use of these services than those in higher social groups. In this area, at least, it appeared that the NHS was pro-poor. There is a more mixed picture in relation to hospital services, with evidence of services being provided in proportion to deprivation in some areas but not in others. On the basis of its review of the evidence, the Acheson Report commented, 'For many ... NHS hospital treatments, there is little evidence of systematic inequities in access between deprivation groups' (Acheson Report, 1998, p. 113). The most recent review of the evidence notes that 'the picture overall is a confusing one' (Dixon *et al.*, 2003, p. 18), at least in part because of variations in the quality of research, and it concludes that on balance there are inequities in utilisation in key areas of health service provision. These inequities were found in relation to preventative services and hospital services, including cardiac surgery and elective surgical procedures such as hip replacements, hernias and treatment of gallstones.

Inequities in access are also evident in relation to the care available to groups such as older people, people with learning disabilities and the mentally ill. We noted in Chapter 1 that concerns about the quality of care provided to these groups was one of the factors behind the reorganisation of the NHS in 1974. The issue was brought to prominence in 1967 when a pressure group known as Aid for the Elderly in Government Institutions published a book called *Sans Everything – A Case to Answer,* containing allegations of ill-treatment to elderly patients in psychiatric and geriatric care (Robb, 1967). The Minister of Health asked regional hospital boards to set up independent enquiries and the general conclusion of the enquiries was that the allegations were unfounded.

A rather different picture emerged from the report of the committee of enquiry set up to investigate conditions at Ely Hospital, a hospital for people with learning disabilities in Cardiff. The committee found that many of the allegations of ill-treatment of patients were true, and that there were serious deficiencies at Ely. A number of recommendations were made for improving standards at Ely and at long-stay hospitals generally, including the establishment of a system of inspection to ensure that the local managers of services were aware of what was required (Ely Report, 1969). The Secretary of State at the time of Ely, Richard Crossman, used the report to give greater priority to long-stay services. The Hospital Advisory Service was set up to provide the system of inspection recommended by the committee of enquiry, although it was presented as a means of giving advice rather than an inspectorate. In addition, Crossman earmarked funds to be spent specifically on hospitals for people with learning disabilities. These earmarked funds were later extended to other services, although earmarking for this purpose came to an end in 1974. At the same time, the DHSS issued advice to hospital boards and committees on measures which could be taken at little cost to raise standards of care. The momentum generated by Crossman was maintained through the publication of a series of further reports into conditions at long-stay hospitals. Partly in response to these inquiries, the DHSS published White Papers setting out the future direction in which services should move; and in terms of overall service development the Department gave priority to these services in the consultative document on *Priorities* published in 1976. These actions were an attempt to allocate a greater share of resources to an area of the NHS which it was recognised had fallen behind required standards (Martin, 1984).

Progress towards achieving the kinds of priorities set out in 1976 has been slow and uneven. Part of the difficulty of achieving national priorities is that NHS bodies may not share the objectives of the DH. The claims of other groups, particularly in the acute hospital sector, may be pressed strongly at the local level, and may push service development in a different direction from that desired by central government. As we noted in Chapter 8, the implementation of national priorities can therefore be problematic. This point can be illustrated in relation to services for people with a learning disability, where a review of progress made in implementing the policies set out in the White Paper, *Better Services for the Mentally Handicapped,* noted that the percentage of NHS revenue allocated to these services declined between 1974/75 and 1977/78. The review commented:

> the financial data for health services suggests that the constraints since 1974, together with demographic pressures and the need to rationalise acute services in order to release revenue for development, meant that health authorities could do little to sustain the previous increase in expenditure on mental handicap services other than their increasing contribution through Joint Finance. (DHSS, 1980c, p. 62)

Undoubtedly one of the reasons for this is that, despite the priority given by the DH, these services are relatively weak in the struggle for scarce resources that occurs in the NHS. Put another way, the micro politics of the NHS may run counter to the macro politics leading to a gap between intention and action.

A fourth area in which access to care has emerged as an issue is the time patients spend waiting for hospital treatment. Waiting lists for surgery have existed ever since the establishment of the NHS and they continue to pose a challenge to policy-makers and NHS managers. In examining this issue, it is important to recognise that of patients admitted from waiting lists, half are admitted within six weeks, and over two-thirds within three months. Analysis has shown that five specialties account for around three-quarters of patients waiting, and at various times initiatives within the NHS have succeeded in cutting both waiting lists and waiting times, in some cases significantly. Although there are differences between areas in the experience of patients waiting for treatment, from an equity perspective a more important consideration is the ability of some patients to access treatment through the private sector rather than having to wait for an NHS operation.

As Yates (1987 and 1995) has shown, there is in fact a perverse incentive for hospital specialists in that their income from private practice is in part dependent on the existence of NHS waiting lists and the willingness of some people to pay for treatment to avoid waiting. This derives from the bargain struck between Bevan and the medical profession at the inception of the NHS after which Bevan famously claimed to have stuffed the mouths of specialists with gold to entice them into the NHS (see Chapter 1). The effects are still felt today with private practice coexisting with NHS work, and patients who are able to pay for treatment receiving this treatment in a matter of days as opposed to months. Only under the Labour Government in the 1970s did this issue become a matter of political controversy, and even then attention focused more on the existence of private beds in NHS hospitals than the employment contract of specialists. One of the effects of the reforms to the NHS initiated by the Thatcher government was an expansion of private provision by NHS trusts and this means that paradoxically the NHS is currently a major provider of acute services to private patients. The consequence is to make even more stark the inequities in access that arise from the persistence of private practice within the NHS.

Reducing waiting lists has been a high priority for both Conservative and Labour governments. Figure 9.3 illustrates the long-term trends in the number of people on waiting lists in England. The Blair government that came to power in 1997 promised to reduce the number of people on inpatient waiting lists by 100 000 and it achieved this objective by allocating extra resources for this purpose and exerting pressure through the management line. The focus of attention shifted from waiting lists to waiting times on publication of *The NHS Plan*. The targets set out in the

Figure 9.3   *Inpatient waiting lists in England*

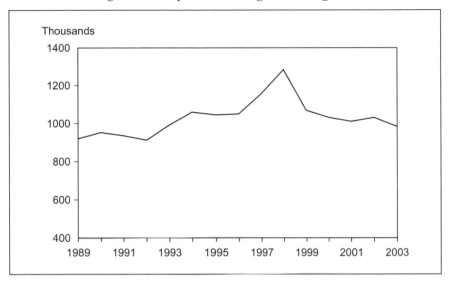

plan included a maximum waiting time of six months for inpatient admission and 13 weeks for an outpatient appointment by the end of 2005. Progress towards these targets was illustrated by the achievement of a maximum waiting time for almost all patients in England of 9 months for inpatient treatment and 17 weeks for outpatients by the end of March 2004. The focus on access to services also encompassed appointments with GPs and the time spent in hospital accident and emergency departments. More ambitious waiting time targets were set for high priority services such as cancer and heart disease, reflecting the importance attached to these clinical conditions.

One of the reasons that waiting for treatment has been singled out as a priority is a concern that an increasing number of people may choose to 'go private' if they are unable to receive treatment in the NHS in a reasonable time, and that this may undermine support for the NHS as a universal service. Another reason is evidence that waiting is a major concern for the public and the aspect of NHS provision of which they are most critical. At a time when taxes have risen to fund the additional investment made in the NHS, the government has been particularly concerned to show that increases in expenditure are producing better results in areas of service provision that are of importance to the public. To this end, the Modernisation Agency focused much of its effort on supporting the NHS to achieve the waiting time targets. In so doing, it placed particular emphasis on assisting NHS staff to work more smartly by redesigning services to make them more efficient and more convenient for patients. This included a series of 'Action on' programmes targeted at specialties like orthopaedics and ENT where access presented particular challenges.

One of the first redesign programmes led by the Agency (and its predecessor, the National Patients' Access Team) was an initiative to offer patients the opportunity of booking the time of their hospital appointments as a way of reducing uncertainty and increasing convenience. Following the piloting of this programme, the government decided to extend booking throughout the NHS. The targets in this area envisaged that all day cases and two-thirds of first outpatient and inpatient elective admissions would be booked by March 2004 on the way to all such appointments being booked by December 2005. The policy on waiting and booking was developed further in 2002 with the establishment of pilot programmes to extend the range of choices available to patients. The first two pilots focused on patients waiting longer than six months for heart surgery and patients in London waiting longer than six months in a number of specialties. Subsequently, the government announced that all patients waiting longer than six months for elective surgery would be offered choices from the summer of 2004 and it launched a consultation exercise to discuss how choice could be extended to other areas of service provision. The policy on access and choice was supported by a drive to increase the proportion of operations carried out as day cases and to increase the capacity for elective surgery. The latter included making greater use of spare capacity in private hospitals and commissioning a number of new diagnostic and treatment centres specialising in elective work. A number of NHS patients also travelled overseas for treatment as part of a pilot undertaken in 2002. To support patients to make choices, a database showing waiting times in NHS hospitals was made available on the internet (www.nhs.uk).

The unrelenting focus on improving access had two adverse effects. The first was to encourage some NHS managers to report inaccurate information on waiting times in their hospitals. The extent to which this happened was examined by the National Audit Office and the Audit Commission. Both organisations found evidence of the mismanagement and misreporting of waiting list data at a small number of NHS trusts. The second adverse effect, to return to our earlier discussion, was that the overriding priority attached to cutting waiting times meant that resources were not available for other purposes, such as improving services for older people and people with mental illness and learning disabilities. To be sure, the additional funding made available to the NHS by the Blair government meant that these other services were able to develop, but they did not benefit to the same extent as acute hospital services. This again illustrates the inevitability of priority-setting in the NHS, a theme to which we return in the final chapter.

Conclusion

In this chapter we have traced the evolution of audit and evaluation of health policy. A wide range of arrangements are currently involved in the audit of health service performance in contrast to the early phases of the NHS when these functions were underdeveloped. We have seen how the results of audit feed back into policy-making, an example being the report by the Health Services Commissioner which led to changes of policy in relation to continuing care. We have also noted that for audit to influence policy-making, ministers and civil servants must be predisposed to act on the results. In this respect, the rejection of the recommendations of the Black Report by a Conservative government stands in contrast to the willingness of a Labour government to change the principles of NHS resource allocation in the light of evidence about continuing inequalities in the distribution of the budget between regions.

Data on the performance of the NHS demonstrate improvements in health and health care since its inception. Nevertheless, there are a number of inequities in access to services, affecting different geographical areas, social classes and care groups. Of particular importance in the recent history of the NHS have been waiting lists and waiting times for treatment. The ability of some people to avoid NHS queues by paying to go private is one of the most obvious inequities in the United Kingdom health care system, and the priority given to improving access and increasing patient choice is an attempt to address this. Successive governments have sought to reduce waiting lists and waiting times and the available data indicate progress towards the targets set out in *The NHS Plan*.

The wider question raised by this chapter is whether the audit explosion and the growth of regulation signal a fundamental change to the management of the NHS. At the time of writing, audit and regulation have been overlaid on a system that retains many of the traditional characteristics of bureaucratic control and performance management that were discussed in the previous chapter. Not only this, but also some of the features of the discarded internal market have reappeared in a new guise. The result is a complex mix of performance management, regulation and competition. The establishment of the Healthcare Commission and the policy of shifting the balance of power within the NHS, together with the entry of new providers and the introduction of a system of paying providers by results, seems to herald the emergence of a regulated market in which less reliance is placed on performance management. These are issues to which we will return in the final chapter.

Chapter 10

Power in Health Services

Our examination of the auditing and evaluation of health policy in Chapter 9 revealed various inequalities in health and health services. In seeking to explain these inequalities, it is helpful to analyse the distribution of power in health care systems. In other words, explaining the distribution of benefits within health services requires us to ask who controls those services and who influences the allocation of resources? In so doing, it is important to examine the relationship between the state and organised interests in the health policy community. There are a number of theoretical approaches to answering these questions, and we now go on to discuss these.

Pluralism

The essence of the pluralist democratic theory of power is that the resources which contribute to power are widely distributed among different groups. As we noted in Chapter 6, pluralists argue that no one group is dominant, and each is able to exercise some influence (see for example Dahl, 1961). Power is in fact shared between official groups in governmental agencies and outside interests exerting pressure on these agencies. This helps to ensure there is no consistent bias in the allocation of values, although pluralists would recognise that groups vary in their ability to exercise power. Developments in health services and health policy are explained in terms of the interplay between pressure groups. Since there is no dominant interest, pluralists analyse the distribution of power in relation to particular issues, studying who wins and who loses through often detailed examination of the preferences of different interests and the extent to which decisions match up with expressed preferences. The question of who has power is an empirical question for the pluralists, to be answered by means of case studies of particular policy areas. A range of factors may be important, including party manifestos, key individuals, official reports and the activities of pressure groups, but their relative influence must be studied in specific cases.

Examples of studies of the NHS which have their roots in the pluralist democratic tradition are Willcocks' (1967) examination of the creation of the NHS and Eckstein's (1960) analysis of the operation of the BMA. Each author analyses the way in which decisions are reached in a system of pressure group politics, and each is able to show how the outcomes were the result of compromise between the various interests involved. Professional interests vie with consumer interests, and civil servants with politicians, but alliances change, leading to the fragmentation of power which pluralists observe. The strength of pluralist theory is the richness of detail provided about decision-making and the high degree of sophistication which has often been achieved in the analysis of individual, group and organisational influences on policy processes.

However, pluralism does not provide a completely adequate theory of power. For example, in earlier chapters we noted the key position occupied by the medical profession in the organisation of health services, and our discussion of how policies are made and implemented in the NHS suggests certain inadequacies in the pluralist position. In particular, the strength of producer groups and the relative weakness of consumer groups cast doubt on the pluralists' argument that any group can make itself heard effectively at some stage in the decision-making process, and that no group is dominant (Ham, 1977). Accordingly, attention needs to be paid to the work of Alford, who has maintained that it is important to analyse the nature of structural interests within health services.

Structuralist approaches

Alford argues that structural interests are those interests which gain or lose from the form of organisation of health services (Alford, 1975a). There are three sets of structural interests: dominant, challenging and repressed. Dominant interests are the professional monopolists; challenging interests are the corporate rationalisers; and repressed interests are the community population. Dominant interests are served by existing social, economic and political institutions, and therefore only need to be active when their interests are challenged. Alford argues that the medical profession is dominant in health services, but the profession may be challenged by corporate rationalisers such as health planners and administrators. Again, patient and consumer groups representing the community population may seek to move out of their repressed position by organising to articulate their interests. These struggles between structural interests are not the same as the competition for power between pressure groups. Pressure group competition may well take place within structural interests, as between, for example, different groups of doctors. These conflicts are important, but they leave unchallenged the principle of professional monopoly and dominance. Pressure group politics coexist with struggles between structural interests, and may explain how particular issues are resolved. Structural interests are, however, more significant in influencing the overall distribution of benefits, and in shaping the main contours of power relationships.

The value of Alford's framework has been demonstrated in a study of policy-making in the NHS (Ham, 1981), and the inequalities in power he highlights indicate a position close to elitist interpretations of the power structure. In the health sector, professional control of knowledge, recruitment and training, as well as claims to professional autonomy over the content of work, provide the basis of the medical profession's power. Its organisation through powerful pressure groups in continuous contact with governmental agencies, coupled with involvement at all stages in the system of administration, enhance this power. Structuralist approaches recognise the existence of pressure group politics but contend that studies which remain at the level of groups are incomplete.

Marxist approaches

A different approach is offered by Marxists who argue that medical care in societies like Britain must be seen as part of the capitalist mode of production (Doyal, 1979). Within capitalism, Marxists contend that there is an important division between the owners of the means of production and those who have to sell their wage labour. It is the capitalist mode of production which gives rise to class relations of production, and Marxists go on to argue that the economically dominant class is also politically dominant. The state therefore acts in the long-term interests of the dominant class, and performs a number of functions.

In O'Connor's terms, the state assists in the process of capital accumulation, and also performs the function of legitimation (O'Connor, 1973). State expenditures are directed towards these ends, and are made up of social capital and social expenses. State expenditures on health services comprise partly social capital, in so far as health services involve the reproduction of a healthy labour force, and partly they comprise social expenses, in so far as health services help to maintain non-working groups and promote social harmony. State involvement in the provision of health services stems from two sources: action by the dominant class to reduce the costs of labour power and to prevent social unrest; and action by the subordinate class to win concessions. However, Marxists argue that there may develop a fiscal crisis for the state when the demand for expenditure on health services outstrips the ability of the state to fund that expenditure. At this point a restructuring of public expenditure may occur to the disadvantage of state health services. Marxists would interpret this as an attack on the interests of the subordinate class, even though health services are seen as a form of social control (Gough, 1979).

Within this theoretical perspective, inequalities in service provision between client groups are explained in terms of the lack of productivity of the mentally ill, people with learning disabilities and older people. It is suggested that because these groups cannot make a significant contribution to the development of the economy, they will receive a lower quality service than productive groups. Similarly, social class inequalities in health are interpreted by Marxists as evidence of the continuing influence of economic factors on health and the persistence of class divisions within society. The distribution of benefits within health services is therefore explained by reference to class conflict.

At a macro level of analysis a number of authors have used Marxist theory to explain developments in health policy. Yet a convincing theory of power must also be able to explain the processes of policy-making and implementation described in Chapters 7 and 8. Marxist approaches are much weaker at this level of analysis, and Marxist studies of particular decisions, issues or health care organisations are little developed. In contrast, pluralist theories, with their focus on the role of pressure groups and bargaining and negotiation within policy communities, offer a range of insights into the dynamics of health policy-making, while structuralist theories provide a way of explaining differences in influence between pressure groups. This suggests that what is required is an approach which builds on the strength of each of the theoretical positions discussed here.

The key issue, then, is to develop 'mediating frameworks to connect macro-theory with specific policy issues' (Dunleavy, 1981, p. 4). One approach to this is through the examination of dominant value systems in particular policy areas and their influence on policy. More specifically, by analysing the operation of professional ideologies in health services, it may be possible to establish links between the way issues are defined and resources allocated, the nature of structural interests and the distribution of power, and macro theories of the state (Ham, 1980). The difficulties of doing this are considerable, but a start can be made by exploring the role of the medical profession and the way in which the profession's view of health has come to occupy a dominant position.

Concepts of health

There are many different concepts of health. Margaret Stacey has identified three dimensions along which these concepts vary: individual or collective; functional fitness or welfare; preventative or curative (Stacey, 1977). Stacey notes that in Western societies the individualistic concept of health tends to dominate, and it is usually associated with ideas of functional fitness and curative approaches. This concept seeks the causes of illness within the biological systems of individuals, and it attempts to provide a specific cure for illness in order to make individuals fit for work. Alongside the individualistic concept of health, Stacey notes the existence of a collective concept which emphasises the importance of prevention. The collective concept seeks the causes of illnesses within the environmental, economic and social systems in which people live, and attempts to prevent illness arising by tackling the unhealthy aspects of those systems. Stacey also notes the existence of a welfare concept of health, emphasising the importance of relieving pain and providing care.

While these concepts coexist, it is the individualistic, functional fitness, curative approach which is the most influential. This approach has been characterised as the medical model of health, a model in which doctors have a central role and hospitals play a major part. It has been suggested that the model has two components: a disease component, which holds that illness results from pathological processes in the biochemical functions of the body; and an engineering component, which sees the body as a machine to be repaired by technical means (Illsley, 1977). The medical model emphasises specific, individual causes of illness and searches for specific individual cures for these illnesses. Acceptance of the medical model is important, first, in justifying the preeminent position of the medical profession in health matters, and second, in helping to explain the pattern of investment in health services. Within the NHS, the bulk of resources is allocated to personally orientated, general and acute hospital services. Much less importance has been attached to collective, preventative and welfare approaches to health.

Using an historical perspective, Fox (1986) has shown how the medical model replaced the collective concept of health in the early decades of the twentieth century. As a consequence, the focus of health policy shifted from public health measures and the relief of poverty to the organisation of medical services. Fox uses the phrase 'hierarchical regionalism' to describe the principles on which health policy evolved. These principles include the view that the causes of illness and disease are discovered in medical schools. For most of the twentieth century, a key aim of policy has been to ensure that the results of medical science are made available to the population through hierarchies of services organised on a regional basis. In these hierarchies, specialist hospital services play a major part.

Alternative approaches, such as those emphasising the social and environmental influences on health, have received less attention. However, this may be changing as the medical model comes under increasing challenge. The challenge to medical dominance in the health field has been spearheaded by writers such as McKeown, who have questioned the significance of the medical contribution in bringing about improvements in health. McKeown's work has demonstrated that improved nutrition, purer water supplies, behavioural changes limiting family size and leading to the better spacing of births, and improved methods of sewage disposal, have been mainly responsible for the advances in health which have occurred in the last 200 years. These factors contributed to the decline in infectious diseases, and assisted in reducing death rates and increasing life expectancy. In contrast, medical science had very little impact until the introduction of vaccines and certain drugs in the twentieth century. Yet McKeown argues that even these interventions came at a time when overall death rates were already in decline as a result of earlier environmental and behavioural changes. On the basis of his analysis, McKeown contends that:

> medical science and services are misdirected, and society's investment in health is not well used, because they rest on an erroneous assumption about the basis of human health. It is assumed that the body can be regarded as a machine whose protection from disease and its effects depends primarily on internal intervention. The approach has led to indifference to the external influences and personal behaviour which are the predominant determinants of health. (McKeown, 1976, p. xiv)

McKeown's work has had a major influence in the development of the health field concept articulated by Lalonde (1974). This concept analyses illness and disease in terms of four elements: human biology, the environment, life-style and health care organisation. Human biology includes aspects of health, such as ageing, which are developed within the body as a result of the basic biology of man. The environment comprises matters relating to health external to the body, over which the individual has little or no control. Life-style refers to the decisions by individuals which affect health and over which they have control. And health care organisation consists of the arrangements made to provide organised health services to individuals. Like McKeown, Lalonde suggests that while most efforts to improve health have centred on medical interventions through health care organisation, it is the other three elements which are more important in identifying the causes of sickness and death. In particular, Lalonde points to the need for people to adopt healthy life-styles in order to prevent illness arising.

This is very much in line with the policy on public health adopted by the government in the 1970s. As we noted in Chapter 4, the DHSS used the work of people like McKeown to argue that greater emphasis should be given to prevention, and that individuals should look after themselves by giving up smoking, adopting an appropriate diet, taking exercise, and so on. This individualistic approach to prevention does not seriously threaten the medical model, and it has been criticised for 'blaming the victim'. A growing body of research indicates that life-style may be less significant than the environment (defined as the social, economic and cultural factors that have a bearing on health) in influencing illness and disease and that a collective approach to health is needed if progress is to be made in tackling contemporary health problems. This was the argument of the Black Report and other studies have drawn attention to the industrial and environmental causes of cancer (Doyal *et al.*, 1983), the impact of unemployment on health (Brenner, 1979), and to the various ways in which the processes of production, distribution and consumption contribute to illness and disease (Draper, Best and Dennis, 1977). These studies constitute a significant challenge to the medical model, not least because they imply a reduced role for doctors, and they have begun to influence health policy. In particular, as we noted in Chapter 9, policies to tackle health inequalities adopted since 1997 have included actions directed at the broader determinants of health. It must be added, though, that medicine has remained remarkably resilient in the face of criticism, and continues to provide the dominant explanation of health problems in contemporary Western societies.

What are the implications of this analysis for the earlier discussion of power in health care systems? What we hope to have shown is that the medical model, as the dominant (though not the only) value system in the health field, exercises a key influence on the definition of issues and the allocation of resources. The question this raises is whose interests are served by the medical model? Stacey (1977) has reminded us that concepts do not stand alone, they must be understood in terms of the power of different groups. Let us then return to the examination of theories of power for help in explaining the dominance of the medical model.

Power, interests and ideology

In the pluralist framework, concepts of health and the role of medicine are not seen as having special significance. The medical profession is viewed as one interest among many, albeit in most studies a key interest; and concepts of health are implicitly assumed to have emerged out of the underlying consensus on which pluralist theories are based. Within this consensus, prevailing concepts of health are no more than a reflection of the shifting balance of power between interests. The fact that they have remained the same over time is seen by pluralists as an indication of the large measure of agreement between these interests on the meaning of health and the manner in which services should be provided. The question that needs to be asked about this interpretation is whether the consensus which pluralists observe is genuine or false. In other words, is the consensus the result of spontaneous agreement among different groups in the population, or does it derive from manipulation by dominant groups?

This question is not easily resolved. Pluralists would argue that people's expressed preferences are the only reliable guide to their interests, and the fact that these preferences demonstrate strong support for the medical profession is in itself sufficient to show that the consensus on values is genuine. In contrast, critics of pluralism would argue that people's real interests may differ from their expressed preferences, in which case the possibility of a false consensus being manipulated by dominant groups cannot be ruled out. The problem with this approach is how to establish the existence of real interests which are different from expressed preferences (Saunders, 1979). One line of analysis in the health field would be to develop McKeown's work, which, as we have noted, has suggested that society's investment in health is not well-used because it is based on the medical model. What this indicates is that people's real interests might be better served by an alternative pattern of investment. That is, improved health might result from a reorientation away from personally orientated, hospital-based health care towards a system in which more emphasis was given to the social causes of illness and disease. If this could be demonstrated, then a rather different explanation of the interests served by dominant concepts of health would be needed.

Such an explanation is provided by structuralists. For structuralists, dominant concepts of health serve the interests of the medical profession because they legitimate the profession's claim to control in health services. In other words, prevailing concepts of health are explained by the position of the medical profession as a dominant structural interest and its success in getting individualistic definitions of illness and disease accepted. The dominance of medicine is in turn explained historically in terms of the success of physicians, surgeons and apothecaries in winning state approval for their position, and in turning their occupations into professions having exclusive control over their area of work (Wilding, 1982; Stacey, 1992). Medical dominance does not imply a conspiracy against subordinate groups. Rather, it reflects the power of doctors, their control of key resources such as expertise and knowledge, and their ability to achieve acceptance for their own concept of health. This concept of health makes sense to groups in the population other than doctors, but as we have shown, it is not the only concept, and it is not necessarily the concept which best serves the interests of the population.

Like structuralists, Marxists would challenge the pluralists' position that consensus is genuine, but would see dominant concepts of health not as an indication of the power of the medical profession, but as evidence of the control exercised by the dominant class. In particular, Marxists argue that the individual, disease-based model of curative medicine helps to maintain the position of dominant groups by masking the real causes of illness which lie within the social and economic system of capitalism. As Navarro has put it:

> the social utility of medicine is measured primarily in the arena of legitimation. Medicine is indeed socially useful to the degree that the majority of people believe and accept the proposition that what are actually politically caused conditions can be individually solved by medical intervention. From the point of view of the capitalist system, this is the actual utility of medicine – it contributes to the legitimation of capitalism. (Navarro, 1976, p. 208)

For Marxists, the medical model is a key linking concept explaining not only how issues are defined and benefits distributed in the policy process, but also highlighting underlying class divisions within society. The conclusion to be drawn from the Marxist analysis is that the prevailing concept of health serves class interests, that power is weighted heavily in favour of those interests, and that doctors, although seemingly in a powerful position, merely administer the health care system on behalf of dominant groups.

It thus emerges that Marxists and structuralists see different interests being served by dominant concepts of health. Structuralists argue that the medical profession has power in its own right, not simply power deriving from its utility to dominant groups. In contrast, Marxists argue that medical power results from class power. The Marxist position is well summarised by Navarro, who criticises writers such as Alford for:

> their failure to recognise that those elites (for example medicine) are in reality segments of a dominant class and that, when they are considered in a systemic and not just a sectorial fashion, they are found to possess a high degree of cohesion and solidarity, with common interests and common purposes for transcending their specific differences and disagreements. (Navarro, 1976, pp. 189–90)

The question which needs to be raised about this argument is whether all conflicts are 'in reality' class conflicts, and if so how disagreements between the state and the medical profession can be explained. A key theme of this book has been the challenge to medical dominance in the NHS since the 1980s as politicians have questioned the autonomy of doctors and have pursued policies which have been strongly opposed by the BMA and other interest groups. In the final section of this chapter we analyse the significance of these developments and what they tell us about power in health services.

Theories and practice

The underlying determinism of Marxist approaches has increasingly been challenged by writers who have pointed to developments in policy and practice which cannot adequately be explained by these approaches. Saunders, for example, has argued that state expenditure on health services may be dysfunctional rather than automatically serving the interests of dominant groups (Saunders, 1981). The fiscal crisis of the state that began in the 1970s has illustrated the importance of Saunders' criticism, and has indicated that while expenditure on areas of collective consumption like the NHS may benefit professional interests, it may be against the interests of dominant groups, whose main purpose is to maintain capital accumulation. A similar point is made by Cawson (1982) who argues that the growth of public expenditure has been fuelled by the bargaining processes between the state and producer groups. Cawson explains this in terms of the development of a corporate sector in the British political system in which producer groups like the BMA are intimately involved both in the making of policy and its implementation. Cawson predicts that expenditure cuts will be resisted by producer groups and that governments faced with a fiscal crisis will seek to reduce the burden of public expenditure by privatising services.

Although this has happened in some policy areas, a comparative study of welfare reform in the USA and the United Kingdom (Pierson, 1994) has highlighted the political difficulties in cutting back public services, including health care, and has shown how governments used a variety of indirect strategies to bring about change rather than risk confrontation and electoral unpopularity. These strategies were pursued in part because of the strength of existing bureaucratic and professional institutions and their ability to resist change. Health policy in Britain in the 1980s and 1990s exemplifies this and demonstrates that the response to the fiscal crisis that developed at that time was mediated by the influence of pressure groups and other interests. While there was some growth in the contribution of the private health sector in this period, privatisation of NHS services was limited to non-clinical areas such as catering, cleaning and laundry services which were opened up to competitive tendering, and increases in charges for prescriptions, dental care and ophthalmic services. The indirect strategies pursued were of greater significance and included the use of private finance to pay for new capital projects, the unannounced transfer of long-term care from the NHS to social services and to private funders and providers, and the use of private hospitals for the treatment of some NHS patients. These policies all stemmed from a concern to control public expenditure at a time when changes in the economy and in political alignments undermined the postwar consensus on the expansion of the welfare state and led to the examination of more radical alternatives.

Yet, in making this point, it should also be noted that the Thatcher government considered but rejected moving away from tax funding of the NHS to private funding both because of the political costs associated with such a move and evidence that alternative methods of funding appeared to offer little benefit. In other words, the fiscal crisis that prompted a review of policy did not lead automatically to the response predicted by some analysts. Rather, the eventual outcome represented a compromise between the ideological instincts of politicians in power and their assessment of what was feasible and desirable. It was this that led the Thatcher government to focus on ways of increasing efficiency and of curtailing professional power. In so doing, the government had to overcome the objections of the BMA and related organisations and it had to persuade civil servants in the Department of Health to support policies that unsettled established routines in the health policy community. To this extent, corporatist relationships in the health sector made it more difficult for a reforming government of the centre-right to pursue those policies that it instinctively favoured.

In relation to health services, the reforms initiated since the Griffiths Report can be seen as an attempt to strengthen the hand of managers in their challenge to medical dominance. The appointment of general managers, and the call for doctors to be more closely involved in management, were both designed to introduce greater control over the activities of the medical profession and to influence the behaviour of consultants in their position as the key influencers of resources in the NHS. What is more, the recommendation in the Griffiths Report that arrangements for public consultation on decisions should be streamlined was interpreted by some observers as an attempt to maintain community interests in their repressed position. As Day and Klein noted at the time, one of the implications was that conflict between managers and professionals was more likely to occur, particularly if clinical freedom was questioned and challenged (Day and Klein, 1983). Coincidentally, publication of the Griffiths Report occurred within days of a claim that clinical freedom had died, 'crushed between the rising costs of new forms of investigation and treatment and the financial limits inevitable in an economy that cannot expand indefinitely' (Hampton, 1983, p. 1238). While this obituary appeared premature, the medical profession was not slow to recognise the threat posed by Griffiths and to argue that doctors should take on the general management role whenever possible.

In practice, the appointment of doctors as general managers was the exception rather than the rule, and the introduction of general management did lead to a more active management style in which managers were increasingly involved in questioning medical priorities (Flynn, 1991). The extent to which this resulted in a shift in the frontier of control between managers and doctors is disputed with the balance of evidence maintaining that change was limited. To quote Harrison, who has made an extensive study of general management:

> the basic sources of (in Alford's terms) the doctors' structural monopoly remain unchanged. It is still general practitioners who provide the selection for consultants to work on. It is still consultants who decide which, and how many patients to see, and how to diagnose and treat them ... The prime determinant of the pattern of the health services is still, just as before Griffiths, what doctors choose to do. (Harrison, 1988, p. 123)

The Griffiths reforms were taken a stage further by *Working for Patients*. The White Paper built on the introduction of general management and sought to reinforce measures already taken to increase the accountability of the medical profession. As a consequence, general managers took part in the appointment of hospital consultants, negotiated job plans with each consultant, and participated in deciding which consultants should receive distinction awards. In parallel, new disciplinary procedures were introduced for hospital doctors, the resource management initiative was extended throughout the NHS, and clinical audit received higher priority.

The separation of purchaser and provider responsibilities and the introduction of contracts posed a challenge to medical dominance. The establishment of health authorities and GP fundholders as purchasers created a countervailing power to established interests in NHS trusts, and over time this had an impact on priority-setting and resource allocation. To some degree, the effect was to shift influence within the medical profession, for example between hospital doctors and GPs, and to some degree it enhanced the role of managers in relation to doctors. Again, though, the impact of these changes should not be exaggerated. Just as with the introduction of general management, the effect on roles and relationships within the NHS was complex as patterns of pluralistic bargaining among doctors mediated the implementation of these changes and defeated attempts to explain their impact from any single perspective. Put another way, while the relative position of structural interests changed only at the margins, there were shifts *within* each set of interests which had an influence on policy-making, as in the enhanced priority attached to public health and primary care.

The policies pursued by the Blair government elected in 1997 take a stage further the search for ways of making doctors more accountable for their performance. These policies build on both general management and the separation of purchaser and provider responsibilities and focus particularly on the introduction of new forms of regulation to raise standards within the NHS. Specifically, doctors are required to take part in clinical audit and to work within the guidelines set at a national level by the National Institute for Clinical Excellence. The establishment of the Healthcare Commission provides a means of independent examination of clinical performance, and the publication of comparative data on clinical outcomes marks the beginning of an attempt to open up variations in standards to public scrutiny. The genesis of these policies lies in part in examples of failures of clinical performance within the NHS, but it is also the latest manifestation of a long-term trend to enhance professional accountability.

In examining this trend, Moran (1999) notes that the relationship between government and professionals has traditionally been characterised by state sanctioned self-regulation, and he describes this as 'pre-democratic'. Reforms to the way in which professionals are governed have resulted from social and cultural changes, including the emergence of a more demanding and less deferential public. As a consequence:

> closely integrated oligarchies dominated by professional and corporate interests, operating with a substantial degree of independence from the core institutions of the state, are being replaced: by looser, more open, more unstable networks; by networks in which professional and corporate elites still exercise great power but in a more contested environment than hitherto; and by an institutional setting in which the core institutions of the state exercise much tighter surveillance and control than hitherto (Moran, 1999, p. 178).

As this observation makes clear, the private government of standards by the medical profession has come under challenge with the state acting in response to changing social attitudes to strengthen accountability. Despite this, it would be wrong to argue that state power has replaced medical power. In Alford's terms, dominant structural interests retain considerable power with corporatist patterns of policy-making coexisting with the more open pluralist arrangements described by Moran. In the process, the state's role in health policy-making has increased, but it would be too simple to see relationships between actors in zero-sum terms. Health policy in Britain has been characterised by more active government, increased lobbying by groups representing patients and the public, and a medical profession that has retained a position of considerable power and influence in the face of unprecedented questioning and challenge.

While this chapter has emphasised the need to locate changes in health services in their wider social, economic and political context, there are occasions when health care institutions may themselves shape the structure and functions of the state. At a time when health services consume a large and often growing share of national income in most developed countries, the actions of policy-makers and the organisations in which they operate are increasingly influenced by the dynamics of health services. Under the Blair government, this has been exemplified by the close involvement of the Prime Minister and the Chancellor of the Exchequer in health policy and the commitment made by the government to unprecedented increases in NHS funding. This commitment has had a significant impact on other spending programmes by preempting resources that might have been used in alternative ways, and it has led to changes in the machinery of government as the Treasury and No 10 Downing Street have set up new forms of scrutiny, like public service agreements and the Prime Minister's Delivery Unit, to review how resources are being used (see Chapter 6). Understanding the *reciprocal* relationship between health services and the state is therefore an increasingly important area of analysis for students of health policy.

Conclusion

At first sight, pluralist theories offer a convincing explanation of the distribution of power within health services. After all, the NHS comprises a large number of different groups competing for resources, and most decisions result from bargaining between these groups. Furthermore, health policies tend to involve small adjustments to what has gone before, and a variety of interests are often involved in policy-making. This is in part the picture which has emerged from the discussion of health policy-making and implementation in earlier chapters, and it fits the description of political activity put forward in the pluralist model.

Marxist theories challenge the assumptions behind pluralism and provide an alternative explanation. Instead of focusing on immediate conflicts between pressure groups, Marxists seek to relate health care systems to the economic systems within which they are located. By analysing the underlying processes at work, Marxists argue that health services are shaped by dominant groups, whose interests are served by prevailing concepts of health and illness. Health services help to legitimate capitalism and to promote capital accumulation. Pluralists are unable to perceive this because they concentrate on surface struggles and neglect deeper class conflicts. Furthermore, pluralists take dominant concepts of health for granted, and do not question seriously the beneficial impact of medicine or the possibility that conflict may be limited to a narrow range of issues through ideological domination.

In contrast to both approaches, Alford's theory of structural interests looks beyond the surface politics of pressure group conflicts and finds not class struggle but professional dominance. This approach recognises that the world of everyday politics may well approximate to pluralist theories, but it goes further to identify wide discrepancies in power in relation to dominant, challenging and repressed structural interests. Alternative concepts of health are acknowledged to exist, and prevailing concepts reflect the ability of dominant groups to get their definitions accepted. Within this framework, it is possible to encompass both the strengths of pluralist theory, recognising the diversity and variety of pressure group behaviour, and some of the insights of the Marxist analysis, acknowledging that what appears to be going on may obscure underlying conflicts between key interests.

It is suggested, then, that future work might usefully build on this framework and seek to further explicate the 'problematic and contingent' (Alford, 1975b, p. 153) nature of relationships between individual and group action on particular issues of health policy, the role of structural interests, and the characteristics of the state. Our earlier analysis of professional ideologies in the health care system provided some hints on how this might be done, and further empirical studies are required. Above all, it is the interaction of the different levels of analysis which is in need of further investigation. Sophisticated studies of specific policy issues need to be related to the action and inaction of structural interests and the changing role and functions of the state (nationally and internationally) if a complete understanding of the complexities of health policy is to be obtained.

Harrison's analysis of the introduction of general management into the NHS (Harrison, 1994) has illustrated how a variety of theoretical perspectives can help to explain particular initiatives, thereby paving the way for other studies. As we argued at the beginning of the book, individuals and groups may have an impact on policy, but under conditions not of their own choosing. This has been demonstrated by Smith (1999) in his analysis of power within government and Smith's contention that actors are central but are constrained by context and structure reinforces these arguments. Articulating the relationship between action and structure is therefore of the utmost importance, and the discussion in this chapter has pointed to some directions in which work might proceed. This includes exploring the way in which actors influence structure as well as vice versa.

Chapter 11

Looking to the Future

In this final chapter, we look beyond the NHS to international experience of health services. We also examine the changing role of the private sector in Britain and the shifting balance between hierarchies, markets and networks. The focus then moves to trends in society, demography, and technology that may have an impact on health and health services, and the implications for health care rationing The chapter concludes by examining the policies of different political parties on the future of the NHS.

Britain in the international context

A number of studies have analysed the NHS in the international context. The focus of these studies includes the health of the population, patient experience of health services, and quality of care. In this section of the chapter, we summarise the evidence on these issues and assess how the performance of the NHS compares with that of health services in other countries.

The health of the population

Although the health of the population of England is good by global standards, comparisons with other developed countries are less favourable. An analysis carried out for the Wanless Review of public health used routinely available data to compare England with Australia, Denmark, Canada, Finland, France, Germany, the Netherlands and Sweden (Wanless, 2003b). The analysis showed that, among this group of countries, life expectancy at birth was lower for women than in any of the other countries except Denmark. For men, the position was more favourable, with England having better life expectancy at birth than Denmark, Finland and Germany. In the case of another widely used measure of population health, potential years of life lost before age 70, for men the United Kingdom performed less well than Sweden, the Netherlands and Canada, and for women less well than all countries except Denmark.

The same analysis showed that compared to other countries, England has relatively high rates of death from respiratory diseases, circulatory disease, and, in women, cancer. More positively, the rate of decline in premature deaths (under the age of 65) from cancers and heart disease in the United Kingdom has been rapid. Comparison with EU countries over the period 1970 to 2000 shows that lung cancer rates among men have fallen substantially and are now below the EU average. There have also been major reductions in premature deaths from breast cancer in women, although these remain above the EU average. Focusing on trends during the 1990s, the improvement in premature mortality from all causes is marginally better than the improvement in the EU average (all data from the WHO–Health for All database). These trends have given rise to the argument that Britain is no longer the 'sick man' of Europe (Office of Health Economics, 2003), even though on many indicators the health of the population is not yet as good as that of other countries.

Patient experience

Surveys carried out by the Picker Institute and the Commonwealth Fund have investigated the experiences of patients in a number of countries. The Picker Institute study focused on hospital patients and covered the United States, Germany, Sweden, and Switzerland, as well as the United Kingdom, between 1998 and 2000. There were similarities between countries in the types of problems reported by patients with continuity of care and transition being the most frequently reported. Other problems concerned information, emotional support, respect for patients' preferences, and involvement of family and friends. Overall, the highest satisfaction ratings were reported by patients in Switzerland and the lowest by patients in the United Kingdom (Coulter and Cleary, 2001).

The Commonwealth Fund's surveys have examined citizens' and patients' views about health services in Australia, Canada, New Zealand, the United Kingdom and the United States over a number of years. In contrast to the Picker Institute's survey, the Commonwealth Fund portrayed the United Kingdom in a relatively favourable light with 25 per cent of people reporting that the NHS worked well and required only minor change, compared with between 9 and 20 per cent in other countries. The main concerns of British respondents were lack of government funding and waiting times for treatment. The survey concluded:

> as the British National Health Service (NHS) celebrates its fiftieth year, the public is happier than any other we surveyed ... Although the public notes, as it has for a decade, that the system is underfunded and waiting times for nonemergency surgery are long, Britons are least likely to call for rebuilding their health care system and are among the least likely to be worried about future health care needs. (Donelan *et al.*, 1999, p. 215)

The 1998 survey identified inequities in access to health care in the United States, Australia and New Zealand but not in the United Kingdom and Canada. Inequity was defined in terms of differences in the use of services by individuals with above average incomes and those with below average incomes (Schoen *et al.*, 2000). Survey respondents were asked about access to medical care when needed, the likelihood of visiting a doctor, and the likelihood of having a regular source of care. They were also asked about waiting times for non-emergency surgery and problems in paying medical bills. The authors commented that:

> the United Kingdom stands out for the similarity of care experiences between above and below average adults. Notably on no measures are British below average income experiences more negative than those reported by above average income adults. Moreover, reflecting their health needs, below average income adults in Britain are more likely to have visited a physician in the past year and have a regular physician. (p. 83)

The other notable conclusion was that, in comparison with the other countries studied:

> The British are both more satisfied with their system overall, and less divided among themselves. Indeed, Britain is the only country where lower income families are more likely to call for keeping the status quo (p. 81)

These findings were echoed in the 1999 Commonwealth Fund survey that focused on older people. Respondents in Britain were least likely to feel that the health care system needed to be completely rebuilt and were most likely to report that the system worked well and needed only minor changes. Similarly, access to care was reported to be good except for waiting times for non-emergency surgery. The one area where the United Kingdom did not perform as well as some other countries was in relation to quality of care where the views of older people tended to be more negative than in other countries.

In these and later surveys, differences in payments made directly by patients emerged as an important theme. These differences had an impact on access to care and underlined the benefit for patients in the United Kingdom of having a universal and comprehensive health service that was mainly free at the point of use. It was on this basis that the 2001 Commonwealth Fund survey concluded that the United Kingdom had the highest degree of equity of all the countries studied (Blendon *et al.*, 2002). The 2002 Commonwealth Fund survey focused on adults with health problems and found that the United Kingdom had the lowest level of medication errors or medical mistakes. It also reported that the United

Kingdom had the lowest overall level of dissatisfaction with the health care system. On the other hand, sicker adults in the United Kingdom were most critical of the communication skills of physicians, and, along with United States respondents, were least likely to rate doctors as excellent or good (Blendon *et al.*, 2003).

The most recent comparative survey of patient experience examined issues concerning communication, information, involvement and choice in eight countries (Coulter and Magee, 2003). Conducted during 2002, the survey found that patients in the United Kingdom were generally positive about their experiences. For example, the United Kingdom performed better than all other countries when patients were asked whether doctors gave them time to ask questions, listened to patients and gave clear explanations. The United Kingdom also ranked first when patients were asked whether doctors involved them as much as they wanted in decisions about their care. On the other hand, the United Kingdom performed much less well in relation to choice, ranking equal sixth on this aspect of patient experience. Public attitudes towards the NHS can be compared with attitudes to the health care systems in other EU countries using data from the Eurobarometer Survey. Carried out in 15 countries in 2002, this showed that people in Austria were most satisfied with their health care system and people in Greece and Portugal least satisfied. Levels of satisfaction in the United Kingdom were slightly below the EU average.

Quality of care

Evidence on patient experience contributes to analysis of the quality of health care and of variations in quality between countries. In exploring this issue, it is important to emphasise the relative paucity of data on quality, certainly compared with data on population health, and the need for caution in interpreting the information that is available. Although organisations like the Commonwealth Fund and the OECD are taking steps to fill the gaps that exist, comparisons of quality of care between countries are much less well developed than comparisons of population health, health services financing and staffing levels.

Recognising this, some of the best evidence on quality concerns survival rates among patients diagnosed with cancer. The latest available data, examining five-year survival rates in 22 countries up to 1999, show that outcomes in the United Kingdom from many cancers are not as good as those found in most other European countries, even though survival rates are improving (Sant *et al.*, 2003). One of the reasons for this is the relatively low level of cancer services provision in the NHS and associated waiting for diagnosis and treatment. The Calman-Hine Report and *The NHS Cancer Plan* have started to address these issues but there is a time lag between increased investment and improved outcomes. More recent data from the Office of National Statistics show continuing improvements in survival rates in England but it is not yet possible to compare these data with those from other countries.

Outcomes following breast cancer were studied by the OECD in an analysis of the quality of care in a number of countries in relation to ageing related diseases (OECD, 2003b). This analysis confirmed that the United Kingdom had lower survival rates following breast cancer than the other countries included in the study and it also showed that outcomes following heart attacks and stroke were relatively poor. On the other hand, a review of the quality of care in Germany, the United States and the United Kingdom conducted by McKinsey reported that the UK performed well in the case of people with diabetes. This was attributed to the greater use of patient self-management with more effective identification and treatment of people with severe diabetes. The McKinsey review found that the United Kingdom did less well in the treatment of lung cancer and breast cancer (McKinsey Global Institute, 1996).

Another aspect of quality is the coverage achieved in programmes of vaccination and immunisation. Childhood immunisation is particularly important in preventing infectious diseases. Like other countries, the United Kingdom has traditionally achieved high levels of coverage (over 90 per cent) and this continues to be the case for diptheria, tetanus and pertussis. There is a different pattern in the case of measles where public concern about the combined measles, mumps and rubella vaccine has resulted in a fall in coverage from 92 per cent in 1995/96 to 82 per cent in 2001/02. This has given rise to concern that the population may lose the protection offered by 'herd immunity' and that measles may reemerge as an important health challenge.

The performance of the NHS

In its assessment of health systems performance, the World Health Organisation sought to rank countries along a number of dimensions (World Health Organisation, 2000). These dimensions were the health of the population, responsiveness to the population, and fairness of financial contribution. On this basis, the United Kingdom was ranked 18 out of 191 on health system performance, lower than France that came out first but higher than Sweden, Germany and Denmark. The United Kingdom scored particularly well on fairness of financial contribution, a finding that is consistent with other research on equity of health financing (Wagstaff *et al.*, 1999) and with the Commonwealth Fund's surveys reported above. By comparison, the United Kingdom scored less well on responsiveness to the population. Again, this is consistent with the evidence from the Picker

Institute and Commonwealth Fund's studies. In interpreting these results, it should be noted that the WHO's methods and data for assessing performance have been heavily criticised (Musgrove, 2003), and they should therefore be used with caution.

Differences in levels of health financing and delivery may help to explain why the performance of health services in the United Kingdom does not match that of some other developed countries on some indicators. International comparisons indicate that, until the increases to the NHS budget that have occurred recently, expenditure on health services was lower than in many of these countries (OECD, 2003a). The United Kingdom also has fewer doctors and less high technology equipment such as scanners in relation to the population served than most other comparable countries. These capacity constraints help to account for the existence of long waiting times in the United Kingdom. The Wanless Review of the long-term funding needs of the NHS used OECD research that showed a relationship between health care resources and health outcomes (Or, 2001) to support its argument for a sustained increase in NHS funding.

Viewing the NHS in the international context helps to put into perspective the discussions earlier in this book. The evidence summarised here suggests that the NHS has traditionally been a low-cost health service that has performed well on equity and poorly on responsiveness. The population has access to more or less comprehensive services without having to be concerned about the cost of most care at the time of use and yet is worried about waiting for treatment should this be necessary. The health of the population lags somewhat behind that of most comparable countries, although recent trends indicate a narrowing of the gap between the United Kingdom and these countries. The evidence also indicates a mixed picture on patient experience with some surveys showing the NHS in a favourable light and others indicating that the United Kingdom does not do as well as other countries. As far as quality of care is concerned, on indicators like cancer survival rates, the United Kingdom falls short of the achievements of most other developed countries. The weaknesses of the NHS can in part be seen as a consequence of its strengths in that the ability of successive governments to control public expenditures on health care has resulted in capacity constraints that contribute to problems of access and responsiveness. As Abel-Smith once commented with a hint of irony, the NHS might no longer be the envy of the world but it was certainly the envy of the world's finance ministers (Abel-Smith, 1994).

The aspect of the NHS that is arguably most admired by other countries is primary care. The existence of GPs as the first point of contact and as the gatekeepers between patients and specialists is often cited as one of the factors that contribute to the achievements of the NHS. The key research in this area is the work of Starfield who compared 11 systems in the 1980s. Starfield demonstrated that primary care in the United Kingdom was both more prominent than in other countries and accounted for the ability of the United Kingdom to deliver comprehensive services for a comparatively low level of expenditure (Starfield, 1992). Survey evidence has shown that the services of GPs are rated highly by patients and more positively than hospital services. Patient registration with GPs together with continuity of care over time and the ability of primary care teams to offer a wide range of services are some of the most important strengths of general practice in the United Kingdom.

Convergence in health care reform?

A clear conclusion to emerge from international comparisons is the existence of widespread public dissatisfaction in almost all systems. For example, the 1998 Commonwealth Fund survey found that in all countries studied there was public dissatisfaction with the performance of health services, and a belief that major reform was needed, even though the British public was least critical. The Commonwealth Fund's 2000 survey showed that the dissatisfaction expressed by the public is shared by physicians, albeit to a lesser extent (Blendon *et al.*, 2001), and appears not to be directly related to differences in *methods* of financing and delivery. A distinction is often drawn between Beveridge-type systems, such as the NHS, whose principal features are general taxation and public ownership; Bismarckian systems of the kind found in many parts of Europe which combine social insurance and mixed forms of ownership; and systems like the United States where private insurance and private provision predominate, albeit with public financing still playing a significant part. In all of these systems there is evidence of concern about health services' performance and continuing debate about alternatives.

In response to public and physician dissatisfaction, policy-makers in many countries have introduced changes to the financing and delivery of health services (OECD, 1992 and 1994b; Ham, 1997b; Saltman, Figueras and Sakallarides, 1998). The epidemic of reform that has resulted has included policies to contain costs, strengthen efficiency and responsiveness, and set priorities in a more systematic manner. As earlier chapters have demonstrated, the United Kingdom has examples of all of these policies. In many countries, the process of reform has involved new policies being overlaid on existing initiatives, and approaches that had been discarded being picked up anew as governments are replaced and fashions change. Although there are similarities between systems in the approaches adopted, the extent of convergence should not be exaggerated (Ham, 1997b).

Analysis of reforms undertaken in different countries indicates that the main concern of policy-makers in the late 1970s and early 1980s was cost containment (see Table 11.1). The policies introduced at that time, including global budgets for hospitals and limits on doctors' fees, helped to slow the increase in health care spending. In the late 1980s and early 1990s, greater attention was given to increasing efficiency and improving the responsiveness of services to users through the use of market like mechanisms and budgetary incentives. More recently, the focus has shifted to rationing and priority-setting, including policies designed to give higher priority to public health and health technology assessment. There is also a world wide interest in the quality of care and patient safety in the light of evidence of gaps between what it is possible to achieve and what is delivered in practice.

Table 11.1   *Trends in health care reform*

PHASE ONE	Late 1970s/early 1980s
Theme	Cost containment at the macro level
Policy instruments	Prospective global budgets for hospitals Controls over hospital building and the acquisition of medical equipment Limits on doctor's fees and incomes Restrictions on the numbers undertaking education and training
PHASE TWO	Late 1980s/early 1990s
Theme	Micro efficiency and responsiveness to users
Policy instruments	Market-like mechanisms Management reforms Budgetary incentives
PHASE THREE	Late 1990s
Theme	Rationing and priority-setting
Policy instruments	Public health Primary care Managed care Health technology assessment Evidence based medicine

Source: Reproduced from Ham (ed.) *Health Care Reform*, Open University Press, 1997 with the kind permission of The Open University Press/McGraw-Hill Publishing Company.

The issue of convergence has also arisen in the context of the growing involvement of the European Union (EU) in health policy. In the past, the impact of the EU on health policy has resulted either from actions to encourage the free movement of people, goods, services and capital, or through public health initiatives, rather than policies directed at health services. Examples of the former include the working time directive, under which the time worked by doctors in training has been reduced considerably to enable the United Kingdom to comply with EU law. Examples of the latter include action on major public health priorities such as the control of tobacco advertising and sponsorship and initiatives on drug misuse and infectious diseases. Health care is a responsibility of member states rather than the EU, although recent decisions of the European Court of Justice have lent support to patients who have received treatment in EU countries other than their own (Mossialos and Palm, 2003). These decisions require national governments to fund hospital treatment in other EU countries if patients would suffer an undue delay in receiving treatment in their own countries. Following a decision in the High Court in 2003 that the NHS should fund the care of a woman who had travelled to France for a hip operation, it is expected that the movement of patients across national borders to receive hospital care will increase.

Questions have also been raised as to whether EU competition law applies to health care services at a time when health care reforms have included the introduction of market principles in some countries. This law was invoked in the BetterCare judgement in 2002 in which a private company supplying nursing and residential care in Northern Ireland successfully challenged the price it was paid for providing care to the NHS (Pollock and Price, 2003b). Similar questions have arisen in relation to the World Trade Organisation (WTO) whose aim is to promote economic growth and stability through the extension of free markets (Price, Pollock and Shaoul, 1999; Pollock and Price, 2000 and 2003a). It has been argued that the activities of the WTO are increasingly embracing public services like health care and are opening up these services to competition and privatisation. These activities have as yet had no impact on health policy in Britain but, as examples of globalisation and its effects, illustrate the potentially significant role of international agencies in the future.

To return to the discussion in Chapter 10, they serve as a timely reminder of the need to locate the dynamics of health policy in their social, economic and international context. We explore the relationship between health services and this wider context in the rest of this chapter, beginning with an analysis of the role of the private sector. In so doing, we make use of Moran's analysis of the health care state (Moran, 1999) in which the activities of the state are explored in three arenas. The first arena concerns relationships with industrial and commercial interests and is referred to as the arena of 'production politics'. The second involves relationships with patients and users and is described as 'governing consumption'. And the third focuses on relationships with doctors and other professionals and is termed 'governing professionals'.

The private sector

One of the recurring themes in the international debate about health care reform is the respective roles of the public and private sectors. In relation to the financing of health services, research shows that public financing is more equitable than private financing and now accounts for around 72 per cent of total health expenditures in OECD countries (OECD, 2003a). While all systems use a mix of public and private financing, only in a few countries have governments actively encouraged the expansion of private financing. Australia is one of those countries and the introduction of tax relief has led to an expansion of private medical insurance. Elsewhere, there have been moves to increase user charges for some services, but charges make a minor contribution to health expenditures in almost all developed countries. Only in central and eastern Europe have radical changes to financing been introduced with social insurance replacing tax as the main form of financing in some systems, and private payments becoming the main way of paying for health care in others (Preker, Jakab and Schneider, 2002). Outside central and eastern Europe, the main focus of reform has been on the delivery of health care rather than methods of financing, and here too there has been debate about the private sector playing a bigger part than in the past.

In fact, there are wide variations between systems in the ownership of health care facilities with the United Kingdom being unusual in the extent to which hospitals are owned and managed by government. Elsewhere, hospital ownership is in the hands of local authorities (for example, in the Nordic countries), not-for-profit private organisations (often with a religious or charitable association) or more exceptionally for-profit companies. In a number of systems, steps have been taken to give public hospitals greater autonomy (Preker and Harding, 2003), sometimes as part of more broadly-based changes to introduce competition between providers. These changes often include a concern to increase the responsiveness of health services and offer patients more choice. Debate about the privatisation of health care provision has been particularly heated in countries like the United Kingdom, Canada and Sweden where there is a long-established commitment to equity in health care provision.

As far as finance is concerned, the share of health expenditures deriving from private payments has increased steadily through the lifetime of the NHS and currently accounts for around 18 per cent of the total (Laing and Buisson, 2003; OECD, 2003a). Although a lower proportion than in most developed countries, the rising share of private funding over the last 25 years illustrates the strength of demand for health care, particularly when increases in public funding are constrained by political decisions on the state of the economy and relative priorities for public spending. The demand for health care affects services provided by the NHS as well as complementary and alternative therapies. In the language of health economics, health care is a luxury good, and both individuals and countries tend to spend more on health care as they become richer.

Research has shown that private funding encompasses a wide range of services (Keen, Light and Mays, 2001). Figure 11.1 illustrates that the biggest items are over-the-counter medicines, private medical insurance and NHS user charges. Private medical insurance covered a small proportion of the population until the 1980s when there was a rapid increase in subscribers. The increase came to an end in 1990 and the proportion of the population with private medical insurance subsequently stabilised at around 11 per cent. The provision of tax relief on insurance policies for older people by the Thatcher government appeared to have little effect on the demand for cover. Approximately two-thirds of those with insurance come under company schemes and the remainder pay individually. The trend in recent years has been for the number of individual subscribers to fall from previous levels as the cost of insurance has increased. In parallel, there has been a significant rise in the number of people choosing to pay for private medical treatment out of pocket. Self-pay, as it is known, now accounts for around 22.5–25 per cent of the market (Laing and Buisson, 2003).

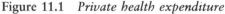

Figure 11.1   *Private health expenditure*

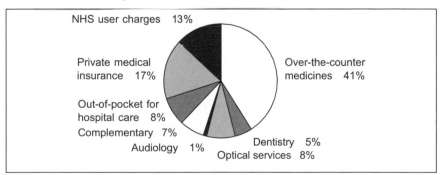

Source: Keen, Light and Mays (2001).

Private medical insurance does not provide comprehensive cover to subscribers. Rather, it pays for consultations with medical specialists and the costs of certain hospital investigations and treatments. Emergency care, primary care, and maternity services are usually excluded, as are preexisting medical conditions. The principal benefit of private medical insurance is to enable subscribers to avoid waiting for NHS appointments and to choose the specialist and hospital providing treatment. Going private may also give patients access to more modern environments and a higher standard of amenity such as food and privacy. Two companies, BUPA and PPP, have over 60 per cent of the share of the insurance market.

User charges for NHS services were first imposed in 1951 for dental services provided out of hospital and for some ophthalmic services, followed by prescription charges a year later. The controversy generated by the imposition of charges led Aneurin Bevan to resign from the Labour Government. Free eye tests were abolished in 1989, although as with prescriptions certain groups in the population are exempt from paying charges. There has been a significant increase in the private funding of dentistry since 1992 when the government sought to claw back what it claimed were overpayments to dentists under a new contract agreed in 1990. As a result of the government's decision, and the limits placed on the fees for carrying out NHS work, dentists in some parts of the country will only treat patients privately. This has given rise to problems for patients in accessing NHS dentistry and the adoption of policies to ensure that all patients at least have access to emergency dental care on the NHS. Despite these policies, the progressive removal of some dental services from some parts of the country has come to symbolise the way in which rationing through the back door is having an increasing impact on the NHS.

The example of dentistry points up another feature of health care in the United Kingdom: the opportunities for some providers to earn income from both public and private sources. The position of hospital specialists in this regard has attracted most attention To persuade specialists to work in the NHS, Aneurin Bevan agreed an arrangement in which consultants could choose to work part time for the NHS and the remainder of their time undertaking private work. Bevan famously remarked that in so doing he had 'stuffed their mouths with gold' (see Chapter 1), and certainly the rewards from private work for consultants working in specialties such as plastic surgery, orthopaedics, and anaesthetics can be high. Figures for 1999 estimated that the average net private income per NHS consultant varied from £7572 in pathology to £75 413 in plastic surgery (Laing and Buisson, 2003). There may also be conflicts of interest in so far as these consultants have an incentive to maintain waiting lists for NHS treatment in order to create a demand for private work.

The mixed nature of public and private provision applies to institutions as well as the professionals providing care. In the case of NHS hospitals, there is often provision for patients to be treated privately, either in the pay beds established at the outset of the NHS, or in the private wings developed during the 1990s as a way of NHS hospitals supplementing their income from public sources by treating private patients. NHS income from private patients in the United Kingdom was estimated to be £388 million in 2002/03 (Laing and Buisson, 2003). For their part, private hospitals earn some of their income from treating NHS patients. In 2002, it was estimated that the NHS spent £185 million on acute non-psychiatric services.

Williams and colleagues have studied trends in the use of private hospitals in a series of studies. Their work has shown that the proportion of elective treatment paid for privately in England and Wales has remained constant at around 13–14 per cent throughout the 1980s and 1990s (Williams *et al.*, 2000a and b). Around ten per cent of private patients were treated in NHS hospitals, and one per cent of NHS patients were treated in private hospitals. Almost half of NHS-funded patients were abortion cases. Between 1992/93 and 1997/98 the number of cases treated in private hospitals increased by 22 per cent. Within this increase there was a reduction in the number of inpatient cases and a large rise in the number of day cases. The number of NHS funded patients increased by 164 per cent to almost 85 000 in 1997/98. Overall, Williams and colleagues concluded that over the period studied 'the demand for privately funded treatment in independent hospitals rose in all parts of the country and in most age groups' (Williams *et al.*, 2000a, p.71).

As part of the drive to reduce waiting lists and waiting times, the Blair government has encouraged primary care trusts to make use of spare capacity in private hospitals. The government agreed a concordat with the private sector in 2000 designed to increase the use of private facilities for the treatment of NHS patients. Four years later it is not clear that this has made a major difference to the income of private hospitals, for whom NHS patients now account for less than 10 per cent of revenue. Nevertheless, the coexistence of public and private patients in both public and private hospitals illustrates the blurring of the boundaries between the two sectors.

The ownership of private hospitals in Britain is concentrated in three main groups – General Healthcare Group (BMI), BUPA Hospitals Limited, and Nuffield Hospitals – and together these account for almost 60 per cent of beds in the private sector. Private hospitals differ from NHS hospitals both in their size and in the range of work they undertake. Most private hospitals are small by NHS standards and they provide a limited range of outpatient, day case and inpatient procedures. Bed occupancy rates are much lower than in the NHS and only a minority of hospitals have facilities like intensive care units and resident medical staff that enable them to carry out more complex treatments. A number of new providers entered the market as part of the development of diagnostic and treatment centres by the Blair government, including groups from north America and South Africa. The aim of these treatment centres is to contribute to the reduction in waiting times for elective surgery by providing additional capacity for the treatment of NHS patients. Early indications suggested that the arrival of new entrants was stimulating existing private sector providers to review their position in the market to enable them to compete successfully.

Private financing and provision are important in relation to the care of older people as well as in relation to acute services. Indeed, as a result of changes made in the 1990s, private providers dominate this market and are funded through a mixture of public and private payments. Following the Report of the Royal Commission on Long Term Care, in 1999, the Blair government decided that nursing care should be free but that the remaining costs (covering personal care and hotel costs) should be funded on a means-tested basis. Older people of limited means therefore have all of their costs covered, whereas others make a partial or full contribution to these costs. Restrictions on the fees paid by local authorities to care homes have resulted in a reduction in care home capacity in some parts of the country. Fees were increased in response in an attempt to stabilise the market. Around 64 per cent of care home residents were funded by local authorities in 2001, and five per cent were funded by the NHS (Laing and Buisson, 2003). The latter were residents requiring nursing care and it seems likely that the number of people supported in this way will increase as a result of recent reports from the Ombudsman that have criticised the NHS for not fulfilling its obligations to people for continuing care (see Chapter 4). One of the features of the care homes market is the higher fees paid by self-payers who comprise over 30 per cent of residents in these homes.

Looking to the future, it seems likely that the role of private financing and provision will continue to be a central part of the health policy debate. Both *The NHS Plan* and the Wanless Report on health service funding concluded that public financing was equitable and efficient and should continue to be the main way of paying for health care. This conclusion is supported by research evidence (Evans, 2002) and by the fact that policy-makers in most developed countries have chosen to use tax financing and social insurance to cover the bulk of health care expenditures. Although it is sometimes argued that the weaknesses of health services in the United Kingdom are the result of low levels of private expenditure on health care, independent analyses have highlighted the drawbacks associated with a larger role for the private sector in financing health care. The conclusion of these analyses is that the arguments for extra private spending are finely balanced (Propper and Green, 2001).

As we have seen, private expenditure has become more significant in the case of dental services and long-term care, and the government's critics have argued that public financing should be increased to enable these services to be available on the same basis as other NHS provision. Against this, the Wanless Report floated the idea that charges should be imposed for non-clinical services provided within the NHS (Wanless, 2002). This suggested that the debate about the mix of public and private financing might resurface. In practice, the idea that new charges might be levied received little attention in relation to the main recommendation of the Wanless Report that public financing of health care should be increased significantly. As long as public expenditure on the NHS continues to rise at the rate recommended by Wanless, it seems unlikely that arguments for a bigger role for private finance will be taken forward. If, on the other hand, increases in public spending on the NHS revert to the historic trend, whether because of economic constraints or political choices, then debate on this issue will again be joined.

In considering the future role of private finance, the attitude of different generations to private medical insurance is highly relevant. A study by Propper, Rees and Green (2001) found that younger people were more likely to purchase private insurance than older people. As they commented:

> younger individuals who have grown up in an era where the political aim has been to 'roll back the frontier of the state' may be more willing to contemplate bypassing the NHS system than their older counterparts ... This change in propensity to 'go private' may in time erode support for tax finance of the NHS, or open the way to greater political acceptability of greater private finance for health care (p. 196).

The importance of this observation is as a reminder that the future of the NHS will be affected by changes in the society in which it is embedded. While public support for the NHS remains strong, and while health services are a high priority for additional public spending in the eyes of the population, then the future of the NHS seems assured. However, the emergence of a younger generation with higher expectations of public services and less willing to accept waiting and variations in care, may make it difficult to sustain a universal, tax funded health service if the NHS fails to keep up with these expectations.

The future for private providers is different. As we have seen, since 2000 the Blair government has actively encouraged the greater use of the private sector for the treatment of NHS patients and it has stimulated the entry of new providers through the diagnostic and treatment centre programme. The government has also promoted the idea of NHS Foundation Trusts as a way of encouraging the emergence of a new form of provider located between the public and private sectors. Opposition parties have been equally pragmatic about the role of the private sector and have argued that NHS Foundation Trusts should be given greater freedoms than proposed. In this area, then, there is considerable convergence in the debate, the main exception being among the trades unions representing NHS staff who have argued against what they perceive to be the creeping privatisation of services.

The trades unions have also been vocal critics of the private finance initiative (PFI) pursued by both Conservative and Labour governments. The PFI has become the main way of paying for major building projects since the middle of the 1990s and has resulted in the opening of several new NHS hospitals. Despite this, it continues to be the subject of debate, with critics arguing that PFI is a more expensive way of paying for new buildings than public capital, and that the additional costs have resulted in the building of hospitals with insufficient capacity (Gaffney *et al.*, 1999). These critics also maintain that hospitals built through PFI are forced to seek other sources of income to cover their costs and that the private companies involved in PFI schemes are earning excess profits from the taxpayer (Pollock *et al.*, 1999). A further argument is that PFI locks the NHS into long term contracts to pay for services and buildings that may not always be appropriate for the duration of these contracts. Whatever the merits of these arguments, and they continue to be hotly debated (Health Committee, 2002), the PFI provides further evidence of the blurring of the boundaries between the public and private sectors in the United Kingdom health care system.

Hierarchies, networks and markets

The emergence of a mixed economy of health and social care provision has given rise to discussion of whether the concept of the NHS as a hierarchical organisation is still valid. Drawing on the literature on organisational analysis, Le Grand (2002) notes that in stylised terms there are three main types of organisations. Hierarchies use managerial command-and-control mechanisms to allocate resources; markets allocate resources through competitive processes; and networks rely on social relationships that involve trust and cooperation. Although the NHS is often described as a command-and-control system, Le Grand argues that for much of its history it was characterised by professional networks operating in the context of self-regulation combined with weak central controls. Markets came to prominence in the 1990s under Margaret Thatcher and John Major but were used alongside hierarchies and networks in an attempt to improve efficiency and responsiveness.

The importance of hierarchical controls was never greater than in the period after the election of the Blair government in 1997. The establishment of NICE, the promulgation of national service frameworks, the setting of national targets, and the strengthening of performance management led to a command-and-control approach that was much more directive than anything that had been attempted before. In parallel, the government took steps to create arrangements for inspection and regulation, particularly through the establishment of the Commission for Health Improvement and the National Care Standards Commission, and their successor the Healthcare Commission. Subsequently, following publication of *Delivering the NHS Plan*, elements of competition were added to the policy mix. The renewed emphasis placed on the market was most apparent in the encouragement given to patient choice linked to a system in which money was to follow patients. The government also acted to develop greater plurality of provision through the creation of NHS Foundation Trusts and the establishment of diagnostic and treatment centres.

What will be the impact of this policy mix? Drawing on experience of the internal market in the 1990s, Le Grand (2002) notes the problems that may arise when different organisational models are combined. As the author has argued elsewhere (Ham, 1997a), the internal market was in reality a politically managed market in which competitive incentives were severely attenuated by the controls exercised by government. By extension, the Blair government may retain hierarchical controls alongside the greater use of regulation and inspection and the reintroduction of competition. In other words, rather than regulation replacing hierarchies and markets, as some commentators have suggested (Walshe, 2003), elements of all three will be used and the professional networks that have been so much in evidence since the inception of the NHS will also continue to be important. Experience in other sectors in the 1980s and the 1990s (Hood *et al.*, 1999) suggests that the risk in such an approach is the NHS may suffer from a surfeit of different models.

In practice, much hinges on the extent to which patient choice and the system of financial flows introduced to support choice provide the drive to improve performance that has previously come from intervention by government. Given that choice was confined to elective services to begin with, it seemed likely that elements of competition would co-exist with regulation and government direction in order to achieve the improvements sought by the Blair government. The unanswered question then was the balance that would emerge between regulation and government direction in a context in which, in its second term, the Blair government was not only seeking to shift the balance of power within the NHS but was also exploring ways of reducing the number of targets imposed on public services like the NHS. The strengthening of regulation through the establishment of the Healthcare Commission, involving a greater measure of independence compared with its predecessors and the power to report publicly on the performance of the NHS, promised to shift the emphasis even further away from government. This shift was reinforced by the move in 2003 to reduce the size of the Department of Health by one-third (see Chapter 7). Against this, there was no evidence that the steps taken to strengthen the oversight of public services by the Prime Minister and Chancellor through the work of the Delivery Unit and the use of public service agreements would be reversed, suggesting that hierarchical controls would continue to be used alongside regulation.

These developments lend support to the argument that health care reform, even where it embraces a stronger role for competition, also tends to increase the role of the state (Freeman, 2000). Support for this argument can be found in the arena of the health care state referred to by Moran as 'governing professionals' (Moran, 1999). One of the recurring themes of this book is the influence exercised by doctors at all levels of the NHS and the limited impact to date of management and market-oriented reforms on medical power. State sanctioned self-regulation through the General Medical Council and other means has been the main mechanism used to govern doctors at the national level. Self-regulation has been mirrored by an emphasis on doctors being accountable for their own work and that of their peers within the NHS. These collegial processes are typical of what Mintzberg describes as professional bureaucracies (Mintzberg, 1983) and only recently has the private government of professional standards and practices been challenged.

The trigger for this was the inquiry into failures of paediatric heart surgery at Bristol Royal Infirmary (Kennedy Report, 2001). An editorial in the *British Medical Journal*, borrowing from Yeats, proclaimed that in the light of these failures all had changed, 'changed utterly' (Smith, 1998). The events at Bristol, together with other examples of weaknesses in self-regulation and mutual processes of control, such as the case of Harold Shipman, a GP who allegedly murdered over 200 patients, provided the basis for government to strengthen the governing of professionals in ways that would not otherwise have been possible. This action included the establishment of a new Council for the Regulation of Health Care Professionals, regular appraisal of doctors, and revalidation of all doctors. In parallel, the government encouraged the entry of new providers to the NHS in a direct challenge to the market power exercised by hospital consultants, particularly in relation to private practice.

What remains unclear is the impact of these changes on power relationships in health care. In this context, Tuohy's analysis of the dynamics of change in the health care arena in the United States, the

United Kingdom and Canada offers some pointers to possible developments (Tuohy, 1999). Tuohy argues that health care in the United
Kingdom is an example of a hierarchical, state system with elements of
collegial processes. The market-oriented reforms of the 1990s had a limited
impact because their effects were attenuated by hierarchical controls and
professional relationships and networks. By extension, it can be suggested
that the reforms implemented by the Blair government will similarly be
modified in the course of implementation by the strength of existing
institutional arrangements. Moves to strengthen the governance of
professionals may therefore increase medical accountability without
fundamentally changing relationships between the structural interests that
shape health policy. Less predictable is the impact of patient choice and
provider plurality where the influence of existing institutional arrangements is being challenged more directly than at any time since the
inception of the NHS.

Changing social attitudes

The aspiration to create a health service that is patient-centred may not
have been invented by the Blair government but as the NHS entered the
twenty-first century it became a major theme of health policy. One of the
reasons for this, as discussed earlier in the chapter, is that the record of the
NHS in delivering responsive services has often been poor. Another
consideration, and one that became increasingly important under the Blair
government, was the perception that changing social attitudes and rising
public expectations made it imperative that the NHS should become more
patient-centred if it wanted to remain a universal service. Alan Milburn,
Secretary of State for Health between 1999 and 2003, put this argument in
the following way:

> Sixty years ago when the NHS was formed it was the era of the ration
> book. People expected little say and experienced precious little choice.
> Today we live in a quite different world; a consumer age; the computer
> age; the informed and inquiring society. People demand services tailored
> to their individual needs. People want choice and expect quality ... To
> meet that challenge we've got to move away from the one size fits all,
> take it or leave it, top down health service of the 1940s towards an NHS
> that embraces devolution, diversity and choice – precisely so that
> services can be more responsive to the way the world is today. Unless we
> do so, more and more people will simply walk away from public services
> eroding the national consensus that supports them. (Milburn, 2003)

Support for Milburn's argument comes from the work of Propper and colleagues, referred to earlier (Propper, Rees and Green, 2001). As they argued, the emergence of a younger generation with higher expectations of public services posed a challenge to a universal, tax-funded health service where the emphasis had traditionally been on responding to need as defined by professionals rather than demand as expressed by users. This challenge in turn reflected long-term trends in governing consumption in the health care state and the difficulty of sustaining a system of implicit rationing by professionals in an increasingly consumerist age (Moran, 1999).

Further evidence of the importance of changing attitudes comes from the British Social Attitudes' Survey. Conducted annually, the survey has tracked attitudes towards the NHS over a 20 year period (Exley and Jarvis, 2003). Figure 11.2 shows that, with the exception of 1983 when satisfaction with the NHS was unusually high, *net* satisfaction has fluctuated between 14 per cent of the population having negative views in 1996 to 13 per cent having positive views in 1999. In recent years, the proportions of people who were satisfied and dissatisfied were broadly the same. The services provided by GPs are viewed most positively followed by inpatient services, outpatient services, and accident and emergency services (for which data have only recently been collected). Net satisfaction with each of these services is always higher than satisfaction with the NHS as a whole in a context in which satisfaction has generally drifted downwards over time.

Importantly, recent users of the NHS tend to be more satisfied than those who have not used the NHS, while dissatisfaction tends to increase with levels of household income and educational attainment. People with experience of private care were more critical than others. Satisfaction also varies by region with people living in London and the south east more dissatisfied than people in other parts of the country, while older people are more satisfied than younger people. What factors lie behind these variations?

Appleby and Rosete (2003) argue that two factors are at work. First, older people are more likely to have used the NHS and their attitudes are therefore consistent with the argument that users are more satisfied than those who have not used the NHS. Second, there is also a cohort effect at work with younger generations having different attitudes and expectations from previous generations. Despite this, there was no evidence from the British Social Attitudes' Survey of any weakening of the commitment to retain the NHS as a universal, tax funded service. Evidence such as this raises questions about the claim of Labour politicians that the NHS risks becoming 'a poor service for the poor' (Propper and Green, 2001).

Leaving this claim on one side, there is little doubt that patients and the public expect to be more involved in their care than in the past and to

Figure 11.2 *Satisfaction with individual services and with the NHS overall*

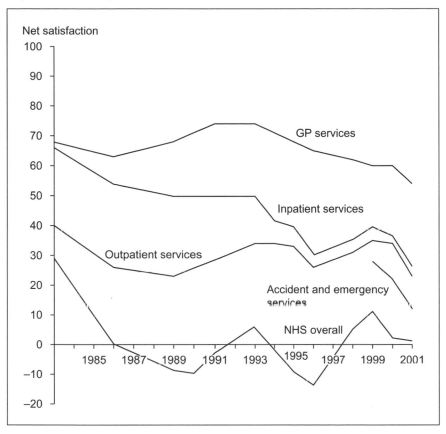

share in decision-making with health care professionals. In this sense, there has been a major shift from the time of the establishment of the NHS when patients deferred to professional judgements, and were willing to accept that doctor knew best (Coulter, 2002; Muir Gray, 2002). The Kennedy Report (2001) highlighted the need for doctors and other health care professionals to involve patients in decision-making and to gain their informed consent, and the report added momentum to the drive to make services more patient centred. This drive included initiatives like the Expert Patient programme in which patients were trained and supported to play a bigger part in their own care. The programme drew on evidence that patients with chronic medical conditions like arthritis achieved better outcomes when they were involved in managing their illness.

Equally important was the policy of increasing the choices available to patients. Initially, this policy was developed in two pilot programmes designed to give patients who had waited longer than six months for heart surgery in England and for a number of elective operations in London the opportunity to use an alternative provider. The success of these pilots led to the extension of choice to all elective services and to a consultation exercise designed to influence how patient choice could be increased in other areas like primary care and maternity services. The consultation exercise led to publication of a consultative document, *Building on the Best* (DH, 2003f), setting out proposals in relation to these other areas and also proposing to increase the availability of information to support choice.

Alongside choice, policy-makers have sought to strengthen patient voice in the NHS. In part this has been pursued through the abolition of community health councils and their replacement with patients' forums and patient advocacy and liaison services, and in part it has entailed more systematic attempts to survey the views of patients. The survey programme initiated by the Blair government has involved studies of general practice patients in 1998 and again in 2001/02, a survey of coronary heart disease patients, a survey of cancer patients, and a survey of patients treated in acute hospitals. These surveys are a rich source of information about patient experience and offer a much more detailed assessment than traditional studies of patient satisfaction.

In the case of the survey of general practice patients, the results showed that in some respects patients' views had become more critical between the time of the first survey in 1998 and the second survey in 2001/02. The main areas of concern related to longer waiting times, difficulties in contacting the GP's surgery and the response to calls made out of hours. Differences between ethnic groups had also widened with White respondents having the most favourable views and South Asian respondents the most critical. Issues of concern identified by patients in the survey of acute hospitals included not receiving sufficient information or explanation about their condition or treatment, not always obtaining clear answers from doctors and nurses, and not being given information about danger signals or potential side-effects. Notwithstanding these criticisms, the surveys of general practice patients and the survey of patients treated in acute hospitals all reported high overall levels of satisfaction with the NHS. The survey of patients treated in acute hospitals was analysed on an NHS trust basis, and the results contributed to the system of star ratings described in Chapter 9. Full details can be found on the Department of Health's website (www.dh.gov.uk/nhspatients).

Reviewing the various initiatives taken by the Blair government, Coulter has offered the following assessment:

> Progress in the last three years since the publication of the NHS Plan has been considerable, but there is still a long way to go. The strategy for patient and public involvement requires a more co-ordinated approach

to ensure that different aspects of the programme reinforce each other...It will be crucial to engage clinicians more actively in this agenda and to support them with training and organisational resources so that real change in their relationships with patients becomes possible (Coulter, 2003, p. 199).

Changing demographic patterns

Another factor that will influence health and health services in the future is changes in the population. Increases in life expectancy and declining fertility rates will combine to alter the balance between older and younger people. The ageing of the population will increase the demand for health care while the growth of single-person and lone-parent households may reduce the capacity of families to share responsibility for care. Reductions in the size of the working population and an increase in the dependency ratio (that is the ratio of people aged under 16 and over 65 as a proportion of the working age population) will put pressure on policy-makers in raising sufficient funds via tax to meet rising demands. Also, the NHS as an employer will face increasing competition from other sectors for staff.

Changes to the retirement age may offset some of these pressures, as may reductions in morbidity among older people, should these occur. On the latter point, recent evidence from the United States suggests that disability among older people is declining (Manton and Gu, 2001; Freedman, Martin and Schoeni, 2002). This evidence lends support to the compression of morbidity thesis (Fries, 1980) which suggests that it is not inevitable that the number of years of disability has to increase in line with increases in life expectancy. Data from the UK are more mixed than those from the USA with evidence from the General Household Survey of increases in self-reported morbidity (see Chapter 9) as well as indications from the Health Survey for England that the prevalence of disability among men is declining (Bajekal and Prescott, 2003). On balance, as the Wanless Report on health services funding noted in its analysis, over the next 20 years demographic trends are likely to have a significant impact on future levels of demand and expenditure for health care. The conclusion of the Wanless Report is supported by an analysis by the OECD suggesting that expenditure on health care is likely to increase even if disability levels decline (Jacobzone, Cambois and Robine, 2000).

As the population ages, there will be an increasing emphasis on chronic illnesses. The incidence of chronic conditions increases with age and older people are more likely to have more than one of these conditions. As we noted in Chapter 9, medical advances have enabled illnesses that were previously fatal like heart disease and cancers to be treated and for patients to live with these illnesses for some considerable time. Also, chronic conditions like diabetes and arthritis present major challenges and require a rather different approach from that which has dominated the NHS since its establishment These chronic conditions are not amenable to episodic treatment in hospitals when patients become acutely ill. Rather, they require high standards of primary care delivering continuity of treatment and support to patients. Effective chronic disease management also benefits from the involvement of patients themselves in their care.

This has implications for the organisation and configuration of health services. Specifically, it is likely to lead to greater interest in the integration of services to enable care to be delivered in the most appropriate way. Integration may well extend to social care and housing in view of the role of these services alongside health care, particularly for older people. The challenge for policy-makers is then to find ways of accommodating different approaches in relation to different services. In the case of elective care, policies to improve access and to promote choice are focusing increasingly on the introduction of new providers and the encouragement of contestable markets. In contrast, policies to strengthen the management of chronic diseases are leading to the development of more collaborative models of service provision based on networks rather than markets. This underlines the point made earlier, namely that the policy mix will need to be carefully calibrated to avoid a repetition of the difficulties that occurred in the NHS in the 1990s.

The growing importance of chronic illnesses emphasises yet again the need for the NHS to give priority to the prevention of these illnesses as well as their effective treatment. Prevention is increasingly focusing on behavioural and lifestyle factors in view of the importance of nutrition, exercise and physical activity in contributing to heart disease, cancer, diabetes and other conditions (Summerfield and Babb, 2003). In parallel, action by government in areas such as tobacco control and the prevention of alcohol misuse is receiving greater attention, as is action to reduce health inequalities, including those affecting minority ethnic groups. The fully engaged scenario outlined in the Wanless report on the future financing of the NHS gave particular emphasis to the role of individuals and communities in bringing about population health improvements, and NHS bodies are increasingly working with other statutory agencies to take this agenda forward. Nowhere is this more important than in relation to obesity which poses one of the most significant challenges to the health of the population and where a focus on prevention is widely recognised to be a high priority for the future. In recognition of these challenges, the Blair government launched a public consultation on prevention and public health at the beginning of 2004 and it was expected that a White Paper would be published at the end of the consultation.

A recent analysis by the World Health Organisation has reviewed the risks contributing to morbidity and mortality (World Health Organisation, 2002). In developed countries, the principal risks in terms of their contribution to the disease burden were identified as tobacco (12.2 per cent of the total), blood pressure (10.9 per cent), alcohol (9.2 per cent), cholesterol (7.6 per cent) and being overweight (7.4 per cent). The World Health Organisation reviewed the range of strategies available for reducing these risks and placed a particular emphasis on population-wide approaches. These approaches included policies to reduce tobacco consumption, such as tobacco taxes, bans on advertising, and restrictions on smoking in public places, and action to reduce levels of cholesterol and of salt intake. In parallel, strategies to reduce the risks for individuals were identified, such as screening for blood pressure and cholesterol, and the use of effective drugs to treat high-risk individuals. The significance of tobacco as a risk factor is underlined by evidence from the UK that cigarette smoking accounts for around half the difference in survival to age 70 between socio-economic groups I to V (Wanless, 2003b).

Changing demographic and disease patterns will have an impact on the politics of the NHS. The ageing population and the increasing importance of chronic diseases will result in the emergence of more vocal patients' groups representing the interests of people who have a long-term interest in their medical condition. Whereas in the past it has been argued that patient and public participation or voice in health care is constrained by the episodic nature of much illness, the trends reviewed here point in a different direction. These trends will shape the governing of consumption in the health care state and may result in new divisions, for example between people who are older, sicker and more reliant on the NHS, and those who are younger, healthier and less in need of health care. The commitment to fund a universal and comprehensive health service may then come under strain. The challenge for those who provide health care will be to meet the needs of an increasingly heterogeneous population by adopting consistently high standards while also treating each patient as an individual. It is here that medical advances may have a contribution to make.

Medical advances

We noted earlier that new medical technologies are less widely available in the United Kingdom than in most comparable countries because of expenditure constraints. The increases in NHS funding made available under the Blair government are beginning to change this. For example, *The NHS Cancer Plan* has led to the acquisition of many new scanners for the diagnosis of cancer, and the recommendations of NICE have resulted in the more active promulgation of new drugs and other technologies that have gone through NICE's appraisal process. Medical advances tend to increase health care costs as well as improve health (see Chapter 9) and this was one of the factors that led the Wanless Report on future financing to argue for a sustained increase in funding to enable the NHS to catch up with other countries and then to keep up with them in delivering responsive and high quality services.

Looking to the future, advances in genetics are likely to result in greater understanding of the causes of illness and eventually to the development of new forms of diagnosis and treatment. Similarly, new drugs will open up further possibilities for treatment of the major medical conditions such as cancer, heart disease, and mental illness. Developments in pharmacogenomics will bring together understanding of genetics with pharmaceutical advances to enable drugs to be used more effectively, for example by tailoring their use to the genetic make-up of patients. Alongside these developments, the increased application of information technology to health care will change the way in which care is provided.

The potential impact of information technology is illustrated by developments such as NHS Direct Online and digital television. These developments already enable people to have easier and faster access at home to health information and advice. In the future, they may be developed to allow health care professionals to monitor patients in their homes through video links and the electronic transfer of information about the health of patients. In this way, many chronic illnesses like diabetes may be managed in the community. Advances in information technology will also enable doctors and other health care professionals to communicate more effectively, for example through the greater use of telemedicine, and they may help to improve the quality of care via the development of expert clinical decision support systems. In parallel, patients themselves will make increasing use of the internet to gain access to information and advice, reinforcing the trend towards more informed and demanding use of services.

Changes in technology are likely to accelerate the development of more integrated approaches to the delivery of health services. Integration may take a variety of forms, including the forging of stronger links between professionals and institutions at the same level (horizontal integration) and between professionals and institutions at different levels (vertical integration). This trend is already apparent in the emergence of service networks in areas such as cancer care, and in the way in which primary care practices are working more closely together in relation to out-of-hours provision. Integration will be particularly important in the prevention and treatment of chronic illnesses where the contribution of primary care and secondary care is needed to achieve the best outcomes for patients. Integration also needs to involve patients, carers and families as co-producers in health care in a world in which patients are increasingly recognised to be experts in their own conditions and will expect customised care.

The trends we have described will change the role of acute hospitals in the NHS. Technological innovations will enable more operations to be carried out as day cases and for hospital lengths of stay to be reduced further. Services that in the past have been provided in acute hospitals will increasingly be available in other settings, such as diagnostic and treatment centres and enhanced primary care facilities. Examples include minor surgery, outpatient services and many forms of diagnosis. Again this underlines the importance of acute hospitals being planned as part of integrated service networks, as envisaged in the latest statement of government policy on the future of acute hospitals (DH, 2003c). Not only this, but also smaller acute hospitals will increasingly be expected to work in collaboration with larger hospitals in order to ensure an effective division of services between different types of hospital. Collaboration between hospitals will enable access to services to be balanced by the provision of specialist care in the most appropriate setting.

Medical advances are likely to alter the dynamics of production politics in the health care state. Government has always had mixed views about the companies involved in the manufacture of health technologies, on the one hand offering encouragement because of their contribution to economic development, and on the other hand constraining the acquisition of new technologies because of the implications for NHS expenditure. The establishment of agencies like NICE to appraise technologies is an attempt to square the circle. Here then is an illustration of how the interdependence of the state and health services leads to the reshaping of the machinery of government, an example that underlines the reciprocal nature of the relationship between government and health services (Moran, 1999).

Rationing

The combination of factors reviewed in this chapter leads naturally into a discussion of health care priority-setting or rationing. Various studies have described the approach taken to rationing in different countries (Klein, Day and Redmayne, 1996; Ham, 1997c; Ham and Robert, 2003). In some systems, such as the state of Oregon, explicit rationing has involved defining a list of services to be funded. In other systems, policy-makers have shied away from excluding services from public funding and have focused instead on trying to ensure that resources are allocated to treatments that offer demonstrable benefit to patients. This is the approach adopted in New Zealand where the committee set up to define the core services to be funded in that country's health care system declined to undertake this task and instead made recommendations on the services that should receive priority in the budget-setting process. In addition, the committee organised a series of consensus conferences on particular treatments or conditions, it developed guidelines for the provision of services, and it worked with clinicians to agree criteria to determine priority for access to elective surgical procedures.

A number of countries have approached rationing by seeking to define the values that should inform priority-setting. Norway was one of the first countries to go down this route and its example finds echoes in the reports of priority-setting committees in the Netherlands and Sweden. For example, the Swedish Parliamentary Priorities Commission proposed an ethical platform for rationing based on three values: human dignity, equity or solidarity, and efficiency. In the Commission's view, human dignity, or respect for the rights of individuals, was of overriding importance, and meant that discrimination based on age, birth weight, lifestyle and similar considerations would not normally be allowed. Furthermore, the equity principle was intended to ensure that the needs of vulnerable groups and people with disabilities received priority. Only after dignity and equity had been taken into account did the Commission feel it was appropriate to consider the efficiency of different treatments.

These national approaches to rationing have emerged in response to the increasing pressures confronting health care systems and the reluctance of clinicians to continue taking responsibility for the consequences of rationing decisions. As Moran has noted, the dynamics of governing consumption in health care have involved a shift over time from doctors rationing care implicitly to greater explicitness in decision-making. The challenge this has thrown up is that:

> choices have to be made in a world where the control systems exercised by the old medical oligarchies have been weakened, and where it is increasingly difficult to manipulate the consuming citizen by either cultural or institutional mystification (Moran, 1999, p. 188).

It would be wrong to infer from this that politicians have replaced doctors as the main agents of rationing. International experience indicates the difficulties that arise in explicit, national approaches, and the resilience of blame diffusion strategies (Ham and Coulter, 2001). For example, policy-makers in the Netherlands faced criticism where explicit rationing meant excluding some services from funding, and this led to a retreat from rationing through exclusions. Instead, greater emphasis was given to rationing by guidelines, with professional networks playing a major part in the development and promulgation of guidelines. In the process, the onus has been placed on decision-makers at the sub-national level to work with professional networks in the implementation of guidelines and in priority setting. This was also the approach adopted in the NHS in the 1990s when health authorities were at the forefront of rationing. Cases like that of Child B, a 10-year-old girl with leukaemia who was denied funding for an experimental treatment by the Cambridge and Huntingdon Health Authority, came to symbolise the dilemmas facing health authorities in balancing the needs of individuals against those of communities (Ham and Pickard, 1998).

In this context, the decision of the Blair government to adopt a more explicit approach to rationing at the national level through NICE and national service frameworks could be seen as swimming against the tide of international developments in so far as other countries are retreating from such an approach. What is distinctive about NICE, however, is the creation of an agency at arm's length from government to take a lead on rationing. The existence of such an agency provided policy-makers with some distance from decisions that risked attracting criticism and unpopularity. Also, the introduction of NICE at a time when the NHS budget was growing at historically unprecedented levels, meant that it was possible to absorb the effects of its decisions, even though most of these decisions added to the pressures on the NHS. The unanswered question was what would happen when the increase in resources slowed down.

Assuming that there is a commitment to maintain the NHS as a universal service, and that the political costs of exclusions remain too high, then a limited list of options is on offer. In keeping with experience of social policy reform in the 1980s and 1990s (Pierson, 1994), it seems likely that rationing will occur largely through the back door, following the examples of dentistry and long-term care described elsewhere in this book. Also, traditional devices such as rationing by delay, dilution and diversion will continue to be used. If this assessment is accurate, then the danger is that such an approach may undermine trust in government. This could occur if the public perceive that the scope of the NHS is being limited not through open debate and discussion but through a series of incremental and largely invisible decisions that cumulatively have a significant impact on the services they assumed would be available to them. Here is a further illustration of the impact that health services may have on government and one that in the longer term could have profound implications for the political system as a whole.

An alternative view is that the existence of NICE and the development of greater explicitness in rationing will help to expose areas of underfunding and generate pressure for sustained increases in NHS funding beyond those already announced. Support for this view comes from experience in systems like Oregon, Israel and New Zealand where explicit rationing did have this effect. The issue then is the willingness of governments and electorates to provide through the tax system the volume of resources needed to fund medical advances deemed to be effective. This suggests that some difficult choices lie ahead, not just within the NHS but in government as a whole in debates about relative spending priorities and the level of taxes needed to pay for these priorities.

One way of squaring the circle is for government to set the national framework for rationing and to continue to rely on primary care trusts to make judgements about relative priorities at the local level. One of the difficulties in this strategy is the decision in 2003 to treat NICE guidance as effectively mandatory for the NHS, thereby reducing the discretion available to primary care trusts to arrive at such judgements. The prospect is therefore of increasing tension between the Department of Health and primary care trusts as the Department seeks to achieve greater consistency in the provision of services and primary care trusts attempt to juggle competing (and increasingly non-discretionary) priorities within the constraints of fixed, albeit growing, budgets. This suggests that the dynamics built into governing consumption will be worked out through the organisational politics of the NHS, in particular the relationship between the centre and the periphery. The question then is, 'How will primary care trusts respond to the challenge of rationing and the inevitable tensions created by rising public awareness and expectations, the emphasis placed by government on reducing variations in provision, and the reluctance of doctors to mask the effects of resource constraints through implicit decision-making?'.

Political futures

In response to the policies promulgated by the Blair government, the two main opposition parties in the Westminster parliament have set out their stalls on the future of the NHS. The Conservative Party has examined experience in a number of other countries in developing its approach. In so doing, it has criticised the Blair government for the use of command-and-control mechanisms in the management of the NHS and for the large number of targets that have been set. In their place, the Conservatives have promised to set professionals free and devolve power to managers and clinicians. The commitment to devolution includes continuing with the development of NHS Foundation Trusts and allowing them greater freedoms than proposed under Labour's plans. The Conservatives have also promised to give more power to GPs by devolving responsibility for commissioning to practices. The most radical aspects of the Conservatives' proposals concern choice where under the 'patient passport' scheme patients using the private sector would receive a subsidy of around 60 per cent of the cost of their treatment, along the lines of an approach developed in Finland. The Conservatives have also suggested bringing back tax breaks to encourage more people to take out private medical insurance and have identified company schemes as the most promising way of doing this. These reforms to the financing of the NHS also include proposals to fine patients who fail to keep appointments.

Like the Conservatives, the Liberal Democrats have criticised the hierarchical approach to the management of the NHS adopted by the Blair government and have promised to devolve more responsibility for decision-making. In the Liberal Democrats' plans, devolution would be pursued through the establishment of elected regional assemblies whose responsibilities would include the NHS. The commissioning functions of PCTs would be taken over by local authorities. Patients would be able to choose where they wished to be treated, and they would be supported in this by the provision of information about waiting times and treatment options. On finance, the Liberal Democrats are committed to ending charges for services such as eye and dental tests and phasing out prescription charges, and to earmarking national insurance to the NHS as people's NHS contribution. As part of the devolution of responsibility to regional assemblies and local government, it would be possible to supplement the resources made available by government through locally raised resources. The Liberal Democrats have also emphasised the need to give higher priority to public health and prevention.

Neither the Conservatives nor the Liberal Democrats have argued that the fundamental basis of the NHS should be overturned. To be sure, their policies, if adopted, would herald a further period of reform for the NHS, but the political consensus around a universal, comprehensive, and largely free-at-the-point-of-use NHS appears to be intact. The precise form that the NHS takes will vary depending on the party in power, with the Liberal Democrats committed to a Nordic-style system of elected regional control of the health services, and the Conservatives maintaining that the NHS should focus more on the funding of the NHS with a variety of (increasingly private) providers delivering care. There are also emerging differences in relation to financing with the Conservatives wanting to encourage a bigger role for private expenditure, while the Liberal Democrats are committed to eliminating charges. Despite these differences, none of the major political parties has proposed ending the system in which most of the resources used to pay for health care are raised through public finance, nor have the core principles of the NHS been challenged.

The extent of the common ground between the Conservatives, Labour and the Liberal Democrats can be explained in two ways. First, as we discussed earlier in the chapter, in all countries there is dissatisfaction with the performance of health services, and there are no models that are clearly superior to the NHS judged in terms of what they achieve for the expenditure involved. The Commonwealth Fund's surveys and the World Health Organisation's rankings show that the NHS performs well on equity and cost containment and its weaknesses in relation to responsiveness and quality are a consequence in large part of a funding system that has resulted in long-term underinvestment. Second, notwithstanding the weaknesses of the NHS, survey evidence shows that it remains a highly valued institution and one which politicians challenge at their peril. This was demonstrated by a MORI survey conducted in 1999 which found that the introduction of the NHS was mentioned by 46 per cent of people when asked about the two or three achievements that contributed most to British life in the twentieth century. The next most significant achievements were the establishment of the welfare state and winning the Second World War, mentioned by 18 per cent and 15 per cent of respondents respectively.

Here then is another example of how the NHS influences the process of government and politics. Put bluntly, the size of the NHS and the extent to which it is supported by staff and the public constrains the freedom of manoeuvre of politicians, whatever their ideology. Health care is both a big business and a major issue of public policy, to the degree that the actions of the government of the day are strongly shaped by what is happening in health care, as well as vice versa. If one implication is that politicians are reluctant to propose radical changes to the NHS, another is that the NHS receives increasing attention and resources as governments as a whole (and not just Health Ministers) see that their future is closely intertwined with the public's perception of the NHS. The ever closer involvement of the Prime Minister and the Chancellor in health policy in the period since 1997 exemplifies the degree to which developments in health care have influenced the process of government.

To make this point is to underscore the difficulty of taking politics out of the NHS, as is often proposed. Of course, the discomfort felt by politicians when faced with criticisms of the NHS may lead them to wish that accountability were located elsewhere, but to date no government has followed through the logic and implemented an arm's length arrangement whereby government and the NHS would be insulated from each other, even though this idea is often floated. Indeed, as we have argued throughout this book, the involvement of politicians in the NHS has increased in recent years, and it would appear that a major crisis of confidence in the NHS model would be required to force politicians to entertain radical approaches involving a more limited role for government. The progress made since 2000 in improving the performance of the NHS through investment and reform suggests that such a crisis is not imminent. Looking to the future, the challenge for the NHS is to sustain this progress and to demonstrate to an increasingly critical and demanding public that services can be delivered in more accessible and responsive ways while equity is preserved and enhanced. The NHS also faces the challenge of using the extra resources it has been allocated efficiently in the face of evidence that on some measures efficiency may be declining (Le Grand, 2002). A major issue here is the need to develop better measures of performance that reflect the changing patterns of care discussed earlier in this chapter and that capture improvements in quality.

Conclusion

In this chapter we have reviewed a range of issues that have a bearing on the future of the NHS. International experience illustrates that Britain is not alone in reforming its health services. One of the themes in health care reform is the role of private finance and provision and we have seen how the boundaries between the two sectors have become increasingly blurred. Policy-makers have used a range of different approaches in seeking to improve the performance of health services, including an eclectic mix of hierarchies, networks and markets. In so doing, they have been responding to changing public attitudes and expectations, in particular by trying to make the NHS more responsive to users. Demographic changes will increase the demands on the NHS through the ageing population, and the changing pattern of disease means that chronic illnesses will become more significant in the future. This will add to the pressure to develop models of service provision that integrate care, and will also accentuate the challenge of rationing.

The main political parties share a good deal of common ground on the future of the NHS while disagreeing, sometimes in important ways, on the details. Health policy is shaped by the social, economic and international context in which it is played out, and in turn has an increasing influence on the machinery of government and the political process. In this respect, the future of the NHS and of politics in Britain are inextricably intertwined, the performance of the NHS having an important bearing on the behaviour of government, and politicians having an increasing influence on the funding and provision of health care. For better or worse, the NHS and politics cannot easily be separated, and the politics and organisation of health care will remain a continuing arena of focus for both policy-makers and analysts of the policy process.

Guide to Further Reading

Chapter 1

Further reading suggestions on the development of health services and health policy must necessarily be highly selective. Useful general accounts of the evolution of the welfare state in Britain are provided by Bruce (1968), Fraser (1973), Gilbert (1966, 1970) and Timmins (1995). Studies which look more specifically at the history of the medical profession and health services include those by Abel-Smith (1964), Cartwright (1971), Porter (1997) and Stevens (1966). Eckstein (1958), Lindsey (1962) and Webster (1988;,1996) provide a wealth of material on the period before and after the creation of the National Health Service. Levitt (1979) describes the reorganised structure of the NHS introduced in 1974, and Brown (1979) analyses the impact of the 1974 changes. Klein (2000) offers a good overview of the politics of health services in the period since 1939.

Chapter 2

The background to the Ministerial Review of the NHS is traced in Timmins (1995) and Butler (1992). A summary of the debate which took place during the Review is contained in Ham, Robinson and Benzeval (1990). The government's proposals were contained in three White Papers, *Working for Patients, Caring for People* and *Promoting Better Health* (Secretary of State for Health and others, 1989a, 1989b; Secretary of State for Social Services and others, 1987). Klein's account of the politics of the NHS (Klein, 2000) contains a useful analysis of the events which led up to the Review and the outcome. Ham (1997a) describes the implementation of the reforms, while Le Grand, Mays and Mulligan (1998) review the evidence on the impact of the internal market. Ham (2000) analyses the politics of NHS reform during this period from the perspective of health secretaries.

Chapter 3

The Blair government's proposals were set out in a White Paper, *The New NHS* (Secretary of State for Health, 1997), a White Paper on public health, *Saving Lives: Our Healthier Nation* (Secretary of State for Health, 1999), and a consultation document on quality in the new NHS, *A First Class Service* (Secretary of State for Health, 1998b). Early commentaries on the government's plans were provided in Klein (1998) and Ham (1999). The comprehensive spending review set out plans for the future of NHS spending (Chancellor of the Exchequer, 1998). *The NHS Plan* (Secretary of State for Health, 2000) and *Delivering the NHS Plan* (Secretary of State for Health, 2002) described the government's proposals on investment and reform. Later commentaries on the government's approach can be found in Appleby and Coote (2002), Le Grand (2002), and Leatherman and Sutherland (2003).

Chapter 4

Useful summaries of contemporary issues in health policy are provided in the annual reports of the Department of Health (for example, DH 2003a) and the guidance on planning and priorities issued to the NHS. Information on expenditure trends and the performance of the NHS since its establishment is contained in the compendium of statistics produced by the Office of Health Economics (2003). More specific informaion is best tracked by consulting White Papers and other policy statements issued by the Department of Health. These can be found on the Department's website (www.dh.gov.uk). The Wanless review provides a good analysis and review of the issues involved in funding the NHS (Wanless, 2001 and 2002). Reports from other organisations, like the Audit Commission and the Commission for Healthcare Audit and Inspection, offer a commentary on particular initiatives and the performance of the NHS as a whole. Experience of rationing in the NHS is analysed by Klein, Day and Redmayne (1996).

Chapter 5

Hazell (2003) provides the best starting point for those seeking to understand political devolution as a whole and the impact on health policy in particular (see Greer's chapter in Hazell, 2003). Jervis and Plowden (2003) and Woods (2002 and 2004) discuss the impact of devolution on health policy in detail. The websites for the governments of Scotland (www.scotland.gov.uk), Wales (www.wales.gov.uk) and Northern Ireland (www.nics.gov.uk) contain reports and publications in relation to health and the NHS in these countries

Chapter 6

Jenkins (1978) examines policy analysis using a political and organisational perspective, and Parsons (1995) offers an overview of different perspectives on policy analysis. Beer (1969) provides an important interpretation of the evolution of politics in Britain. Norton (1981) discusses the role of the House of Commons and Richardson and Jordan (1979) focus on the part played by pressure groups in the policy process. Jordan and Richardson (1987) examine the policy process in Britain, and Hennessy (1986, 1989, 1995, 2000) analyses the role of the Cabinet, civil service, Prime Minister, and other institutions. Dunleavy and others (2003) assess recent developments in British politics and should be read alongside Rhodes (1997), Smith (1999), and Marsh, Richards and Smith (2001). Deakin and Parry (2000) provide the best introduction to the role of the Treasury in relation to social policy.

Chapter 7

Brown (1975) has written a good, general account of the workings of the DHSS and the part it played in the management of the NHS, personal social services and social security until the mid-1970s. Detailed information on the organisation of the DHSS is provided by Razell (1980). The Griffiths Report (1983) and the Regional Chairmen's Enquiry (1976) indicate some of the reasons why a change in the organisation of the DHSS was necessary. The Crossman and Castle Diaries give valuable insights into the politician's view of health policy-making in central government (Crossman, 1977; Castle, 1980). Studies of policies on hospital planning (Allen, 1979) and smoking (Popham, 1981) have illustrated the role of ministers, civil servants and pressure groups in the policy process. The Banks Review (1994) summarises developments in the 1980s and 1990s. Day and Klein offer an assessment of more recent changes (Day and Klein, 1997). The author's analysis of the politics of NHS reform in the 1990s (Ham, 2000) analyses the role of health secretaries and the world in which they work.

Chapter 8

Brown (1975, 1979) discusses the historical relationship between the DHSS and health authorities, while Haywood and Alaszewski (1980) analyse the extent to which the NHS Planning System was an effective vehicle for the implementation of central policies. Hunter (1980) explores the dynamics of policy-making in health authorities, and identifies a number of phases in centre–periphery relationships (Hunter, 1983). The author's own examination of policy-making in the NHS between 1948 and 1974 (Ham, 1981) covers similar territory. Klein's (2000) work on the politics of the NHS contains much that is relevant to the student of health policy implementation, as does the author's study of health authorities in the period 1981–85 (Ham, 1986). Harrison (1988; 1994) assesses the impact of the Griffiths Report on general management and the effect this had on the role of managers. Ferlie and colleagues (1996) offer an interpretation of the impact of the new public management on the NHS. McDonald (2002) reviews policy-making in health authorities in the 1990s and McNulty and Ferlie (2002) analyse the impact of doctors on initiatives designed to improve the quality of care. Regen and colleagues (2001) and Wilkin and colleagues (2002) review the evolution of primary care groups and trusts.

Chapter 9

The *Report of the Royal Commission on the NHS* (1979) contains a general review of the impact of the NHS in its first thirty years. The RAWP report (DHSS, 1976a) describes the method used to allocate resources on an equitable geographical basis, and its implementation and impact are reviewed by Mays and Bevan (1987). The Black Report, *Inequalities in Health* (1980), was the first systematic attempt to bring together information on social class differences in health and the use of health services. More recent evidence is reviewed by Drever and Whitehead (1997), the Acheson Report (1998) and the Cross-Cutting Review (2002). The series of inquiries into long-stay hospitals provide powerful evidence of client-group inequalties. Examples are the Ely and Normansfield reports (Ely Report, 1969; Normansfield Report, 1978). Martin (1984) has summarised the reports and has analysed the nature of the problems that exist in this area. Yates (1987 and 1995) has examined waiting lists and the role of private practice. Charlton and Murphy (1997) summarise the evidence on population health. Day and Klein (2001) discuss the role of the Audit Commission and the National Audit Office. Leatherman and Sutherland (2003) provide a comprehensive assessment of the performance of the NHS in relation to quality of care under the Blair government. Walshe (2003) offers a good introduction to regulation in the NHS.

Chapter 10

Pluralist ideas have been applied in the work of Eckstein (1960) and Willcocks (1967). The structuralist argument has been set out by Alford (1975a), and applied to the NHS by the author (Ham, 1981). The Marxist perspective has been most fully developed by Navarro (1976) and Doyal (1979). Stacey (1977) and Illsley (1977) review different concepts of health and the way these concepts have influenced service provision. Outside the health field, Saunders (1979) has written a major study of theories of power and the role of ideology which is of considerable relevance to the student attempting to understand the complexities of health policy-making. Smith's (1999) analysis examines the interplay between actors, institutions, context and structure. Harrison (1994) applies a range of theoretical perspectives to the study of health policy.

Chapter 11

The performance of the NHS in the international context is considered in a range of publications by the OECD and WHO (see, as examples, OECD, 1992, 1994b and 2003a, and WHO, 2000). The Commonwealth Fund's annual surveys offer comparisons of the United Kingdom, Australia, Canada, New Zealand and the United States (www.cmwf.org). Coulter and Magee (2003) compare patient experiences in a number of countries. The annual review published by Laing and Buisson (2003) is the best source of information about the role of the private sector in Britain. International influences on the NHS are disccussed by Mossialos and Palm (2003) in the case of the EU, and Pollock and colleagues in the case of the World Trade Organisation (for example, Pollock and Price, 2003a). Tuohy (1999) provides a detailed historical and comparative analysis of the dynamics of health systems, and Moran (1999) similarly reviews the functions of the health care state. Changing attitudes to the NHS have been tracked in the British Social Attitudes' Survey (Exley and Jarvis, 2003) and patient experiences are reflected in the surveys initiated by the Blair government (www.dh.gov.uk). The Wanless reports (2001, 2002, 2003b) explore changing demographic patterns (www.hm-treasury.gov.uk). Issues to do with health care rationing are discussed by Coulter and Ham (2000) and Ham and Robert (2003).

Bibliography

Note: where no publisher is given, the author indicated is also the publisher.

Abel, L. A. and Lewin, W. (1959) 'Report on Hospital Building', *British Medical Journal Supplement*, 4 April, 109–14.

Abel-Smith, B. (1964) *The Hospitals 1800–1948* (Heinemann).

Abel-Smith, B. (1994) *How to Contain Health Care Costs: An International Dilemma* (University of London).

Acheson Report (1998) *Independent Inquiry into Inequalities and Health* (The Stationery Office).

Alderson, M. R. (1970) 'Social Class and the Health Service', *The Medical Officer*, 17 July, 50–2.

Alford, R. (1975a) *Health Care Politics* (University of Chicago Press).

Alford, R. (1975b) 'Paradigms of Relations between State and Society', in Lindberg, L. N., Alford, R., Crouch, C. and Offe, C. (eds), *Stress and Contradiction in Modern Capitalism* (Lexington Books).

Allen, D. (1979) *Hospital Planning* (Pitman Medical).

Allsop, J. and Mulcahy, L. (1996) *Regulating Medical Work* (Open University Press).

Appleby, J. and Coote, A. (eds) (2002) *Five-Year Health Check* (King's Fund).

Appleby, J. and Rosete, A. (2003) 'The NHS: keeping up with public expectations?', in Park, A., Curtice, J., Thomson, K., Jarvis, L. and Bromley, C. (eds) *British Social Attitudes: the 20th Report* (Sage).

Audit Commission (1997) *The Coming of Age* (The Stationery Office).

Audit Commission (2003) *Achieving the NHS Plan*.

Bachrach, P. and Baratz, M. S. (1970) *Power and Poverty* (Oxford University Press).

Bagehot, W. (1963) [1867] *The English Constitution*, new edn (Fontana).

Baggott, R. (1986) 'Alcohol, Politics and Social Policy', *Journal of Social Policy*, 15 (4), 467–88.

Bajekal, M. and Prescott, A. (2003) *Disability. The Health Survey for England 2001* (The Stationery Office).

Banks, G. T. (1979) 'Programme Budgeting in the DHSS', in Booth, T. A. (ed.), *Planning for Welfare* (Blackwell).

Banks Review (1994) *Review of the Wider Department of Health* (DH).

Banting, K. (1979) *Poverty, Politics and Policy* (Macmillan – now Palgrave Macmillan).

Barrett, S. and Fudge, C. (eds) (1981) *Policy and Action* (Methuen).

Bauld, L. and Judge, K. (eds) (2002) *Learning from Health Action Zones* (Aeneas Press).

Bebbington, A. and Darton, R. (1996) *Healthy Life Expectancy in England and Wales: Recent Evidence* (University of Kent).

Becker, H. (ed.) (1967) *Social Problems: A Modern Approach* (Wiley).

Beer, S. H. (1969) *Modern British Politics*, 2nd edn (Faber).

Bevir, M. and Rhodes, R.A.W. (2003) *Interpreting British Governance* (Routledge).

Birch, R. (1983) 'Policy Analysis in the DHSS: Some Reflections', *Public Administration Bulletin*, no. 43.

Black Report (1980) *Inequalities in Health* (DHSS).

Blackstone, T. (1979) 'Helping Ministers do a Better Job', *New Society*, 19 July, 131–2.

Blendon, R. *et al.* (2001) 'Physicians' Views on Quality of Care: A Five-Country Comparison', *Health Affairs*, 20, 233–43.

Blendon, R. *et al.* (2002) 'Inequities in Health Care: A Five-Country Study', *Health Affairs*, 21, 182–91.

Blendon, R. *et al.* (2003) 'Common Concerns Amid Diverse Systems: Health Care Experience in Five Countries', *Health Affairs*, 22, 106–21.

Bloor, K. and Maynard, A. (1994) 'An Outsider's View of the NHS Reforms', *British Medical Journal*, 309, 352–3.

Botting, B. (ed.) (1995) *The Health of Our Children* (HMSO).

Botting, B. (1997) 'Mortality in Childhood', in Drever, F. and Whitehead, M. (eds), *Health Inequalities, op. cit.*

Bottomley, V. (1995) *The NHS: Continuity and Change* (DH).

Brenner, H. (1979) 'Mortality and the National Economy', *The Lancet*, 15 September, 586–73.

Bridgen, P and Lewis, J. (1999) *Elderly People and the Boundary between Health and Social Care 1946–91: Whose Responsibility?* (The Nuffield Trust).

Brown, G. (2003) *A Modern Agenda for Prosperity and Social Reform* Issued under cover of press release 12/03 by HM Treasury (www.hm-treasury.gov.uk).

Brown, R. G. S. (1975) *The Management of Welfare* (Fontana).

Brown, R. G. S. (1979) *Reorganising the National Health Service* (Blackwell & Robinson).

Bruce, M. (1968) *The Coming of the Welfare State*, 4th edn (Batsford).

Bunker, J. (2001) 'The role of medical care in contributing to health improvements within societies', *International Journal of Epidemiology*, 30, 1260–3.

Bunting, J. (1997) 'Morbidity and Health-related Behaviour of Adults – a Review', in Drever, F. and Whitehead, M. (eds), *Health Inequalities, op. cit.*

Butler, J. (1992) *Patients, Policies and Politics* (Open University Press).

Butler, J. R. with Bevan, J. M. and Taylor, R. C. (1973) *Family Doctors and Public Policy* (Routledge & Kegan Paul).

Butts, M., Irving, D. and Whitt, C. (1998) *From Principles to Practice* (Nuffield Provincial Hospitals Trust).

Calman-Hine (1995) *A Policy Framework for Commissioning Cancer Services* (DH).

Cannon, G. (1984) 'The Cover-up that Kills', *The Times*, 12 June, 13.

Cartwright, F. (1971) *A Social History of Medicine* (Longman).

Castle, B. (1980) *The Castle Diaries 1974–76* (Weidenfeld & Nicolson).

Cawson, A. (1982) *Corporatism and Welfare* (Heinemann).

Central Health Services Council (1969) *The Functions of the District General Hospital* (HMSO).

Central Policy Review Staff (1975) *A Joint Framework for Social Policies* (HMSO).

Chancellor of the Exchequer (1998) *Modern Public Services in Britain*, Cm 4011 (The Stationery Office).

Charlton, J. (1997) 'Trends in all-cause mortality: 1841–1994', in Charlton and Murphy (eds), Vol 1, *op. cit.*

Charlton, J., Fraser, P. and Murphy, M. (1997) 'Medical Advances and Iatrogenesis', in Charlton and Murphy (eds), Vol. 1, *op. cit.*

Charlton, J. and Murphy, M. (eds) (1997) *The Health of Adult Britain 1841–1994*, Vols 1 and 2 (The Stationery Office).

CHI (Commission for Health Improvement) (2001) *NHS Cancer Care in England and Wales.*

CHI (Commission for Health Improvement) (2003) *Getting Better?* (The Stationery Office).

Clode, D. (1977) 'Plans aren't Worth the Paper they are Written on', *Health and Social Services Journal*, 16 September, 1314–16.

Cmnd 9058 (1983) *Financial Management in Government Departments* (HMSO).

Committee on Standards in Public Life (2002) *Defining the Boundaries within the Executive: Ministers, Special Advisers and the Permanent Civil Service.*

Coulter, A. (2002) *The Autonomous Patient* (The Stationery Office).

Coulter, A. (2003) 'Engaging Patients and Citizens', in Leatherman, S. and Sutherland, K. *op. cit.*

Coulter, A. and Cleary, P. (2001) 'Patients' experiences with hospital care in five countries', *Health Affairs*, 20, 244–52.

Coulter, A. and Ham, C. (eds) (2000) *The Global Challenge of Health Care Rationing* (Open University Press).

Coulter, A. and Magee, H. (eds) (2003) *The European Patient of the Future* (Open University Press).

Cross-Cutting Review (2002) *Tackling Health Inequalities* (DH and HM Treasury).

Crossman, R. H. S. (1963) Introduction to Bagehot, W., *The English Constitution* (Fontana) *op. cit.*

Crossman, R. H. S. (1972) *A Politician's View of Health Service Planning* (University of Glasgow Press).

Crossman, R. H. S. (1975) *The Diaries of a Cabinet Minister:* Vol 1, *Minister of Housing 1964–66* (Hamilton & Cape).

Crossman, R. H. S. (1976) *The Diaries of a Cabinet Minister:* Vol 2, *Lord President of the Council and Leader of the House of Commons 1966–68* (Hamilton & Cape).

Crossman, R. H. S. (1977) *The Diaries of a Cabinet Minister:* Vol 3, *Secretary of State for Social Services 1968–70* (Hamilton & Cape).

Cutler, D. and McClellan, M. (2001) 'Is Technological Change in Medicine Worth It?', *Health Affairs*, 20, 11–29.

Dahl, R. (1961) *Who Governs?* (Yale University Press).

Davey Smith, G., Gunnell, D. and Ben-Shlomo, Y. (2001) 'Life-course approaches to socio-economic differentials in cause-specific mortality', in Leon, D. and Walt, G. (eds) *Poverty, Inequality and Health: an international perspective* (Oxford University Press).

Day, P. and Klein, R. (1983) 'The Mobilisation of Consent versus the Management of Conflict: Decoding the Griffiths Report', *British Medical Journal*, 287, 1813–16.

Day, P. and Klein, R. (1997) *Steering but not Rowing?* (The Policy Press).

Day, P. and Klein, R. (2001) *Auditing the Auditors: audit in the national health service* (The Stationery Office).

Deakin, N. and Parry, R. (2000) *The Treasury and Social Policy* (Macmillan – now Palgrave Macmillan).

DH (1991) *The Patient's Charter.*

DH (1994) *The Operation of the NHS Internal Market: Local Freedoms, National Responsibilities.*

DH (1997) *Statement of Responsibilities and Accountabilities.*

DH (1998a) *The Health of the Nation – a Policy Assessed* (The Stationery Office).

DH (1998b) *Partnership In Action.*

DH (1999) *A National Service Framework for Mental Health*

DH (2000a) *Shaping the Future NHS: long term planning for hospitals and related services.*

DH (2000b) *The NHS Cancer Plan.*

DH (2000c) *National Service Framework for Coronary Heart Disease.*

DH (2001a) *Shifting the Balance of Power within the NHS – Securing Delivery.*

DH (2001b) *Valuing People: a new strategy for learning disability for the 21st Century* Cm 5086 (The Stationery Office).

DH (2001c) *National Service Framework for Older People.*

DH (2002) *Chief Executive's Report to the NHS.*

DH (2003a) *Departmental Report 2003* (The Stationery Office).

DH (2003b) *Tackling Health Inequalities: a programme for action.*

DH (2003c) *Keeping the NHS Local.*

DH (2003d) *Delivering Better Heart Services.*

DH (2003e) *Chief Executive's report to the NHS.*

DH (2003f) *Building on the Best*, Cm 6079 (The Stationery Office).

DHSS (1971) *Better Services for the Mentally Handicapped*, Cmnd 4683 (HMSO).

DHSS (1972) *The Facilities and Services of Psychiatric Hospitals in England and Wales 1970*, Statistical and Research Report Series no. 2 (HMSO).

DHSS (1974) *The Facilities and Services of Mental Illness and Mental Handicap Hospitals in England and Wales 1972*, Statistical and Research Report Series no. 8 (HMSO).

DHSS (1975a) *Better Services for the Mentally Ill*, Cmnd 6223 (HMSO).

DHSS (1975b) *Draft Guide to Planning in the NHS.*

DHSS (1975c) *First Interim Report of the Resource Allocation Working Party.*

DHSS (1976a) *Sharing Resources for Health in England* (HMSO).

DHSS (1976b) *Priorities for Health and Personal Social Services in England* (HMSO).

DHSS (1976c) *The NHS Planning System.*

DHSS (1976d) *Prevention and Health: Everybody's Business* (HMSO).

DHSS (1977a) *Prevention and Health*, Cmnd 7047 (HMSO).

DHSS (1977b) *The Way Forward* (HMSO).

DHSS (1979a) *Patients First* (HMSO).

DHSS (1979b) *Review of Health Capital.*

DHSS (1980a) Health Circular (80) 8, *Health Service Development Structure and Management.*

DHSS (1980b) *Hospital Services: The Future Pattern of Hospital Provision in England.*

DHSS (1980c) *Mental Handicap: Progress, Problems and Priorities.*

DHSS (1980d) *Reply by the Government to the Third Report from the Social Services Committee, Session 1979–80,* Cmnd 8086 (HMSO).

DHSS (1981a) *Report of a Study on Community Care.*

DHSS (1981b) *Growing Older,* Cmnd 8173 (HMSO).

DHSS (1981c) *Care in Action* (HMSO).

DHSS (1981d) *Care in the Community.*

DHSS (1981e) *Report on a Study of the Acute Hospital Sector* (HMSO).

DHSS (1981f) *Report on a Study of the Respective Roles of the General Acute and Geriatric Sectors in Care of the Elderly Hospital Patient.*

DHSS (1983a) *Health Care and its Cost* (HMSO).

Dixon, A. et al. (2003) *Is the NHS equitable? A review of the evidence* (LSE).

Dixon, A. and Mossialos, E. (eds) (2002) *Health Care Systems in Eight Countries: trends and challenges* (LSE).

Dixon, J., Inglis, S. and Klein, R. (1999) 'Is the English NHS Underfunded?', *British Medical Journal,* 318, 20 February, 522–6.

Doll, R. (1974) *To Measure NHS Progress* (Fabian Society).

Donelan, K. et al. (1999) 'The Cost of Health System Change: public discontent in five nations', *Health Affairs,* 18, 206–16.

Doyal, L. with Pennell, I. (1979) *The Political Economy of Health* (Pluto Press).

Doyal, L. et al.. (1983) *Cancer in Britain* (Pluto Press).

Draper, P., Best, G. and Dennis, J. (1977) 'Health and Wealth', *Royal Society of Health Journal,* 97, 65–70.

Drever, F. and Bunting, J. (1997) 'Patterns and Trends in Male Mortality', in Drever, F. and Whitehead, M. (eds), *Health Inequalities, op. cit.*

Drever, F. and Whitehead, M. (eds) (1997) *Health Inequalities* (The Stationery Office).

Dunleavy, P. (1981) 'Professions and Policy Change: Notes Towards a Model of Ideological Corporatism', *Public Administration Bulletin,* no. 36, 3–16.

Dunleavy, P., Gamble, A. Heffernanan, R. and Peele, G. (eds) (2003) *Developments in British Politics,* 7th edn (Palgrave).

Dunnell, K. (1997) 'Are we Healthier', in Charlton and Murphy (eds), Vol 2, *op. cit.*

Easton, D. (1953) *The Political System* (Knopf).

Eckstein, H. (1958) *The English Health Service* (Harvard University Press).

Eckstein, H. (1960) *Pressure Group Politics* (Allen & Unwin).

Edelman, M. (1971) *Politics as Symbolic Action* (Markham).

Edelman, M. (1977) *Political Language* (Academic Press).

Ely Report (1969) *Report of the Committee of Enquiry into Allegations of Ill-treatment of Patients and Other Irregularities at the Ely Hospital, Cardiff,* Cmnd 3975 (HMSO).

Enthoven, A. (1985) *Reflections on the Management of the NHS* (Nuffield Provincial Hospitals Trusts).

Evans, R. G. (2002) 'Financing health care: taxation and the alternatives', in Mossialos, E. et al. (eds) *Funding Health Care: options for Europe* (Open University Press).

Exley, S. and Jarvis, L. (2003) *Trends in Attitudes to Health Care 1983 to 2001* (National Centre for Social Research).

Expenditure Committee (1971) Employment and Social Services Sub-Committee, *Minutes of Evidence*, 31 March 1971, session 1970–1. HC 323ii (HMSO).

Expenditure Committee (1972) *Relationship of Expenditure to Needs*, eighth report from the Expenditure Committee, session 1971–2 (HMSO).

Ferlie, E., Ashburner, L., Fitzgerald, L. and Pettigrew, A. (1996) *The New Public Management in Action* (Oxford University Press).

Ferri, E., Bynner, J. and Wadsworth, M. (2003) *Changing Britain, Changing Lives* (Institute of Education).

Flynn, R. (1991) 'Coping with Cutbacks and Managing Retrenchment in Health', *Journal of Social Policy*, 20 (2), 215–36.

Fowler, N. (1991) *Ministers Decide* (Chapmans).

Fox, D. (1986) *Health Policies Health Politics* (Princeton University Press).

Fraser, D. (1973) *The Evolution of the British Welfare State* (Macmillan – now Palgrave Macmillan).

Freedman, V.A., Martin, L.G. and Schoeni, R.F. (2002) 'Recent Trends in Disability and Functioning Among Older Adults in the United States', *Journal of the American Medical Association*, 288, 3137–46.

Freeman, R. (2000) *The Politics of Health in Europe* (Manchester University Press).

Fries, J.F. (1980) 'Aging, natural death and the compression of morbidity', *New England Journal of Medicine*, 303, 130–5.

Gaffney, D., Pollock, A., Price, D. and Shaoul, J. (1999) 'NHS capital expenditure and the private finance initiative – expansion or contraction?', *British Medical Journal*, 319, 3 July, 48–51

Gilbert, B. B. (1966) *The Evolution of National Insurance in Great Britain* (Michael Joseph).

Gilbert, B. B. (1970) *British Social Policy 1914–39* (Batsford).

Godber, G. (1975) *The Health Service: Past, Present and Future* (Athlone Press).

Godber, G. (1981) 'Doctors in Government', *Health Trends*, 13.

Gough, I. (1979) *The Political Economy of the Welfare State* (Macmillan – now Palgrave Macmillan).

Greer, S. (2003) 'Policy Divergence. Will it change something in Greenock?', in Hazell, *op. cit.*

Griffiths, C. and Brock, A. (2003) 'Twentieth Century Mortality Trends in England and Wales', *Health Statistics Quarterly*, 18, 5–18.

Griffiths, C. and Fitzpatrick J. (2001) *Geographic Variations in Health* (The Stationery Office).

Griffiths, R. (1992) 'Seven Years of Progress – General Management in the NHS', *Health Economics*, 1(1), 61–70.

Griffiths Report (1983) *NHS Management Inquiry* (DHSS).

Griffiths Report (1988) *Community Care: Agenda for Action* (HMSO).

Guillebaud Committee (1956) *Report of the Committee of Enquiry into the Cost of the National Health Service*, Cmd 9663 (HMSO).

Halper, T. (1989) *The Misfortunes of Others: End-Stage Renal Disease in the United Kingdom* (Cambridge University Press).

Ham, C. J. (1977) 'Power, Patients and Pluralism', in Barnard, K. and Lee, K. (eds), *Conflicts in the NHS* (Croom Helm).

Ham, C. J. (1980) 'Approaches to the Study of Social Policy Making', *Policy and Politics*, (1), 55–71.

Ham, C. J. (1981) *Policy Making in the National Health Service* (Macmillan – now Palgrave Macmillan).

Ham, C. J. (1984) 'Members in Search of an Identity', *Health and Social Service Journal*, 23 February, 222–3.

Ham, C. J. (1986) *Managing Health Services* (School for Advanced Urban Studies, University of Bristol).

Ham, C. J. (1993) 'Priority Setting in the NHS: Reports from Six Districts', *British Medical Journal*, 367, 435–8.

Ham, C. J. (1996) *Public, Private or Community? What Next for the NHS* (DEMOS).

Ham, C. J. (1997a) *Management and Competition in the NHS* (Radcliffe Medical Press).

Ham, C. J. (ed.) (1997b) *Health Care Reform: Learning from International Experience* (Open University Press).

Ham, C. J. (1997c) 'Priority setting in health care: learning from international experience' *Health Policy*, 42, 49–66

Ham, C. J. (1999) 'The Third Way in Health Care Reform: Does the Emperor have any Clothes?' *Journal of Health Services Research and Policy*, 4(3), 1–6.

Ham, C. J. (2000) *The Politics of NHS Reform 1988–97* (King's Fund).

Ham, C. J. (2001) 'The Changing Organisation of Health and Social Care Across the UK', in Open University, *Critical Practice in Health and Social Care* (OU K302 course materials)

Ham, C. J. (2003) 'Betwixt and Between: Autonomization and Centralization of UK Hospitals, in Preker, A. and Harding, A. (eds) *op. cit.*

Ham, C. J. and Coulter, A. (2001) 'Explicit and implicit rationing: taking responsibility and avoiding blame for health care choices', *Journal of Health Services Research and Policy*, 6, 163–69.

Ham, C. J., Kipping, R. and McLeod, H. (2003) 'Redesigning Work Processes in Health Care: Lessons from the National Health Service', *The Milbank Quarterly*, 81(3) 415–39.

Ham, C. J. and Pickard, S. (1998) *Tragic Choices in Health Care* (King's Fund).

Ham, C. J. and Robert, G. (eds) (2003) *Reasonable Rationing* (Open University Press).

Ham, C. J., Robinson, R. and Benzeval, M. (1990) *Health Check* (King's Fund Institute).

Ham, C. J., Smith, J. and Temple, J. (1998) *Hubs, Spokes and Policy Cycles* (King's Fund).

Hampton, J. R. (1983) 'The End of Clinical Freedom', *British Medical Journal*, 287, 1237–8.

Hansard (1986) 'NHS (General Managers)', written answers, 26 June, col. 298.

Harrison, S. (1988) *Managing the National Health Service* (Chapman & Hall).

Harrison, S. (1994) *National Health Service Management in the 1980s* (Avebury).

Haywood, S. (1983) *District Health Authorities in Action* (University of Birmingham).

Haywood, S. and Alaszewski, A. (1980) *Crisis in the Health Service* (Croom Helm).

Haywood, S. and Hunter, D. (1982) 'Consultative Processes in Health Policy in the United Kingdom: A View from the Centre', *Public Administration*, 69, 143–62.

Hazell, R. (ed.) (2003) *The State of the Nations 2003* (Imprint Academic).

Health Committee (2002) *The Role of the Private Sector in the NHS, First Report from the Health Committee, Session 2001–02* (The Stationery Office).

Health Services Commissioner (2003) *NHS Funding for Long Term Care. Second Report – Session 2002–2003*, HC 399 (The Stationery Office).

Heclo, H. (1974) *Modern Social Politics in Britain and Sweden* (Yale University Press).

Heclo, H. (1978) 'Issue Networks and the Executive Establishment', in King, A. (ed.), *The New American Political System* (American Enterprise Institute).

Heclo, H. and Wildavsky, A. (1981) *The Private Government of Public Money*, 2nd edn (Macmillan – now Palgrave Macmillan).

Hennessy, P. (1986) *Cabinet* (Basil Blackwell).

Hennessy, P. (1989) *Whitehall* (Seeker & Warburg).

Hennessy, P. (1995) *The Hidden Wiring* (Victor Gollancz).

Hennessy, P. (2000) *The Prime Minister* (Penguin).

Hood, C. (1991) 'A Public Management for All Seasons', *Public Administration*, 69, 3–19.

Hood, C., Scott, C., James, O., Jones, G. and Travers, T. (1999) *Regulation Inside Government* (Oxford University Press).

Hunter, D. (1980) *Coping with Uncertainty* (Research Studies Press).

Hunter, D. (1983) 'Centre–Periphery Relations in the National Health Service: Facilitators or Inhibitors of Innovation?', in Young, K. (ed.), *National Interests and Local Governments* (Heinemann).

Illsley, R. (1977) 'Everybody's Business? Concepts of Health and Illness', in Social Science Research Council, *Health and Health Policy Priorities for Research* (SSRC).

Irvine, D. (2003) *The Doctors' Tale: Professionalism and Public Trust* (Radcliffe Medical Press).

Jacobzone, S., Cambois, E. and Robine, J. (2000) *Is the Health of Older Persons in OECD Countries Improving Fast Enough to Compensate for Population Ageing?* (OECD).

Jenkins, W. I. (1978) *Policy Analysis* (Martin Robertson).

Jervis, P. and Plowden, W. (2003) *The Impact of Political Devolution on the UK's Health Services* (The Nuffield Trust).

Jones, K. (1972) *A History of the Mental Health Services* (Routledge & Kegan Paul).

Jordan, A. G. and Richardson, J. J. (1987) *British Politics and the Policy Process* (Unwin Hyman).

Joss, R. and Kogan, M. (1995) *Advancing Quality: Total Quality Management in the National Health Service* (Open University Press).

Judge, K., Mulligan, J. and New, B. (1997) 'The NHS: New Prescriptions Needed?', in Jowell, R. *et al..* (eds), *British Social Attitudes: The 14th Report* (Social and Community Planning Research).

Kavanagh, D. and Seldon, A. (1999) *The Powers Behind the Prime Minister* (HarperCollins).

Kaye, V. (1977) 'The Team Spirit', *Health and Social Services Journal*, 16 September.

Keen, J., Light, D. and Mays, N. (2001) *Public–Private Relations in Health Care* (King's Fund).

Kelly, S. and Baker, A. (2000) 'Healthy life expectancy in Great Britain, 1980–96, and its use as an indicator in United Kingdom Government strategies', *Health Statistics Quarterly*, 07, 32–6.

Kennedy Report (2001) *The Report of the Public Inquiry into children's heart surgery at the Bristol Royal Infirmary 1984–1995*, CM 5207 (1) (The Stationery Office).

Kingdon, J. W. (1995) *Agendas, Alternatives and Public Policies*, 2nd edn (HarperCollins).

King's Fund Institute (1988) *Health Finance: Assessing the Options* (King's Fund Institute).

Klein, R. (1982) 'Performance Evaluation and the NHS: A Case Study in Conceptual Perplexity and Organisational Complexity', *Public Administration*, 60, 385–404.

Klein, R. (1983) *The Politics of the National Health Service* (Longman, 2nd edn 1989).

Klein, R. (1995) *The New Politics of the NHS*, 3rd edn (Longman).

Klein, R. (1998) 'Why Britain is Reorganising its National Health Service – Yet Again', *Health Affairs*, 17, 111–25.

Klein, R. (2000) *The New Politics of the NHS*, 4th edn (Prentice-Hall).

Klein, R., Day, P. and Redmayne, S. (1996) *Managing Scarcity* (Open University Press).

Labour Party (1995) *Renewing the NHS* (The Labour Party).

Laing and Buisson (2003) *Laing's Healthcare Market Review 2003–2004*.

Lalonde, M. (1974) *A New Perspective on the Health of Canadians* (Government of Canada).

Laming Report (2003) *The Victoria Climbie Inquiry* (The Stationery Office).

Lawson, N. (1992) *The View from No. 11* (Bantam Press).

Leatherman, S. and Sutherland, K. (2003) *The Quest for Quality in the NHS* (The Stationery Office).

Le Grand, J. (1978) 'The Distribution of Public Expenditure: The Case of Health Care', *Economica*, 45, 125–42.

Le Grand, J. (2002) 'The Labour Government and the National Health Service', *Oxford Review of Economic Policy*, 18 (2), 137–53.

Le Grand, J., Mays, N. and Mulligan, J. (eds) (1998) *Learning from the NHS Internal Market* (King's Fund).

Lee-Potter, J. (1997) *A Damn Bad Business* (Gollancz).

Levitt, R. (1979) *The Reorganised National Health Service*, 3rd edn (Croom Helm).

Lewis, J. (1986) *What Price Community Medicine?* (Wheatsheaf Books).

Likierman, A. (1988) *Public Expenditure* (Penguin Books).

Lindblom, C. E. (1965) *The Intelligence of Democracy* (The Free Press).

Lindblom. C. E. (1977) *Politics and Markets* (Basic Books).

Lindsey, A. (1962) *Socialized Medicine in England and Wales* (University of North Carolina Press).

Mackenbach, J.P. and Bakker, M.J. (2003) 'Tackling socioeconomic inequalities in health: analysis of European experiences', *The Lancet*, 362, 1409–14.

Mackintosh, J. P. (1974) *The Government and Politics of Britain*, 3rd revised edn (Hutchinson).

Malone-Lee. M. (1981) 'Where Loyalties Differ', *Health and Social Services Journal*, 26 November, 1448–9.

Manton, K.G. and Gu, X. (2001) 'Changes in the prevalence of chronic disability in the United States black and non-black population above age 65 from 1982 to 1999', *Proceedings of the National Academy of Sciences*, 98, 6354–9.

March, J. and Olsen, J. (1989) *Rediscovering Institutions: The Organisational Basis of Politics* (Free Press).

Marsh, D., Richards, D. and Smith, M. (2001) *Changing Patterns of Governance in the United Kingdom* (Palgrave).

Martin, J. P. (1984) *Hospitals in Trouble* (Blackwell).

Maxwell, R. (1984) 'Quality Assessment in Health', *British Medical Journal*, 288, 1470–2.

Maynard, A. and Bloor, K. (1996) 'Introducing a Market to the United Kingdom's National Health Service', *The New England Journal of Medicine*, 334, 604–8.

Mays, N. and Bevan, G. (1987) *Resource Allocation in the Health Service* (Bedford Square Press).

Mays, N., Goodwin, N., Killoran, A. and Malbon, G. (1998) *Total Purchasing. A step towards Primary Care Groups* (King's Fund).

McDonald, R. (2002) *Using Health Economics in Health Services* (Open University Press).

McKinsey Global Institute (1996) *Health Care Productivity*.

McKeown. T. (1976) *The Role of Medicine* (Nuffield Provincial Hospitals Trust).

McNulty, T. and Ferlie, E. (2002) *Reengineering Health Care* (Oxford University Press).

Middlemas, K. (1979) *Politics in Industrial Society* (André Deutsch).

Milburn, A. (2003) *Social Market Foundation Speech*, 30 April.

Ministry of Health (1946) *NHS Bill. Summary of the Proposed New Service*, Cmd 6761 (HMSO).

Ministry of Health (1967) *First Report of the Joint Working Party on the Organisation of Medical Work in Hospitals* (HMSO).

Mintzberg, H. (1983) *Structure in Fives: Designing Effective Organisations* (Prentice-Hall).

Moore, J. (1988) *Protecting the Nation's Health*, issued under cover of DHSS press release 88/97.

Moran, M. (1999) *Governing the Health Care State* (Manchester University Press).

Mossialos, E. and Dixon, A. (2002) 'Funding health care: an introduction', in Mossialos, E. *et al.* (eds) *Funding Health Care: options for Europe* (Open University Press).

Mossialos, E. and Palm, W. (2003) 'The European Court of Justice and the free movement of patients in the European Union', *International Social Security Review*, 56, 3–29.

Muir Gray, J.A. (2002) *The Resourceful Patient* (eRosetta Press).

Musgrove, P. (2003) 'Judging health systems: reflections on WHO's methods', *The Lancet*, 361, 1817–20.

NAHA (1987) *Autumn Survey 1987* (NAHA).

Nairne, P. (1983) 'Managing the DHSS Elephant: Reflections on a Giant Department', *Political Quarterly*, 243–56.

National Assembly for Wales (2001) *Improving Health in Wales* (National Assembly for Wales).

Navarro, V. (1976) *Medicine Under Capitalism* (Prodist).

NHS Alliance (2003) *Engaging GPs in the New NHS*.

NHS Executive (1996) *Seeing the Wood, Sparing the Trees*.

Nixon, J. and Nixon, N. (1983) 'The Social Services Committee: A Forum for Policy Review and Policy Reform', *Journal of Social Policy*, 12 (3), 331–55.

Normansfield Report (1978) *Report of the Committee of Inquiry into Normansfield Hospital*, Cmnd 7357 (HMSO).

Norton, P. (1981) *The Commons in Perspective* (Martin Robertson).

Norton, P. (1997) 'Parliamentary Oversight', in Dunleavy, P., Gamble, A., Holliday, I. and Peele, G. (eds) (1997), *Developments in British Politics*, 5th edn (Macmillan – now Palgrave Macmillan).

Nuffield Provincial Hospitals Trust (1946) *The Hospital Surveys: The Domesday Book of the Hospital Services* (Oxford University Press).

O'Connor, J. (1973) *The Fiscal Crisis of the State* (St Martin's Press: also Macmillan, 1981).

OECD (1992) *The Reform of Health Care: A Comparative Analysis of Seven OECD Countries* (OECD).

OECD (1994a) *OECD Economic Surveys: United Kingdom 1994* (OECD).

OECD (1994b) *The Reform of Health Care Systems: A Review of Seventeen OECD Countries* (OECD).

OECD (2003a) *Health at a Glance* (OECD).

OECD (2003b) *A Disease-based Comparison of Health Systems* (OECD).

Office of Health Economics (1989) *Compendium of Health Statistics*, 7th edn (OHE).

Office of Health Economics (2002) *Compendium of Health Statistics*, 14th edn (OHE).

Office of Health Economics (2003) *Compendium of Health Statistics*, 15th edn (OHE) and accompanying press release, 'Latest Figures Show the Health of most of the Nation is Catching up with Europe'.

Office of National Statistics (2002) *Living in Britain* (The Stationery Office).

Or, Z. (2001) *Exploring the Effects of Health Care on Mortality across OECD Countries* (OECD).

Osmond, J. (2003) 'From Corporate Body to Virtual Parliament. The Metamorphosis of the National Assembly for Wales', in Hazell *op. cit.*

Owen, D. (1991) *Time to Declare* (Michael Joseph).

Packwood, T., Keen, J. and Buxton, M. (1991) *Hospitals in Transition* (Open University Press).

Paige, V. (1987) 'The Development of General Management within the NHS', *The Health Summary*, June, 6–8.

Parsons, W. (1995) *Public Policy* (Edward Elgar).

Pater, J. E. (1981) *The Making of the NHS* (King's Fund).

Pettigrew, A., Ferlie, E. and McKee, L. (1992) *Shaping Strategic Change* (Sage).

Pierson, P. (1994) *Dismantling the Welfare State?* (Cambridge University Press).

Pollock, A., Dunnigan, M., Gaffney, D., Price, D. and Shaoul, J. (1999) 'Planning the "new" NHS: downsizing for the 21st century', *British Medical Journal*, 319, 17 July, 179–84.

Pollock, A. and Price, D. (2000) 'Rewriting the regulations: how the World Trade Organisation could accelerate privatisation in health-care systems', *The Lancet*, 356, 1995–2000.

Pollock, A. and Price, D. (2003a) 'The public health implications of world trade negotiations on the general agreement on trade in services and public services', *The Lancet*, 362, 1072–5.

Pollock, A. and Price, D. (2003b) 'The BetterCare Judgment – a challenge to health care', *British Medical Journal*, 326, 236–7.

Popham, G. T. (1981) 'Government and Smoking: Policy Making and Pressure Groups', *Policy and Politics*, (3), 331–47.

Porter, R. (1997) *The Greatest Benefit to Mankind* (HarperCollins).

Powell, J. E. (1966) *A New Look at Medicine and Politics* (Pitman).

Power, M. (1994) *The Audit Explosion* (DEMOS).

Preker, A. and Harding, A. (eds) (2003) *Innovations in Health Service Delivery* (The World Bank).

Preker, A., Jakab, M. and Schneider, M. (2002) 'Health financing reforms in central and eastern Europe and the former Soviet Union', in Mossialos, E. *et al.* (eds) *Funding Health Care: options for Europe* (Open University Press).

Price, D., Pollock, A. and Shaoul, J. (1999) 'How the World Trade Organisation is shaping domestic policies in health care', *The Lancet*, 354, 1889–92.

Propper, C. (1996) 'Market Structure and Prices: The Response of Hospitals in the UK National Health Service to Competition', *Journal of Public Economics*, 61, 307–35.

Propper, C. (1998) *Who Pays For and Who Gets Health Care?* (The Nuffield Trust).

Propper, C., Burgess, S. and Gossage, D. (2003) *Competition and Quality: Evidence from the NHS Internal Market 1991–1999* (University of Bristol).

Propper, C. and Green, K. (2001) 'A Larger Role for the Private Sector in Financing UK Health Care: the Arguments and the Evidence' *Journal of Social Policy*, 30 (4), 685–704.

Propper, C., Rees, H. and Green, K. (2001) 'The Demand for Private Medical Insurance in the UK: A Cohort Analysis' *The Economic Journal*, vol. 111, C180–C200.

Public Accounts Committee (1977) *Ninth Report from the Public Accounts Committee Session 1976–77*, HC 532 (HMSO).

Public Accounts Committee (1981) *Seventeenth Report from the Public Accounts Committee Session 1980–81: Financial Control and Accountability in the NHS*, HC 255 (HMSO).

Public Administration Committee (2001) *Fourth Report of the Select Committee on Public Administration 2000–01*, HC 293 (The Stationery Office).

Razell, E. (1980) *Improving Policy Analysis in the DHSS*, Civil Service College Working Paper no. 19.

Regen, E. (2002) *Driving Seat or Back Seat? GPs's views on and involvement in primary care groups and trusts* (University of Birmingham).

Regen, E., Smith, J., Goodwin, N., McLeod, H. and Shapiro, J. (2001) *Passing on the baton: final report of a national evaluation of primary care groups and trusts* (University of Birmingham).

Regen, E., Smith, J., and Shapiro, J. (1999) *First off the Starting Blocks: Lessons from GP Commissioning Pilots for PCGs* (University of Birmingham).

Regional Chairmen's Enquiry (1976) *Regional Chairmen's Enquiry into the Working of the DHSS in Relation to Regional Health Authorities* (DHSS).

Rhodes, R. A. W. (1979) 'Research into Central–Local Relations in Britain. A Framework for Analysis', appendix 1, in Social Science Research Council, *Central–Local Relationships* (SSRC).

Rhodes, R. A. W. (1997) *Understanding Governance* (Open University Press).

Richardson, J. J. and Jordan, A. G. (1979) *Governing under Pressure* (Martin Robertson).

Riddell, P. (2001) 'New look behind the revolving doors of power', *The Times*, 13 June.

RIPA (Royal Institute of Public Administration) (1980) *Policy and Practice: The Experience of Government* (RIPA).

Robb. B. (ed.) (1967) *Sans Everything – A Case to Answer* (Nelson).

Roberts. J. (1990) 'Kenneth Clarke: Hatchet Man or Remoulder?', *British Medical Journal*, 301. 1383–6.

Robinson, R. and Le Grand, J. (eds) (1994) *Evaluating the NHS Reforms* (King's Fund Institute).

Royal Commission on the National Health Service (1979) *Report*, Cmnd 7615 (HMSO).

Saltman, R., Figueras, J. and Sakallarides, C. (1998) *Critical Challenges for Health Care Reform in Europe* (Open University Press).

Sant, M. *et al.* (2003) 'Eurocare-3: survival of cancer patients diagnosed 1990–94 – results and commentary', *Annals of Oncology*, 14 (Supplement 5), v61–v118.

Saunders, P. (1979) *Urban Politics* (Hutchinson).

Saunders, P. (1981) 'Notes on the Specificity of the Local State', in Boddy, M. and Fudge, C. (eds). *The Local State: Theory and Practice* (University of Bristol, School for Advanced Urban Studies).

Schoen, C. *et al.* (2000) 'Health insurance markets and income inequality: findings from an international health policy survey', *Health Policy*, 51, 67–85.

Scottish Executive (2000) *Our National Health* (The Stationery Office).

Scottish Executive (2001) *Rebuilding our National Health Service*.

Scottish Executive (2003) *Partnership for Care: Scotland's Health White Paper* (The Stationery Office).

Secretary of State for Health and others (1989a) *Working for Patients* (HMSO).

Secretary of State for Health and others (1989b) *Caring for People* (HMSO).

Secretary of State for Health (1992) *The Health of the Nation*, Cm. 1986 (HMSO).

Secretary of State for Health (1996) *The National Health Service. A Service With Ambitions*, Cm 3425 (The Stationery Office).

Secretary of State for Health (1997) *The New NHS. Modern. Dependable* (The Stationery Office).

Secretary of State for Health (1998a) *Our Healthier Nation*, Cm 3852 (The Stationery Office).

Secretary of State for Health (1998b) *A First Class Service* (The Stationery Office).

Secretary of State for Health (1999) *Saving Lives: Our Healthier Nation*, Cm 4386 (The Stationery Office).

Secretary of State for Health (2000) *The NHS Plan* Cm 4818–I (The Stationery Office).

Secretary of State for Health (2002) *Delivering the NHS Plan* Cm 5503 (The Stationery Office).

Secretary of State for Scotland (1997) *Designed to Care* (The Stationery Office).

Secretary of State for Social Services and others (1987) *Promoting Better Health* (HMSO).

Sikora, K. and Bosanquet, N. (2003) 'Cancer care in the United Kingdom: new solutions are needed', *British Medical Journal*, 327, 1 November, 1044–6.

Smee, C. (1995) 'Self-governing Trusts and GP Fundholders: the British Experience', in Saltman, R. and von Otter, C. (eds), *Implementing Planned Markets in Health Care* (Open University Press).

Smith, B. (1976) *Policy Making in British Government* (Martin Robertson).

Smith, M. (1993) *Pressure, Power and Policy* (Harvester Wheatsheaf).

Smith, M. (1999) *The Core Executive in Britain* (Macmillan – now Palgrave Macmillan)

Smith, P. (2002) 'Performance Management in British Health Care: Will it Deliver?' *Health Affairs*, 21 (3), 103–15.

Smith, R. (1991) 'William Waldegrave: Thinking beyond the New NHS', *British Medical Journal*, 302, 711–14.

Smith, R. (1998) 'All changed, changed utterly', *British Medical Journal*, 316, 1917–18.

Social Services Committee (1980) *The Government's White Papers on Public Expenditure: The Social Services, Third Report from the Social Services Committee, Session 1979–80*, HC 701–2 (HMSO): vol. 1, *Report*; vol. 2 *Minutes of Evidence and Appendices*.

Social Services Committee (1981) *Public Expenditure on the Social Services, Third Report from the Social Services Committee, Session 1980–81*, HC 324–1 (HMSO): vol. I, *Report*; vol. II, *Minutes of Evidence and Appendices*.

Social Services Committee (1984) *Griffiths NHS Management Inquiry Report, First Report from the Social Services Committee, Session 1983–4*, HC 209 (HMSO).

Social Services Committee (1990) *Public Expenditure on Health Matters, Session 1989–90*, HC 484 (HMSO).

Soderlund, N., Csaba, I., Gray, R., Milne, R. and Raftery, J. (1997) 'Impact of the NHS Reforms on English Hospital Productivity: An analysis of the first three years', *British Medical Journal*, 315, 1126–29.

Solesbury, W. (1976) 'The Environmental Agenda', *Public Administration*, Winter, 379–97.

Stacey, M. (1977) 'Concepts of Health and Illness: A Working Paper on the Concepts and their Relevance for Research', in Social Science Research Council, *Health and Health Policy – Priorities for Research* (SSRC).

Stacey, M. (1992) *Regulating British Medicine* (John Wiley).

Starfield, B. (1992) *Primary Care: Concept, Evaluation and Policy* (Oxford University Press).

Stevens, R. (1966) *Medical Practice in Modern England* (Yale University Press).

Stowe, K. (1989) *On Caring for the National Health* (The Nuffield Provincial Hospitals Trust).

Summerfield, C. and Babb, P. (eds) (2003) *Social Trends 33* (The Stationery Office).

Taylor, P. (1984) *The Smoke Ring* (The Bodley Head).

Thwaites, B. (1987) *The NHS: The End of the Rainbow* (The Institute of Health Policy Studies, University of Southampton).

Timmins, N. (1995) *The Five Giants* (HarperCollins).

Timmins, N. (2003) 'Patients paying for healthcare "tripled since 1997 election" ', *Financial Times*, 4 April.

Titmuss, R. (1968) *Commitment to Welfare* (Allen & Unwin).

Tudor-Hart, J. (1971) 'The Inverse Care Law', *The Lancet*, 27 February, 405–12.

Tunstall-Pedoe, H. *et al.* (2000) 'Estimation of contribution of changes in coronary care to improving survival, event rates, and coronary heart disease mortality across the WHO MONICA Project populations', *The Lancet*, 355, 688–700.

Tuohy, C. (1999) *Accidental Logics* (Oxford University Press).

van Doorslaer, E., Rutten, F. and Wagstaff, A. (1993) *Equity in the Finance and Delivery of Health Care: An International Perspective* (Oxford University Press).

Wagstaff, A. *et al.* (1999) 'Equity in the finance of health care: some further international comparisons', *Journal of Health Economics*, 18, 263–90.

Walshe, K. (2003) *Regulating Healthcare* (Open University Press).

Wanless, D. (2001) *Securing Our Future Health: Taking a Long-Term View. Interim Report.* (HM Treasury).

Wanless, D. (2002) *Securing Our Future Health: Taking a Long-Term View. Final Report.* (HM Treasury).

Wanless, D. (2003a) *The Review of Health and Social Care in Wales* (Welsh Assembly Government).

Wanless, D. (2003b) *Securing Good Health for the Whole Population* (HM Treasury).

Webster, C. (1988) *The Health Services Since the War*, Vol. 1 (HMSO).

Webster, C. (1996) *The Health Services Since The War*, Vol. 2 (The Stationery Office).

Webster, C. (1998) *The National Health Service: A Political History* (Oxford University Press).

Whitehead, M. (1987) *The Health Divide* (Health Education Council).

WHO (World Health Organization) (2000) *The World Health Report 2000. Health Systems: Improving Performance.*

WHO (World Health Organization) (2002) *The World Health Report 2002. Reducing Risks, Promoting Healthy Life.*

Wilding, P. (1982) *Professional Power and Social Welfare* (Routledge & Kegan Paul).

Wilkin, D., Coleman, A., Dowling, B. and Smith, K. (2002) *National Tracker Survey of Primary Care Groups and Trusts 2001/2002: Taking Responsibility?* (National Primary Care Research and Development Centre).

Willcocks, A. J. (1967) *The Creation of the National Health Service* (Routledge & Kegan Paul).

Willetts, D. (1987) 'The Role of the Prime Minister's Policy Unit', *Public Administration*, 65, 443–54.

Williams, B. *et al.* (2000a) 'Patients and procedures in short-stay independent hospitals in England and Wales, 1997–1998', *Journal of Public Health Medicine*, 22, 68–73.

Williams, B. *et al.* (2000b) 'Private funding of elective hospital treatment in England and Wales, 1997–8: national survey', *British Medical Journal*, 320, 904–5.

Woods, K. (2002) 'Health Policy and the NHS in the UK 1997–2002', in Adams, J. and Robinson, P. (eds) *Devolution in Practice* (IPPR and ESRC).

Woods, K. (2004) 'Political Devolution and the Health Services in Great Britain', *International Journal of Health Services*, 34, 323–39.

Yates, J. (1987) *Why Are We Waiting?* (Oxford University Press).

Yates, J. (1995) *Private Eye, Heart and Hip* (Churchill Livingstone).

Young, H. (1989) *One of Us* (Macmillan – now Palgrave Macmillan).

Young, H. and Sloman, A. (1982) *No, Minister* (BBC).

Index

282